Bhagavad Gita

Mata Amritanandamayi Center
San Ramon, California, United States

Published by:
Mata Amritanandamayi Center
P.O. Box 613
San Ramon, CA 94583
United States

First Edition: September 2015

In India:
www.amritapuri.org
inform@amritapuri.org

In USA:
www. amma.org

In Europe:
www.amma-europe.org

Contents

Satguru Sri Mātā Amṛitānandamayi Devi Aṣhṭothara Śata Nāmāvali

The Hundred and Eight Names of
Satguru Sri Mata Amritanandamayi

Dhyāna Śloka

dhyāyāmo-dhavalāvaguṇṭhanavatīṁ
tejomayīm-naiṣhṭikīṁ
snigdhāpāṅga-vilokinīm bhagavatīṁ
mandasmita-śrī-mukhīṁ
vātsalyāmṛta-varṣiṇīm sumadhuraṁ
saṅkīrtanālāpinīṁ
śyāmāṅgīṁ madhu-sikta-sūktīṁ
amṛtānandātmikāmīśvarīṁ

1. Oṁ pūrṇa-brahma-svarūpiṇyai namaḥ
2. Oṁ saccidānanda mūrtaye namaḥ
3. Oṁ ātmā-rāmāgragaṇyāyai namaḥ
4. Oṁ yoga-līnāntarātmane namaḥ
5. Oṁ antar-mukha-svabhāvāyai namaḥ
6. Oṁ turya-tuṅga-sthalījjuṣe namaḥ
7. Oṁ prabhā-maṇḍala-vītāyai namaḥ
8. Oṁ durāsada-mahaujase namaḥ
9. Oṁ tyakta-dig-vastu-kālādi-sarvāvaccheda -rāśaye namaḥ
10. Oṁ-sajātīya-vijātīya-svīya-bheda-nirākṛte namaḥ
11. Oṁ-vāṇī-buddhi-vimṛgyāyai namaḥ
12. Oṁ śaśvad-avyakta-vartmane namaḥ
13. Oṁ nāma-rūpādi-śūnyāyai namaḥ
14. Oṁ śūnya-kalpa-vibhūtaye namaḥ
15. Oṁ ṣaḍaiśvarya-samudrāyai namaḥ
16. Oṁ dūrī-kṛta-ṣaḍ-ūrmaye namaḥ
17. Oṁ nitya-prabuddha-saṁśuddha-nirmuktātma- prabhāmuce namaḥ
18. Oṁ kāruṇyākula-cittāyai namaḥ
19. Oṁ tyakta-yoga-suṣuptaye namaḥ
20. Oṁ kerala-kṣmāvatīrṇāyai namaḥ
21. Oṁ mānuṣa-strī-vapurbhṛte namaḥ

22. Oṁ dharmiṣṭa-suguṇānanda damayantī-svayaṁ-bhuve namaḥ
23. Oṁ mātā-pitṛ-cirācīrṇa-puṇya-pūra-phalātmane namaḥ
24. Oṁ niśśabda-jananī-garbha-nirgamādbhuta-karmaṇe namaḥ
25. Oṁ kālī-śrī-kṛṣṇa-saṅkāśa-komala-śyāmala-tviṣe namaḥ
26. Oṁ cira-naṣṭa punar-labdha-bhārgava-kṣetra-sampade namaḥ
27. Oṁ mṛta-prāya-bhṛgu-kṣetra punar-uddhita-tejase namaḥ
28. Oṁ sauśīlyādi-guṇākṛṣṭa-jaṅgama-sthāvarālaye namaḥ
29. Oṁ manuṣya-mṛga-pakṣyādi sarva-saṁsevitāṅghraye namaḥ
30. Oṁ naisargika-dayā-tīrtha-snāna-klinnāntarātmane namaḥ
31. Oṁ daridra-janatā-hasta-samarpita nijāndhase namaḥ
32. Oṁ anya-vaktra-pra-bhuktānna pūrita-svīya-kukṣaye namaḥ
33. Oṁ samprāpta-sarva-bhūtātma svātma-sattānubhūtaye namaḥ

34. Oṁ aśikṣita-svayam-svānta-sphurat-kṛṣṇa-vibhūtaye namaḥ
35. Oṁ acchinna-madhurodāra kṛṣṇa-līlānusandhaye namaḥ
36. Oṁ nandātmaja-mukhāloka nityotkaṇṭhita cetase namaḥ
37. Oṁ govinda viprayogādhi-dāva-dagdhāntarātmane namaḥ
38. Oṁ viyoga-śoka-sammūrcchā-muhur-patita-varṣmaṇe namaḥ
39. Oṁ sārameyādi vihita-śuśrūṣā-labdha buddhaye namaḥ
40. Oṁ prema-bhakti balākṛṣṭa-prādur-bhāvita śārṅgiṇe namaḥ
41. Oṁ kṛṣṇa-loka mahāhlāda-dhvasta śokāntarātmane namaḥ
42. Oṁ kāñcī-candraka-manjīra vaṁśī śobhi svabhū-dṛśe namaḥ
43. Oṁ sārvatrika hṛṣīkeśa sānnidhya laharī-spṛśe namaḥ
44. Oṁ susmera-tan mukhāloka vismerotphulla-dṛiṣṭaye namaḥ
45. Oṁ tat-kānti-yamunā-sparśa-hṛṣṭa romāṅga-yaṣṭaye namaḥ

46. Oṁ apratīkṣita saṁprāpta-devī-
rūpopalabdhaye namaḥ
47. Oṁ pāṇī-padma svapadvīṇā
śobhamānāṁbikādṛśe namaḥ
48. Oṁ devī sadyas-tirodhāna tāpa-vyathita-
cetase namaḥ
49. Oṁ dīna-rodana-nir-ghoṣa-dīrṇa-
dikkarṇa-vartmane namaḥ
50. Oṁ tyaktānna-pāna nidrādi-sarva-
daihika-dharmaṇe namaḥ
51. Oṁ kurarādi-samānīta-bhakṣya-poṣita-
varṣmaṇe namaḥ
52. Oṁ vīṇā-niṣyanti-saṅgīta-lālita-śruti-
nālaye namaḥ
53. Oṁ apāra-paramānanda laharī-magna-
cetase namaḥ
54. Oṁ caṇḍikā-bhīkarākāra darśanālabdha-
śarmaṇe namaḥ
55. Oṁ śānta-rūpāmṛtajharī-pāraṇā
nirvṛtātmane namaḥ
56. Oṁ śāradā-smārakāśeṣa-svabhāva-guṇa-
saṁpade namaḥ
57. Oṁ prati-bimbita-cāndreya-śāradobhaya-
mūrtaye namaḥ

58. Oṁ tannāṭakā bhinayana-nitya-
raṅgayitātmane namaḥ
59. Oṁ cāndreyā-śāradā-kelī-kallolita-
sudhābdhaye namaḥ
60. Oṁ uttejita-bhṛgu-kṣetra-daiva-caitanya
raṁhase namaḥ
61. Oṁ bhūyaḥ-pratyavaruddhārṣa-divya-
saṁskāra-rāśaye namaḥ
62. Oṁ aprākṛtāt-bhūtānanda-kalyāṇa-guṇa-
sindhave namaḥ
63. Oṁ aiśvarya-vīrya-kīrti-śrī-jñāna-
vairāgya-veśmaṇe namaḥ
64. Oṁ upātta-bāla-gopāla veṣa-bhūṣā-
vibhūtaye namaḥ
65. Oṁ smera-snigdha-kaṭakṣāyai namaḥ
66. Oṁ svairādyuṣita-vedaye namaḥ
67. Oṁ piñcha-kuṇḍala-mañjīra vaṁśikā
kiṅkiṇī-bhṛte namaḥ
68. Oṁ bhakta-lokākhilā-bhīṣṭa pūraṇa
prīṇanecchave namaḥ
69. Oṁ pīṭhārūdha-mahādevī-bhāva-
bhāsvara-mūrtaye namaḥ
70. Oṁ bhūṣanāmbara-veṣa-śrī dīpya-
mānāṁga-yaṣṭaye namaḥ

71. Oṁ suprasanna-mukhāṁbhoja-varābhayada pāṇaye namaḥ
72. Oṁ kirīṭa-raśanākarṇa-pūra-svarṇa-paṭī-bhṛte namaḥ
73. Oṁ jihva-līḍha-mahā-rogi-bībhatsa vraṇita-tvace namaḥ
74. Oṁ tvag-roga-dhvaṁsa-niṣṇāta gaurāṅgāpara-mūrtaye namaḥ
75. Oṁ steya-himsā-surāpānā-dyaśeṣādharma-vidviṣe namaḥ
76. Oṁ tyāga-vairagya-maitryādi-sarva sadvāsanā puṣe namaḥ
77. Oṁ pādāśrita-manorūḍha-dussaṁskāra-rahomuṣe namaḥ
78. Oṁ prema-bhakti-sudhāsikta-sādhu-citta-guhājjuṣe namaḥ
79. Oṁ sudhāmaṇi mahā-nāmne namaḥ
80. Oṁ subhāṣita sudhā-muce namaḥ
81. Oṁ amṛtānanda-mayyākhyā-janakarṇa-puṭa-spṛśe namaḥ
82. Oṁ dṛpta-datta-viraktāyai namaḥ
83. Oṁ namrārpita-bhubhukṣave namaḥ
84. Oṁ uthsṛṣṭa-bhogi-saṁgāyai namaḥ
85. Oṁ yogi-saṁga-riraṁsave namaḥ

86. Oṁ abhinandita-dānādi-śubha-karmā-
bhivṛddhaye namaḥ
87. Oṁ abhivandita niśśeṣa sthira-jaṁgama
sṛṣṭaye namaḥ
88. Oṁ protsāhita brahma-vidyā sampradāya-
pravṛttaye namaḥ
89. Oṁ punarāsādita-śreṣṭha-tapovipina-
vṛttaye namaḥ
90. Oṁ bhūyo gurukulā-vāsa-śikṣaṇotsuka-
medhase namaḥ
91. Oṁ aneka-naiṣṭika-brahmacāri nirmātṛ-
vedhase namaḥ
92. Oṁ śiṣya-saṁkrāmita-svīya-projvalat-
brahma-varcase namaḥ
93. Oṁ antevāsi-janāśeṣa-ceṣṭā-pātita dṛṣṭaye
namaḥ
94. Oṁ mohāndha-kāra-sañcāri-lokā-
nugrāhi-rociṣe namaḥ
95. Oṁ tamaḥ-kliṣṭa-mano-vṛṣṭa-svaprakāśa-
śubhāśiṣe namaḥ
96. Oṁ bhakta-śuddhānṭa-raṁgastha bhadra-
dīpa-śikhā-tviṣe namaḥ
97. Oṁ saprīthi-bhukta-bhaktaughanyarpita-
sneha-sarpiṣe namaḥ

98. Oṁ śiṣya-varya-sabhā-madhya dhyāna-yoga-vidhitsave namaḥ
99. Oṁ śaśvalloka-hitācāra-magna dehendriyāsave namaḥ
100. Oṁ nija-puṇya-pradānānya-pāpādāna-cikīrṣave namaḥ
101. Oṁ para-svaryāpana-svīya naraka-prāpti-lipsave namaḥ
102. Oṁ rathotsava-calat-kanyā-kumārī-martya-mūrtaye namaḥ
103. Oṁ vimo-hārṇava nirmagna bhṛgu-kṣetrojjihīrṣave namaḥ
104. Oṁ punassantā-nita-dvaipāyana-satkula-tantave namaḥ
105. Oṁ veda-śāstra-purāṇetihāsa-śāśvata-bandhave namaḥ
106. Oṁ bṛghu-kṣetra-samun-mīlat-para-daivata-tejase namaḥ
107. Oṁ devyai namaḥ
108. Oṁ premāmṛtānandamayyai nityam namo namaḥ

Gita Dhyanam

MEDITATION ON THE GITA

ॐ पार्थाय प्रतिबोधितां भगवता नारायणेन स्वयं
व्यासेन ग्रथितां पुराणमुनिना मध्ये महाभारतम् ।
अद्वैतामृतवर्षिणीं भगवतीमष्टादशाध्यायिनीं
अम्ब त्वामनुसन्दधामि भगवद्गीते भवद्वेषिणीम् ॥

Om Pārthāya pratibodhitāṁ bhagavatā nārāyaṇena svayaṁ
Vyāsena grathitāṁ purāṇa-muninā madhye mahābhāratm
Advaitāmṛta-varṣiṇīṁ bhagavatīm aṣṭādaśādhyāyinīṁ
Amba tvām anusandadhāmi bhagavad-gīte bhava-dveṣiṇīm

1. Om. O Bhagavad Gita, with which Partha was illumined by Lord Narayana Himself, and which was composed within the Mahabharata by the ancient sage, Vyasa, O Divine Mother, the destroyer of rebirth, the showerer of the nectar of Advaita, and consisting of eighteen discourses—upon Thee, O Gita, O affectionate Mother, I meditate!

नमोऽस्तु ते व्यास विशालबुद्धे फुल्लारविन्दायतपत्रनेत्र ।
येन त्वया भारततैलपूर्णः प्रज्वालितो ज्ञानमयः प्रदीपः ॥

Namo'stu te vyāsa viśāla-buddhe
phullāravindāyātapatra-netra
Yena tvayā bhārata-taila-pūrṇaḥ prajvalito
jñānamayaḥ pradīpaḥ

2. Salutations unto thee, O Vyasa, of broad intellect and with eyes like the petals of a full-blown lotus, by whom the lamp of knowledge, filled with the oil of the Mahabharata, has been lighted!

प्रपन्नपारिजातायतोत्रवेत्रैकपाणये ।
ज्ञानमुद्राय कृष्णाय गीतामृतदुहे नमः ॥

Prapanna-parijātāya totra-vetraika-pāṇaye
Jñāna-mudrāya kṛṣṇāya gītāmṛta-duhe namaḥ

3. Salutations to Lord Krishna, the Parijata or the Kalpataru or the bestower of all desires for those who take refuge in Him, the holder of the whip in one hand, the holder of the symbol of divine knowledge and the milker of the divine nectar of the Bhagavad Gita!

सर्वोपनिषदो गावो दोग्धा गोपालनन्दनः ।
पार्थो वत्सः सुधीर्भोक्ता दुग्धं गीतामृतं महत् ॥

Sarvopaniṣado gāvo dogdhā gopāla-nandanaḥ
Pārtho vatsaḥ sudhīr bhoktā dugdhaṁ
gītāmṛtaṁ mahat

4. All the Upanishads are the cows; the milker is Krishna; the cowherd boy, Partha (Arjuna), is the calf; men of purified intellect are the drinkers; the milk is the great nectar of the Gita.

वसुदेवसुतं देवं कंसचाणूरमर्दनम् ।
देवकीपरमानन्दं कृष्णं वन्दे जगद्गुरुम् ॥

Vasudeva-sutaṁ devaṁ kaṁsa-cāṇūra-mardanam
Devakī-paramānandaṁ kṛṣṇaṁ vande jagad-gurum

5. I salute Sri Krishna, the world-teacher, son of Vasudeva, the destroyer of Kamsa and Chanura, the supreme bliss of Devaki!

भीष्मद्रोणतटा जयद्रथजला गान्धारनीलोपला
शल्यग्राहवती कृपेण वहनी कर्णेन वेलाकुला ।
अश्वत्थामविकर्णघोरमकरा दुर्योधनावर्तिनी
सोत्तीर्णा खलु पाण्डवै रणनदी कैवर्तकः केशवः ॥

Bhīṣma-droṇa-taṭā jayadratha-jalā gāndhā-nīlotpalā
Śalya-grāhavatī kṛpeṇa vahinī karṇena velākula
Aśvattāma-vikarṇa-ghora-makarā duryodhanāvartinī
Sottīrṇā khalu pāṇḍavārṇava-nadī kaivartakaḥ keśvaḥ

6. With Kesava as the helmsman, verily was crossed by the Pandavas the battle-river, whose banks were Bhishma and Drona, whose water was Jayadratha, whose blue lotus was the king of Gandhara, whose crocodile was Salya, whose current was Kripa, whose billow was Karna, whose terrible alligators were Vikarna and Asvatthama, whose whirlpool was Duryodhana.

पाराशर्यवचः सरोजममलं गीतार्थगन्धोत्कटं
नानाख्यानककेसरं हरिकथासम्बोधनाबोधितम् ।
लोके सज्जनषट्पदैरहरहः पेपीयमानं मुदा
भूयाद्भारतपङ्कजं कलिमलप्रध्वंसि नः श्रेयसे ॥

Pārāśarya-vacaḥ sarojam amalaṁ gītārtha-gandhotkaṭaṁ
Nānākhyānaka-keśaraṁ hari-kathā-sambodhanābodhitam
Loke sajjana-ṣaṭpadair aharahaḥ pepīyamānaṁ mudā
Bhūyād bhārata-paṇkajaṁ kalimala-pradhvaṁsanaḥ śreyase

7. May this lotus of the Mahabharata, born in the lake of the words of Vyasa, sweet with the fragrance of the meaning of the Gita, with many stories as its stamens, fully opened by the discourses of Hari, the destroyer of the sins of Kali, and drunk joyously by the bees of good men in the world, become day by day the bestower of good to us!

मूकं करोति वाचालं पङ्गुं लङ्घयते गिरिम् ।
यत्कृपा तमहं वन्दे परमानन्दमाधवम् ॥

Mūkaṁ karoti vācālaṁ paṇguṁ laṇghāyate girim
Yat-kṛpā tam ahaṁ vande paramānanda-mādhavam

8. I salute that Madhava, the source of supreme bliss, whose Grace makes the dumb eloquent and the cripple cross mountains!

यं ब्रह्मा वरुणेन्द्ररुद्रमरुतः स्तुन्वन्ति दिव्यैः स्तवै -
र्वेदैः साङ्गपदक्रमोपनिषदैर्गायन्ति यं सामगाः ।
ध्यानावस्थिततद्गतेन मनसा पश्यन्ति यं योगिनो
यस्यान्तं न विदुः सुरासुरगणा देवाय तस्मै नमः ॥

Yaṁ brahmā varuṇendra-rudra-marutaḥ stunvanti divyaiḥ stavair
Vedaiḥ sāṇga-pada-kramopaniṣadair gāyanti yaṁ sāma-gāḥ
Dhyānāvastita-tad-gatena manasā paśyanti yaṁ yogino
Yasyāntaṁ na viduḥ surāsura-gaṇā devāya tasmai namaḥ

9. Salutations to that God whom Brahma, Indra, Varuna, Rudra and the Maruts praise with divine hymns, of whom the Sama-chanters sing by the Vedas and their Angas (in the Pada and Krama methods), and by the Upanishads; whom the Yogis see with their minds absorbed in Him through meditation, and whose ends the hosts of Devas and Asuras know not!

Bhagavad Gita

अथ प्रथमोऽध्यायः - अर्जुनविषादयोगः

Chapter One: Arjuna Viśhada-Yoga

धृतराष्ट्र उवाच ।
धर्मक्षेत्रे कुरुक्षेत्रे, समवेता युयुत्सवः ।
मामकाः पाण्डवाश्चैव, किमकुर्वत संजय ॥१॥

dhṛtarāṣṭra uvāca
dharma-kṣetre kurukṣetre / samavetā yuyutsavaḥ
māmakāḥ pāṇḍavāś caiva / kim akurvata sañjaya

1. Dhritarashtra said: Assembled on the field of Dharma, O Sanjaya, on the field of the Kurus, eager to fight, what did my people and the Pandavas do?

संजय उवाच ।
दृष्ट्वा तु पाण्डवानीकं, व्यूढं दुर्योधनस्तदा ।
आचार्यमुपसंगम्य, राजा वचनमब्रवीत् ॥२॥

sañjaya uvāca
dṛṣṭvā tu pāṇḍavānīkaṁ / vyūḍhaṁ duryodhanas tadā
ācāryam upasaṅgamya / rājā vacanam abravīt

2. Sanjaya said: Then Duryodhana the King, seeing the army of the Pandavas drawn up in battle array, approached his Master and spoke these words:

पश्यैतां पाण्डुपुत्राणामाचार्य महतीं चमूम् ।
व्यूढां द्रुपदपुत्रेण तव शिष्येण धीमता ॥३॥

paśyaitāṁ pāṇḍu-putrāṇām ācārya mahatīṁ camūm
vyūḍhāṁ drupada-putreṇa tava śiṣyeṇa dhīmatā

3. Behold, O Master, this great army of the sons of Pandu, arrayed by your wise pupil, the son of Drupada.

अत्र शूरा महेष्वासाः, भीमार्जुनसमा युधि ।
युयुधानो विराटश्च, द्रुपदश्च महारथः ॥४॥

atra śūrā maheṣvāsā / bhīmārjuna-samā yudhi
yuyudhāno virāṭaś ca / drupadaś ca mahā-rathaḥ

4. Here are men of valour, mighty archers, the equals of Bhima and Arjuna - in battle Yuyudhana, Virata and Drupada, the maharathi.

धृष्टकेतुश्चेकितानः, काशिराजश्च वीर्यवान् ।
पुरुजित्कुन्तिभोजश्च, शैब्यश्च नरपुङ्गवः ॥५॥

dhṛṣṭaketuś cekitānaḥ / kāśirājaś ca vīryavān
purujit kuntibhojaś ca / śaibyaś ca nara-puṅgavaḥ

5. Dhrishtaketu, Chekitana and the valiant king of Kashi, also Purujit, Kuntibhoja and Shaibya, chief among men.

युधामन्युश्च विक्रान्तः, उत्तमौजाश्च वीर्यवान् ।
सौभद्रो द्रौपदेयाश्च, सर्व एव महारथाः ॥६॥

yudhāmanyuś ca vikrānta / uttamaujāś ca vīryavān
saubhadro draupadeyāś ca / sarva eva mahā-rathāḥ

6. Yudhamanyu, the brave; the valiant Uttamauja; also the son of Subhadra and the sons of Draupadi - all of them maharathis.

अस्माकं तु विशिष्टा ये, तान्निबोध द्विजोत्तम ।
नायका मम सैन्यस्य, संज्ञार्थं तान्ब्रवीमि ते ॥७॥

asmākam tu viśiṣṭā ye / tān nibodha dvijottama
nāyakā mama sainyasya / saṁjñārthaṁ tān bravīmi te

7. Know well, o noblest of the twice born, those who are pre-eminent among us. I speak to you of the leaders of my army that you may know them.

भवान्भीष्मश्च कर्णश्च, कृपश्च समितिंजयः ।
अश्वत्थामा विकर्णश्च, सौमदत्तिस्तथैव च ॥८॥

bhavān bhīṣmaś ca karṇaś ca / kṛpaś ca samitiñjayaḥ
aśvatthāmā vikarṇaś ca / saumadattis tathaiva ca

8. Thyself and Bhishma and Karna and Kripa, victor in battle; Ashvatthama and Vikarna and also the son of Somadatta.

अन्ये च बहवः शूराः, मदर्थे त्यक्तजीविताः ।
नानाशस्त्रप्रहरणाः, सर्वे युद्धविशारदाः ॥९॥

anye ca bahavaḥ śūrā / mad-arthe tyakta-jīvitāḥ
nānā-śastra-praharaṇāḥ / sarve yuddha-viśāradāḥ

9. And many other heroes there are, armed with various weapons, all skilled in warfare, who have risked their lives for me.

अपर्याप्तं तदस्माकं, बलं भीष्माभिरक्षितम् ।
पर्याप्तं त्विदमेतेषां, बलं भीमाभिरक्षितम् ॥१०॥

aparyāptaṁ tad asmākaṁ / balaṁ bhīṣmābhirakṣitam
paryāptaṁ tv idam eteṣāṁ / balaṁ bhīmābhirakṣitam

10. Unlimited is that army of ours commanded by Bhishma, whereas this, their army, commanded by Bhima, is limited.

अयनेषु च सर्वेषु, यथाभागमवस्थिताः ।
भीष्ममेवाभिरक्षन्तु, भवन्तः सर्व एव हि ॥११॥

ayaneṣu ca sarveṣu / yathā-bhāgam avasthitāḥ
bhīṣmam evābhirakṣantu / bhavantaḥ sarva eva hi

11. Therefore, stationed in your respective positions on all fronts, support Bhishma alone, all of you!

तस्य संजनयन्हर्षं, कुरुवृद्धः पितामहः ।
सिंहनादं विनद्योच्चैः, शङ्खं दध्मौ प्रतापवान् ॥१२॥

tasya sañjanayan harṣaṁ / kuru-vṛddhaḥ pitāmahaḥ
siṁha-nādaṁ vinadyoccaiḥ / śaṅkhaṁ dadhmau pratāpavān

12. The aged Kuru, the glorious grandsire (Bhishma), gave a loud roar like a lion and blew his conch, gladdening the heart of Duryodhana.

ततः शङ्खाश्च भेर्यश्च, पणवानकगोमुखाः ।
सहसैवाभ्यहन्यन्त, स शब्दस्तुमुलोऽभवत् ॥१३॥

tataḥ śaṅkhāś ca bheryaś ca / paṇavānaka-gomukhāḥ
sahasaivābhyahanyanta / sa śabdas tumulo'bhavat

13. Then quite suddenly conches, horns, kettledrums, tabors and drums blared forth, and the sound was tumultuous.

ततः श्वेतैर्हयैर्युक्ते, महति स्यन्दने स्थितौ ।
माधवः पाण्डवश्चैव, दिव्यौ शङ्खौ प्रदध्मतुः ॥१४॥

tataḥ śvetair hayair yukte / mahati syandane sthitau
mādhavaḥ pāṇḍavaś caiva / divyau śaṅkhau pradadhmatuḥ

14. Then, seated in a great chariot yoked to white horses, Madhava (Lord Krishna) and the son of Pandu (Arjuna) also blew their glorious conches.

पाञ्चजन्यं हृषीकेशो, देवदत्तं धनंजयः ।
पौण्ड्रं दध्मौ महाशङ्खं, भीमकर्मा वृकोदरः ॥१५॥

pāñcajanyaṁ hṛṣīkeśo / devadattaṁ dhanañjayaḥ
pauṇḍraṁ dadhmau mahā-śaṅkhaṁ / bhīma-karmā vṛkodaraḥ

15. Hrishikesha (Lord Krishna) blew Panchajanya, Dhananjaya (Arjuna) blew Devadatta, Bhima of powerful deeds blew his great conch Paundra.

अनन्तविजयं राजा, कुन्तीपुत्रो युधिष्ठिरः ।
नकुलः सहदेवश्च, सुघोषमणिपुष्पकौ ॥१६॥

anantavijayaṁ rājā / kuntī-putro yudhiṣṭhiraḥ
nakulaḥ sahadevaś ca / sughoṣa-maṇipuṣpakau

16. King Yudhishthira, the son of Kunti, blew his conch Anantavijaya; Nakula and Sahadeva blew Sughosha and Manipushpaka.

काश्यश्च परमेष्वासः, शिखण्डी च महारथः ।
धृष्टद्युम्नो विराटश्च, सात्यकिश्चापराजितः ॥१७॥

kāśyaś ca parameṣvāsaḥ / śikhaṇḍī ca mahā-rathaḥ
dhṛṣṭadyumno virāṭaś ca / sātyakiś cāparājitaḥ

17. The King of Kashi, the great archer, and Shikhandi, the maharathi, Dhrishtadyumna and Virata and Satyaki, the unsubdued.

द्रुपदो द्रौपदेयाश्च सर्वशः पृथिवीपते ।
सौभद्रश्चमहाबाहुः शङ्खान्दध्मुः पृथक् पृथक् ॥१८॥

drupado draupadeyāś ca sarvaśaḥ pṛthivī-pate
saubhadraś ca mahā-bāhuḥ śaṅkhān dadhmuḥ pṛthak pṛthak

18. Drupada, as well as the sons of Draupadi, and the mighty-armed son of Subhadra, O Lord of earth, all blew their different conches.

स घोषो धार्तराष्ट्राणां, हृदयानि व्यदारयत् ।
नभश्च पृथिवीञ्चैव, तुमुलो व्यनुनादयन् ॥१९॥

sa ghoṣo dhārtarāṣṭrāṇāṁ / hṛdayāni vyadārayat
nabhaś ca pṛthivīñ caiva / tumulo 'bhyanunādayan

19. That tumultuous uproar, reverberating through earth and sky, rent the hearts of Dhritarashtra's men.

अथ व्यवस्थितान्दृष्ट्वा, धार्तराष्ट्रान्कपिध्वजः ।
प्रवृत्ते शस्त्रसंपाते, धनुरुद्यम्य पाण्डवः ॥२०॥

atha vyavasthitān dṛṣṭvā / dhārtarāṣṭrān kapi-dhvajaḥ
pravṛtte śastra-sampāte / dhanur udyamya pāṇḍavaḥ

20. Then, seeing the sons of Dhritarashtra drawn up in battle order, as missiles were about to fly, the son of Pandu (Arjuna), whose banner bore the image of Hanuman, took up his bow.

हृषीकेशं तदा वाक्यमिदमाह महीपते ।
अर्जुन उवाच ।
सेनयोरुभयोर्मध्ये रथं स्थापय मेऽच्युत ॥२१॥

hṛṣīkeśaṁ tadā vākyam idam āha mahī-pate
arjuna uvāca
senayor ubhayor madhye rathaṁ sthāpaya me 'cyuta

21. Then, Arjuna said: O Lord of earth, Hrishikesha (Lord Krishna), Draw up my chariot between the two armies, O Achyuta.

यावदेतान्निरीक्षेऽहं योद्धुकामानवस्थितान् ।
कैर्मया सह योद्धव्यमस्मिन्रणसमुद्यमे ॥२२॥

yāvad etān nirīkṣe 'haṁ yoddhu-kāmān avasthitān
kair mayā saha yoddhavyam asmin raṇa-samudyame

22. So that I may observe those who stand here eager for battle and know with whom I should fight in this toil of war.

योत्स्यमानानवेक्षेऽहं य एतेऽत्र समागताः ।
धार्तराष्ट्रस्य दुर्बुद्धेर्युद्धे प्रियचिकीर्षवः ॥२३॥

yotsyamānān avekṣe 'haṁ ya ete 'tra samāgatāḥ
dhārtarāṣṭrasya durbuddher yuddhe priya-cikīrṣavaḥ

23. Let me look on those who are assembled here ready to fight, eager to accomplish in battle what is dear to the evil-minded son of Dhritarashtra.

संजय उवाच ।
एवमुक्तो हृषीकेशो, गुडाकेशेन भारत ।
सेनयोरुभयोर्मध्ये, स्थापयित्वा रथोत्तमम् ॥२४॥

sañjaya uvāca
evam ukto hṛṣīkeśo / guḍākeśena bhārata
senayor ubhayor madhye / sthāpayitvā rathottamam

24. Sanjaya said: O Bharata, thus invoked by Gudakesha (Arjuna), Hrishikesha (Lord Krishna), having drawn up the magnificent chariot between the two armies.

भीष्मद्रोणप्रमुखतः सर्वेषां च महीक्षिताम् ।
उवाच पार्थ पश्यैतान्समवेतान्कुरूनिति ॥२५॥

bhīṣma-droṇa-pramukhataḥ sarveṣāṁ ca mahīkṣitām
uvāca pārtha paśyaitān samavetān kurūn iti

25. Before Bhishma and Drona and all the rulers of the earth, said: Partha (Arjuna)! behold these Kurus gathered together.

तत्रापश्यत्स्थितान्पार्थः पितनथ पितामहान्
आचार्यान्मातुलान्भ्रातन्पुत्रान्पौत्रान्सखींस्तथा ॥२६॥

tatrāpaśyat sthitān pārthaḥ pitṝn atha pitāmahān
ācāryān mātulān bhrātṝn putrān pautrān sakhīṁs tathā

26. The son of Pritha (Arjuna) saw there before him uncles and grandfathers, teachers, maternal uncles, brothers, sons and grandsons and many friends as well.

श्वशुरान्सुहृदश्चैव, सेनयोरुभयोरपि
तान्समीक्ष्य स कौन्तेयः, सर्वान्बन्धूनवस्थितान् ॥२७॥
कृपया परयाविष्टो, विषीदन्निदमब्रवीत् ।
अर्जुन उवाच ।
दृष्ट्वेमं स्वजनं कृष्ण, युयुत्सुं समुपस्थितम् ॥२८॥

śvaśurān suhṛdaś caiva / senayor ubhayor api
tān samīkṣya sa kaunteyaḥ / sarvān bandhūn avasthitān

kṛpayā parayāviṣṭo / viṣīdann idam abravīt
arjuna uvāca
dṛṣṭvemām svajanān kṛṣṇa / yuyutsūn samupasthitām

27 & 28. Then that son of Kunti (Arjuna), seeing all these kinsmen thus present, possessed by extreme compassion, spoke thus in grief: Seeing these my kinsmen, O Krishna, gathered, eager to fight,

सीदन्ति मम गात्राणि, मुखं च परिशुष्यति ।
वेपथुश्च शरीरे मे, रोमहर्षश्च जायते ॥२९॥

sīdanti mama gātrāṇi / mukham ca pariśuṣyati
vepathuś ca śarīre me / roma-harṣaś ca jāyate

29. My limbs fail, my mouth is parched, my body quivers and my hair stands on end.

गाण्डीवं स्रंसते हस्तात्त्वक्चैव परिदह्यते ।
न च शक्नोम्यवस्थातुं भ्रमतीव च मे मनः ॥३०॥

gāṇḍīvaṁ sraṁsate hastāt tvak caiva paridahyate
na ca śaknomyavasthātuṁ bhramatīva ca me manaḥ

30. Gandiva (the bow) slips from my hand and even my skin burns all over; I am unable to stand and my mind seems to whirl.

निमित्तानि च पश्यामि, विपरीतानि केशव ।
न च श्रेयोऽनुपश्यामि, हत्वा स्वजनमाहवे ॥३१॥

nimittāni ca paśyāmi / viparītāni keśava
na ca śreyo 'nupaśyāmi / hatvā svajanam āhave

31. And I see adverse omens, O Keshava (Lord Krishna), nor can I see good from killing my kinsmen in battle.

न काङ्क्षे विजयं कृष्ण, न च राज्यं सुखानि च ।
किं नो राज्येन गोविन्द, किं भोगैर्जीवितेन वा ॥३२॥

na kāṅkṣe vijayaṁ kṛṣṇa / na ca rājyaṁ sukhāni ca
kiṁ no rājyena govinda / kiṁ bhogair jīvitena vā

32. I desire not victory, O Krishna, nor a kingdom, nor pleasures. Of what avail will a kingdom be to us, or enjoyments, or even life, O Govinda?

येषामर्थे काङ्क्षितं नो, राज्यं भोगाः सुखानि च ।
त इमेऽवस्थिता युद्धे, प्राणांस्त्यक्त्वा धनानि च ॥३३॥
आचार्याः पितरः पुत्रास्तथैव च पितामहाः ।
मातुलाः श्वशुराः पौत्राः स्यालाः संबन्धिनस्तथा ॥३४॥

yeṣām arthe kāṅkṣitaṁ no / rājyaṁ bhogāḥ sukhāni ca
ta ime 'vastitā yuddhe / prāṇāṁs tyaktvā dhanāni ca

ācāryāḥ pitaraḥ putrās tathaiva ca pitāmahāḥ
mātulāḥ śvaśurāḥ pautrāḥ śyālāḥ sambandhinas tathā

33 & 34. Those for whose sake we desire a kingdom, enjoyments and comforts are here on the battlefield, having resigned their lives and riches. Teachers, uncles, sons and likewise grandfathers, maternal uncles, fathers-in-law, grandsons, brothers-in-law and other kinsmen.

एतान्न हन्तुमिच्छामि, घ्नतोऽपि मधुसूदन ।
अपि त्रैलोक्यराज्यस्य, हेतोः किं नु महीकृते ॥३५॥

etān na hantum icchāmi / ghnato 'pi madhusūdana
api trailokya-rājyasya / hetoḥ kin nu mahī-kṛte

35. O Madhusudana (Lord Krishna), these I do not wish to kill - though they might kill me otherwise - even for the sake of sovereignty of the three worlds, how much less for this world.

निहत्य धार्तराष्ट्रान्नः का प्रीतिः स्याज्जनार्दन ।
पापमेवाश्रयेदस्मान्हत्वैतानाततायिनः ॥३६॥

nihatya dhārtarāṣṭrān naḥ kā prītiḥ syāj janārdana
pāpam evāśrayed asmān hatvaitān ātatāyinaḥ

36. What happiness could come to us from slaying the sons of Dhritarashtra, O Janardana (Lord Krishna)? Only sin could come upon us through killing these aggressors.

तस्मान्नार्हा वयं हन्तुं, धार्तराष्ट्रान्स्वबान्धवान् ।
स्वजनं हि कथं हत्वा, सुखिनः स्याम माधव ॥३७॥

tasmān nārhā vayaṁ hantuṁ /dhārtarāṣṭrān sva-bāndhavān
svajanaṁ hi kathaṁ hatvā / sukhinaḥ syāma mādhava

37. Therefore it would not be right for us to kill the sons of Dhritarashtra, our own kinsmen. How should we be happy after killing our own people, O Madhava?

यद्यप्येते न पश्यन्ति, लोभोपहतचेतसः ।

कुलक्षयकृतं दोषं, मित्रद्रोहे च पातकम् ॥३८॥

yadyapy ete na paśyanti / lobhopahata-cetasaḥ
kula-kṣaya-kṛtaṁ doṣaṁ / mitra-drohe ca pātakam

38. Although, their minds clouded by greed, they see no wrong in bringing destruction to the family and no sin in treachery to friends,

कथं न ज्ञेयमस्माभिः, पापादस्मान्निवर्तितुम् ।
कुलक्षयकृतं दोषं, प्रपश्यद्भिर्जनार्दन ॥३९॥

kathaṁ na jñeyam asmābhiḥ / pāpād asmān nivarttitum
kula-kṣaya-kṛtaṁ doṣaṁ / prapaśyadbhir janārdana

39. How should we not know to turn away from this sin, we who clearly see the wrong in bringing destruction upon the family, O Janardana ?

कुलक्षये प्रणश्यन्ति कुलधर्माः सनातनाः ।
धर्मे नष्टे कुलं कृत्स्नमधर्मोऽभिभवत्युत ॥४०॥

kula-kṣaye praṇaśyanti kula-dharmāḥ sanātanāḥ
dharme naṣṭe kulaṁ kṛtsnam adharmo 'bhibhavaty uta

40. The age-old family dharmas are lost in the destruction of a family. Its dharma lost, adharma overtakes the entire family.

अधर्माभिभवात्कृष्ण, प्रदुष्यन्ति कुलस्त्रियः ।
स्त्रीषु दुष्टासु वार्ष्णेय, जायते वर्णसंकरः ॥४१॥

adharmābhibhavāt kṛṣṇa / praduṣyanti kula-striyaḥ
strīṣu duṣṭāsu vārṣṇeya / jāyate varṇa-saṅkaraḥ

41. When adharma prevails, O Krishna, the women of the family become corrupt, and with the corruption of women, O Varshneya, intermixture of castes happens.

संकरो नरकायैव, कुलघ्नानां कुलस्य च ।
पतन्ति पितरो ह्येषां, लुप्तपिण्डोदकक्रियाः ॥४२॥

saṅkaro narakāyaiva / kula-ghnānāṁ kulasya ca
patanti pitaro hy eṣāṁ / lupta-piṇḍodaka-kriyāḥ

42. This admixture of races leads only to hell, both for the family and its destroyers. Their forefathers fall as well, when the offerings for the Pitruloka cease.

दोषैरेतैः कुलघ्नानां, वर्णसंकरकारकैः ।
उत्साद्यन्ते जातिधर्माः, कुलधर्माश्च शाश्वताः ॥४३॥

doṣair etaiḥ kula-ghnānāṁ / varṇa-saṅkara-kārakaiḥ
utsādyante jāti-dharmāḥ / kula-dharmāś ca śāśvatāḥ

43. Through the wrongs done by the destroyers of the family, in causing the intermixing of castes, the immemorial dharmas of caste and family become lost.

उत्सन्नकुलधर्माणां, मनुष्याणां जनार्दन ।
नरकेऽनियतं वासो, भवतीत्यनुशुश्रुम ॥४४॥

utsanna-kula-dharmāṇāṁ / manuṣyāṇāṁ janārdana
narakea niyataṁ vāso / bhavatīty anuśuśruma

44. Men whose family dharmas have lapsed, so we have heard, O Janardana (Lord Krishna), necessarily live in hell.

अहो बत महत्पापं, कर्तुं व्यवसिता वयम् ।
यद्राज्यसुखलोभेन, हन्तुं स्वजनमुद्यताः ॥४५॥

aho bata mahat-pāpaṁ / karttuṁ vyavasitā vayam
yad rājya-sukha-lobhena / hantuṁ svajanam udyatāḥ

45. Alas! We are resolved to commit great sin in that we are prepared to slay our kinsmen out of greed for the pleasures of a kingdom.

यदि मामप्रतीकारमशस्त्रं शस्त्रपाणयः ।
धार्तराष्ट्रा रणे हन्युस्तन्मे क्षेमतरं भवेत् ॥४६॥

yadi mām apratīkāram aśastraṁ śastra-pāṇayaḥ
dhārtarāṣṭrā raṇe hanyus tan me kṣemataraṁ bhavet

46. It were better for me if the sons of Dhritarashtra, weapons in hand, should slay me, unresisting and unarmed in battle.

संजय उवाच ।
एवमुक्त्वाऽर्जुनः संख्ये, रथोपस्थ उपाविशत् ।
विसृज्य सशरं चापं, शोकसंविग्नमानसः ॥४७॥

evam uktvārjunaḥ saṅkhye / rathopastha upāviśat
visṛjya sa-śaraṁ cāpaṁ / śoka-saṁvigna-mānasaḥ

47. Sanjaya said: Having spoken thus at the time of battle, casting away arrows and bows, Arjuna sat down on the seat of the chariot, his mind overwhelmed with sorrow.

ॐ तत् सत् । इति श्रीमद्भगवद्गीतासु उपनिषत्सु ब्रह्मविद्यायां योगशास्त्रे श्रीकृष्णार्जुन संवादे अर्जुनविषादयोगो नाम प्रथमोऽध्यायः ॥

Om Tat Sat. Iti Śrimad Bhagavad Gitasu Upanishatsu Brahmavidyayām yogaśastre Sri Krishnarjuna samvade Arjuna vishadayogo nama prathamodhyayaḥ

Thus ends the first chapter named "Arjuna Vishada-Yoga" (Arjuna's Dilemma) of the Upanishad of the Bhagavad Gita, the scripture of yoga, dealing with the science of the Absolute in the form of the dialogue between Krishna and Arjuna.

अथ द्वितीयोऽध्यायः - सांख्ययोगः

Chapter Two: Sāṅkhya-Yoga

संजय उवाच ।
तं तथा कृपयाविष्टमश्रुपूर्णाकुलेक्षणम् ।
विषीदन्तमिदं वाक्यमुवाच मधुसूदनः ॥१॥

sañjaya uvāca
taṁ tathā kṛpayāviṣṭam aśru-pūrṇākulekṣaṇam
viṣīdantam idaṁ vākyam uvāca madhusūdanaḥ

1. Sanjaya said: To him thus overcome by compassion, full of sorrow, his eyes distressed and filled with tears, Madhusudana (Lord Krishna) spoke thus:

श्रीभगवानुवाच ।
कुतस्त्वा कश्मलमिदं विषमे समुपस्थितम् ।
अनार्यजुष्टमस्वर्ग्यमकीर्तिकरमर्जुन ॥२॥

śrī bhagavān uvāca
kutas tvā kaśmalam idaṁ viṣame
samupasthitam
anārya-juṣṭam asvargyam akīrtti-karam arjuna

2. The Blessed Lord said: Whence has this blemish, alien to honourable men, causing disgrace and opposed to heaven, come upon you, Arjuna, at this untimely hour?

क्लैब्यं मास्म गमः पार्थ नैतत्त्वय्युपपद्यते ।
क्षुद्रं हृदयदौर्बल्यं त्यक्त्वोत्तिष्ठ परंतप ॥३॥

klaibyaṁ mā sma gamaḥ pārtha naitat tvayy upapadyate
kṣudraṁ hṛdaya-daurbalyaṁ tyaktvottiṣṭha parantapa

3. Partha! Yield not to unmanliness. It is unworthy of you. Shake off this paltry faintheartedness. Stand up, O scorcher of enemies!

अर्जुन उवाच ।
कथं भीष्ममहं संख्ये, द्रोणं च मधुसूदन ।
इषुभिः प्रतियोत्स्यामि, पूजार्हावरिसूदन ॥४॥

arjuna uvāca
kathaṁ bhīṣmam ahaṁ saṅkhye / droṇañ ca madhusūdana
iṣubhiḥ pratiyotsyāmi / pūjārhāv arisūdana

4. Arjuna said: How shall I fight Bhishma and Drona with arrows on the battlefield, O Madhusudana? Worthy of reverence are they, O slayer of enemies!

गुरूनहत्वा हि महानुभावान् श्रेयो भोक्तुं भैक्ष्यमपीह लोके ।
हत्वार्थकामांस्तु गुरूनिहैव भुञ्जीय भोगान्रुधिरप्रदिग्धान्
॥५॥

gurūn ahatvā hi mahānubhāvān
śreyo bhoktuṁ bhaikṣyam apīha loke
hatvārtha-kāmāṁs tu gurūn ihaiva
bhuñjīya bhogān rudhira-pradigdhān

5. It is certainly better to live even on alms in this world than to slay these noble-minded masters; for though they are desirous of gain, having killed them I should enjoy only blood-stained pleasures in this world.

न चैतद्विद्मः कतरन्नो गरीयो यद्वा जयेम यदि वा नो जयेयुः ।
यानेव हत्वा न जिजीविषामस्तेऽवस्थिताः प्रमुखे धार्तराष्ट्राः ॥६॥

na caitad vidmaḥ kataran no garīyo yad vā
jayema yadi vā no jayeyuḥ
yān eva hatvā na jijīviṣāmaste 'vasthitāḥ
pramukhe dhārtarāṣṭrāḥ

6. We do not know which is better for us: that we should conquer them or they should conquer us. The sons of Dhritarashta stand face to face with us. If we killed them we should not wish to live.

कार्पण्यदोषोपहतस्वभावः पृच्छामि त्वां धर्मसंमूढचेताः ।
यच्छ्रेयः स्यान्निश्चितं ब्रूहि तन्मे शिष्यस्तेऽहं शाधि मां त्वां प्रपन्नम् ॥७॥

kārpaṇya-doṣopahata-svabhāvaḥ
pṛcchāmi tvāṁ dharma-sammūḍha-cetāḥ
yac chreyaḥ syān niścitaṁ brūhi tan me
śiṣyas te 'haṁ śādhi māṁ tvāṁ prapannam

7. My nature smitten with the taint of weakness, confused in mind about dharma, I pray Thee, tell me decisively what is good for me. I am Thy disciple; teach me for I have taken refuge in Thee.

न हि प्रपश्यामि ममापनुद्यात् यच्छोकमुच्छोषणमिन्द्रियाणाम् ।
अवाप्य भूमावसपत्नमृद्धं राज्यं सुराणामपि चाधिपत्यम् ॥८॥

na hi prapaśyāmi mamāpanudyād
yac chokam ucchoṣaṇam indriyāṇām
avāpya bhūmāv asapatnam ṛddhaṁ
rājyaṁ surāṇām api cādhipatyam

8. Indeed I do not see what could dispel the grief that dries up my senses, though I should obtain an unrivalled and prosperous kingdom on earth and even lordship of the gods.

संजय उवाच ।
एवमुक्त्वा हृषीकेशं गुडाकेशः परंतपः ।
न योत्स्य इति गोविन्दमुक्त्वा तूष्णीं बभूव ह ॥९॥

sañjaya uvāca
evam uktvā hṛṣīkeśaṁ guḍākeśaḥ parantapaḥ
na yotsya iti govindam uktvā tūṣṇīṁ babhūva ha

9. After speaking these words, Gudakesha, the chastiser of enemies, said to Sri Krishna, O Govinda, I shall not fight, and fell silent.

तमुवाच हृषीकेशः, प्रहसन्निव भारत ।
सेनयोरुभयोर्मध्ये, विषीदन्तमिदं वचः ॥१०॥

tam uvāca hṛṣīkeśaḥ / prahasann iva bhārata
senayor ubhayor madhye / viṣīdantam idaṁ vacaḥ

10. To him, O Bharata (Dhritarashtra), sorrowing in the midst of the two armies, Hrishikesha smilingly spoke these words:

श्रीभगवानुवाच ।
अशोच्यानन्वशोचस्त्वं, प्रज्ञावादांश्च भाषसे ।
गतासूनगतासूंश्च, नानुशोचन्ति पण्डिताः ॥११॥

śrī bhagavān uvāca
aśocyān anvaśocas tvaṁ / prajñā-vādāṁś ca bhāṣase
gatāsūn agatāsūṁś ca / nānuśocanti paṇḍitāḥ

11. The Blessed Lord said: You grieve for those for whom there should be no grief, yet speak as do the wise. Wise men grieve neither for the dead nor for the living.

नत्वेवाहं जातु नासं, न त्वं नेमे जनाधिपाः ।
न चैव न भविष्यामः, सर्वे वयमतः परम् ॥१२॥

na tv evāhaṁ jātu nāsaṁ / na tvaṁ neme janādhipāḥ
na caiva na bhaviṣyāmaḥ / sarve vayam ataḥ param

12. There never was a time when I was not, nor you, nor these rulers of men. Nor will there ever be a time when all of us shall cease to be.

देहिनोऽस्मिन्यथा देहे कौमारं यौवनं जरा ।
तथा देहान्तरप्राप्तिर्धीरस्तत्र न मुह्यति ॥१३॥

dehino 'smin yathā dehe kaumāraṁ yauvanaṁ jarā
tathā dehāntara-prāptir dhīras tatra na muhyati

13. As the dweller in this body passes into childhood, youth and age, so also does he pass into another body. This does not bewilder the wise.

मात्रास्पर्शास्तु कौन्तेय शीतोष्णसुखदुःखदाः ।
आगमापायिनोऽनित्यास्तांस्तितिक्षस्व भारत ॥१४॥

mātrā-sparśās tu kaunteya śītoṣṇa-sukha-duḥkha-dāḥ
āgamāpāyino 'nityās tāṁs titikṣasva bhārata

14. Contacts (of the senses) with their objects, O son of Kunti, give rise to (the experience of) cold and heat, pleasure and pain. Transient, they come and go. Bear them patiently, O Bharata!

यं हि न व्यथयन्त्येते, पुरुषं पुरुषर्षभ ।
समदुःखसुखं धीरं, सोऽमृतत्वाय कल्पते ॥१५॥

yaṁ hi na vyathayanty ete / puruṣaṁ puruṣarṣabha
sama-duḥkha-sukhaṁ dhīraṁ / so 'mṛtatvāya kalpate

15. That man indeed whom these (contacts) do not disturb, who is even-minded in pleasure and pain, steadfast, he is fit for immortality, O best of men!

नासतो विद्यते भावो नाभावो विद्यते सतः ।
उभयोरपि दृष्टोऽन्तस्त्वनयोस्तत्त्वदर्शिभिः ॥१६॥

nāsato vidyate bhāvo nābhāvo vidyate sataḥ
ubhayor api dṛṣṭo 'ntas tv anayos tattva-darśibhiḥ

16. The unreal has no being; the real never ceases to be. The final truth about them both has thus been perceived by the seers of ultimate Reality.

अविनाशि तु तद्विद्धि, येन सर्वमिदं ततम् ।
विनाशमव्ययस्यास्य, न कश्चित्कर्तुमर्हति ॥१७॥

avināśi tu tad viddhi / yena sarvam idaṁ tatam
vināśam avyayasyāsya / na kaścit karttum arhati

17. Know That to be indeed indestructible by which all this is pervaded. None can work the destruction of this immutable Being.

अन्तवन्त इमे देहाः, नित्यस्योक्ताः शरीरिणः ।
अनाशिनोऽप्रमेयस्य, तस्माद्युध्यस्व भारत ॥१८॥

antavanta ime dehā / nityasyoktāḥ śarīriṇaḥ
anāśino 'prameyasya / tasmād yudhyasva bhārata

18. These bodies are known to have an end; the dweller in the body is eternal, imperishable, infinite. Therefore, O Bharata, fight!

य एनं वेत्ति हन्तारं, यश्चैनं मन्यते हतम् ।
उभौ तौ न विजानीतो, नायं हन्ति न हन्यते ॥१९॥

ya enaṁ vetti hantāraṁ / yaś cainaṁ manyate hatam
ubhau tau na vijānīto / nāyaṁ hanti na hanyate

19. He who understands him to be the slayer, and he who takes him to be the slain, both fail to perceive the truth. He neither slays nor is slain.

न जायते म्रियते वा कदाचि - न्नायं भूत्वा भविता वा न भूयः ।
अजो नित्यः शाश्वतोऽयं पुराणो न हन्यते हन्यमाने शरीरे ॥२०॥

na jāyate mriyate vā kadācit
nāyaṁ bhūtvā bhavitā vā na bhūyaḥ
ajo nityaḥ śāśvato 'yaṁ purāṇo
na hanyate hanyamāne śarīre

20. He is never born, nor does he ever die; nor once having been, does he cease to be; unborn, eternal, everlasting, ancient, he is not slain when the body is slain.

वेदाविनाशिनं नित्यं, य एनमजमव्ययम् ।
कथं स पुरुषः पार्थ, कं घातयति हन्तिकम् ॥२१॥

vedāvināśinaṁ nityaṁ / ya enam ajam avyayam
kathaṁ sa puruṣaḥ pārtha / kaṁ ghātayati hanti kam

21. One who knows him to be indestructible, everlasting, unborn, undying, how can that man, O Partha, slay or cause anyone to slay?

वासांसि जीर्णानि यथा विहाय नवानि गृह्णाति
नरोऽपराणि ।
तथा शरीराणि विहाय जीर्णा - न्यन्यनि संयाति नवानि
देही ॥२२॥

vāsāṁsi jīrṇāni yathā vihāya navāni gṛhṇāti
naro 'parāṇi
tathā śarīrāṇi vihāya jīrṇāny anyāni saṁyāti
navāni dehī

22. As a man casting off worn-out garments takes other new ones, so the dweller in the body casting off worn-out bodies takes others that are new.

नैनं छिन्दन्ति शस्त्राणि, नैनं दहति पावकः ।
न चैनं क्लेदयन्त्यापो, न शोषयति मारुतः ॥२३॥

nainaṁ chindanti śastrāṇi / nainaṁ dahati
pāvakaḥ
na cainaṁ kledayanty āpo / na śoṣayati
mārutaḥ

23. Weapons cannot cleave him, nor fire burn him; water cannot wet him, nor wind dry him away.

अच्छेद्योऽयमदाह्योऽयमक्लेद्योऽशोष्य एव च ।
नित्यः सर्वगतः स्थाणुरचलोऽयं सनातनः ॥२४॥

acchedyo 'yam adāhyo 'yam akledyo 'śoṣya eva ca
nityaḥ sarva-gataḥ sthāṇur acalo 'yaṁ sanātanaḥ

24. He is uncleavable; he cannot be burned; he cannot be wetted, nor yet can he be dried. He is eternal, all pervading, stable, immovable, ever the same.

अव्यक्तोऽयमचिन्त्योऽयमविकार्योऽयमुच्यते ।
तस्मादेवं विदित्वैनं नानुशोचितुमर्हसि ॥२५॥

avyakto 'yam acintyo 'yam avikāryo 'yam ucyate
tasmād evaṁ viditvainaṁ nānuśocitum arhasi

25. He is declared to be unmanifest, unthinkable, unchangeable; therefore knowing him as such you should not grieve.

अथ चैनं नित्यजातं, नित्यं वा मन्यसे मृतम् ।
तथापि त्वं महाबाहो, नैनं शोचितुमर्हसि ॥२६॥

atha cainaṁ nitya-jātaṁ / nityaṁ vā manyase mṛtam
tathāpi tvaṁ mahā-bāho / nainaṁ śocitum arhasi

26. Even if you think of him as constantly taking birth and constantly dying, even then, O mighty-armed, you should not grieve like this.

जातस्य हि ध्रुवो मृत्युर्ध्रुवं जन्म मृतस्य च ।
तस्मादपरिहार्येऽर्थे न त्वं शोचितुमर्हसि ॥२७॥

jātasya hi dhruvo mṛtyur dhruvaṁ janma mṛtasya ca
tasmād aparihārye 'rthe na tvaṁ śocitum arhasi

27. Certain indeed is death for the born and certain is birth for the dead; therefore over the inevitable you should not grieve.

अव्यक्तादीनि भूतानि, व्यक्तमध्यानि भारत ।
अव्यक्तनिधनान्येव, तत्र का परिदेवना ॥२८॥

avyaktādīni bhūtāni / vyakta-madhyāni bhārata
avyakta-nidhanāny eva / tatra kā paridevanā

28. Creatures are unmanifest in the beginning, manifest in the middle state and unmanifest again at the end, Oh Bharata! What grief is there in this?

आश्चर्यवत्पश्यति कश्चिदेन - माश्चर्यवद् वदति तथैव चान्यः ।
आश्चर्यवच्चैनमन्यः शृणोति श्रुत्वाप्येनं वेद न चैव कश्चित् ॥२६॥

āścaryavat paśyati kaścid enam-
āścaryavad vadati tathaiva cānyaḥ
āścaryavac cainam anyaḥ śṛṇoti
śrutvāpy enaṁ veda na caiva kaścit

29. One sees him as a wonder, another likewise speaks of him as a wonder, and as a wonder another hears of him. Yet even on (seeing, speaking and hearing) some do not understand him.

देही नित्यमवध्योऽयं, देहे सर्वस्य भारत ।
तस्मात्सर्वाणि भूतानि, न त्वं शोचितुमर्हसि ॥३०॥

dehī nityam avadhyo 'yaṁ / dehe sarvasya bhārata
tasmāt sarvāṇi bhūtāni / na tvaṁ śocitum arhasi

30. He who dwells in the body of everyone is eternal and invulnerable, O Bharata; therefore you should not grieve for any creature whatsoever.

स्वधर्ममपि चावेक्ष्य न विकम्पितुमर्हसि ।
धर्म्याद्धि युद्धाच्छ्रेयोऽन्यत्क्षत्रियस्य न विद्यते ॥३१॥

svadharmam api cāvekṣya na vikampitum arhasi
dharmyād dhi yuddhāc chreyo 'nyat kṣatriyasya na vidyate

31. Even if you consider your own dharma you should not waver, for there is nothing better for a kshatriya than a battle in accord with dharma.

यदृच्छया चोपपन्नं, स्वर्गद्वारमपावृतम् ।
सुखिनः क्षत्रियाः पार्थ, लभन्ते युद्धमीदृशम् ॥३२॥

yadṛcchayā copapannaṁ / svarga-dvāram apāvṛtam
sukhinaḥ kṣatriyāḥ pārtha / labhante yuddham īdṛśam

32. Happy are the kshatriyas, O Partha, who find, unsought, such a battle - an open door to heaven.

अथ चेत्त्वमिमं धर्म्यं, संग्रामं न करिष्यसि ।
ततः स्वधर्मं कीर्तिं च, हित्वा पापमवाप्स्यसि ॥३३॥

atha cet tvam imaṁ dharmyaṁ / saṅgrāmaṁ na kariṣyasi
tataḥ svadharmaṁ kīrttiṁ ca / hitvā pāpam avāpsyasi

33. Now, if you do not engage in this battle, which is in accord with dharma, then casting away your own dharma and good fame, you will incur sin.

अकीर्तिं चापि भूतानि कथयिष्यन्ति तेऽव्ययाम् ।
संभावितस्य चाकीर्तिर्मरणादतिरिच्यते ॥३४॥

akīrttiṁ cāpi bhūtāni kathayiṣyanti te 'vyayām
sambhāvitasya cākīrttir maraṇād atiricyate

34. Moreover men will ever tell of your disgrace, and to a man of honour ill fame is worse than death.

भयाद्रणादुपरतं, मंस्यन्ते त्वां महारथाः ।
येषां च त्वं बहुमतो, भूत्वा यास्यसि लाघवम् ॥३५॥

bhayād raṇād uparataṁ / maṁsyante tvāṁ mahā-rathāḥ
yeṣāṁ ca tvaṁ bahu-mato / bhūtvā yāsyasi lāghavam

35. The great warriors will think you fled from battle out of fear, and they who held you in esteem will belittle you.

अवाच्यवादांश्च बहून्वदिष्यन्ति तवाहिताः ।
निन्दन्तस्तव सामर्थ्यं ततो दुःखतरं नु किम् ॥३६॥

avācya-vādāṁś ca bahūn vadiṣyanti tavāhitāḥ
nindantas tava sāmarthyaṁ tato duḥkhataraṁ nu kim

36. Your enemies will speak many ill words of you and will deride your strength. What greater pain than this!

हतो वा प्राप्स्यसि स्वर्गं, जित्वा वा भोक्ष्यसे महीम् ।
तस्मादुत्तिष्ठ कौन्तेय, युद्धाय कृतनिश्चयः ॥३७॥

hato vā prāpsyasi svargaṁ / jitvā vā bhokṣyase mahīm
tasmād uttiṣṭha kaunteya / yuddhāya kṛta-niścayaḥ

37. Slain, you will reach heaven; victorious, you will enjoy the earth. Therefore, O son of Kunti, stand up, resolved to fight!

सुखदुःखे समे कृत्वा, लाभालाभौ जयाजयौ ।
ततो युद्धाय युज्यस्व, नैवं पापमवाप्स्यसि ॥३८॥

sukha-duḥkhe same kṛtvā / lābhālābhau jayājayau
tato yuddhāya yujyasva / naivaṁ pāpam avāpsyasi

38. Having gained equanimity in pleasure and pain, in gain and loss, in victory and defeat, then come out to fight. Thus you will not incur sin.

एषा तेऽभिहिता सांख्ये, बुद्धिर्योगे त्विमां शृणु ।
बुद्ध्या युक्तो यया पार्थ, कर्मबन्धं प्रहास्यसि ॥३९॥

eṣā te 'bhihitā sāṅkhye / buddhir yoge tv imāṁ śṛṇu
buddhyā yukto yayā pārtha / karma-bandhaṁ prahāsyasi

39. This which has been set before you is understanding in terms of Sankhya; hear it now in terms of Yoga. Your intellect established through it, O Partha, you will cast away the binding influence of action.

नेहाभिक्रमनाशोऽस्ति, प्रत्यवायो न विद्यते ।
स्वल्पमप्यस्य धर्मस्य, त्रायते महतो भयात् ॥४०॥

nehābhikrama-nāśo 'sti / pratyavāyo na vidyate
svalpam apy asya dharmasya / trāyate mahato bhayāt

40. In this (Yoga) no effort is lost and no obstacle exists. Even a little of this dharma delivers from great fear.

व्यवसायात्मिका बुद्धिरेकेह कुरुनन्दन ।
बहुशाखा ह्यनन्ताश्च बुद्धयोऽव्यवसायिनाम् ॥४१॥

vyavasāyātmikā buddhir ekeha kuru-nandana
bahu-śākhā hy anantāś ca buddhayo
'vyavasāyinām

41. In this Yoga, O joy of the Kurus, the resolute intellect is one-pointed, but many-branched and endlessly diverse are the intellects of the irresolute.

यामिमां पुष्पितां वाचं, प्रवदन्त्यविपश्चितः ।
वेदवादरताः पार्थ, नान्यदस्तीति वादिनः ॥४२॥

yām imāṁ puṣpitāṁ vācaṁ / pravadanty
avipaścitaḥ
veda-vāda-ratāḥ pārtha / nānyad astīti vādinaḥ

42. The undiscerning who are engrossed in the letter of the Veda, O Partha, and declare that there is nothing else, speak flowery words.

कामात्मानः स्वर्गपरा, जन्मकर्मफलप्रदाम् ।
क्रियाविशेषबहुलां, भोगैश्वर्यगतिं प्रति ॥४३॥

kāmātmānaḥ svarga-parā / janma-karma-phala-pradām
kriyā-viśeṣa-bahulāṁ / bhogaiśvarya-gatiṁ prati

43. Filled with desires, with heaven as their goal, (their words) proclaim birth as the reward of action and prescribe many special rites for the attainment of enjoyment and power.

भोगैश्वर्यप्रसक्तानां, तयापहृतचेतसाम् ।
व्यवसायात्मिका बुद्धिः, समाधौ न विधीयते ॥४४॥

bhogaiśvarya-prasaktānāṁ / tayāpahṛta-cetasām
vyavasāyātmikā buddhiḥ / samādhau na vidhīyate

44. The resolute state of intellect does not arise in the mind of those who are deeply attached to enjoyment and power and whose thought is captivated by those (flowery words).

त्रैगुण्यविषया वेदा, निस्त्रैगुण्यो भवार्जुन ।
निर्द्वन्द्वो नित्यसत्त्वस्थो, निर्योगक्षेम आत्मवान् ॥४५॥

traiguṇya-viṣayā vedā / nistraiguṇyo bhavārjuna
nirdvandvo nitya-sattva-stho / niryoga-kṣema ātmavān

45. The Vedas' concern is with the three gunas. Be without the three gunas, O Arjuna, freed from duality, ever firm in purity, independent of possessions, possessed of the Self.

यावानर्थ उदपाने, सर्वतः संप्लुतोदके ।
तावान् सर्वेषु वेदेषु, ब्राह्मणस्य विजानतः ॥४६॥

yāvān artha udapāne / sarvataḥ samplutodake
tāvān sarveṣu vedeṣu / brāhmaṇasya vijānataḥ

46. To the enlightened brahmin all the Vedas are of no more use than is a small well in a place flooded with water on every side.

कर्मण्येवाधिकारस्ते, मा फलेषु कदाचन ।
मा कर्मफलहेतुर्भूर्माते सङ्गोऽस्त्वकर्मणि ॥४७॥

karmaṇy evādhikāras te / mā phaleṣu kadācana
mā karma-phala-hetur bhūr / mā te saṅgo 'stv akarmaṇi

47. You have control over action alone, never over its fruits. Live not for the fruits of action, nor attach yourself to inaction.

योगस्थः कुरु कर्माणि, सङ्गं त्यक्त्वा धनंजय ।
सिद्ध्यसिद्ध्योः समो भूत्वा, समत्वं योग उच्यते ॥४८॥

yoga-sthaḥ kuru karmāṇi / saṅgaṁ tyaktvā dhanañjaya
siddhy-asiddhyoḥ samo bhūtvā / samatvaṁ yoga ucyate

48. Established in Yoga, O winner of wealth, perform actions having abandoned attachment and having become balanced in success and failure, for balance of mind is called Yoga.

दूरेण ह्यवरं कर्म, बुद्धियोगाद्धनंजय ।
बुद्धौ शरणमन्विच्छ, कृपणाः फलहेतवः ॥४६॥

dūreṇa hy avaraṁ karma / buddhi-yogād dhanañjaya
buddhau śaraṇam anviccha / kṛpaṇāḥ phala-hetavaḥ

49. Far away, indeed, from the balanced intellect is the action devoid of greatness, O winner of wealth. Take refuge in the intellect. Pitiful are those who live for the fruits (of action).

बुद्धियुक्तो जहातीह, उभे सुकृतदुष्कृते ।
तस्माद्योगाय युज्यस्व, योगः कर्मसु कौशलम् ॥५०॥

buddhi-yukto jahātīha / ubhe sukṛta-duṣkṛte
tasmād yogāya yujyasva / yogaḥ karmasu kauśalam

50. He whose intellect is united (with the Self) casts off both good and evil even here. Therefore, devote yourself to Yoga. Yoga is skill in action.

कर्मजं बुद्धियुक्ता हि, फलं त्यक्त्वा मनीषिणः ।
जन्मबन्धविनिर्मुक्ताः, पदं गच्छन्त्यनामयम् ॥५१॥

karma-jaṁ buddhi-yuktā hi / phalaṁ tyaktvā manīṣiṇaḥ
janma-bandha-vinirmuktāḥ / padaṁ gacchanty anāmayam

51. The wise, their intellect truly united with the Self, having renounced the fruits born of their actions and being liberated from the bonds of birth, arrive at a state devoid of suffering.

यदा ते मोहकलिलं, बुद्धिर्व्यतितरिष्यति ।
तदा गन्तासि निर्वेदं, श्रोतव्यस्य श्रुतस्य च ॥५२॥

yadā te moha-kalilaṁ / buddhir vyatitariṣyati
tadā gantāsi nirvedaṁ / śrotavyasya śrutasya ca

52. When your intellect crosses the mire of delusion, then will you gain indifference to what has been heard and what is yet to be heard.

श्रुतिविप्रतिपन्ना ते यदा स्थास्यति निश्चला ।
समाधावचला बुद्धिस्तदा योगमवाप्स्यसि ॥५३॥

śruti-vipratipannā te yadā sthāsyati niścalā
samādhau acalā buddhis tadā yogam avāpsyasi

53. When your intellect, bewildered by Vedic texts, shall stand unshaken, steadfast in the Self, then will you attain to Yoga.

अर्जुन उवाच ।
स्थितप्रज्ञस्य का भाषा, समाधिस्थस्य केशव ।
स्थितधीः किं प्रभाषेत, किमासीत व्रजेत किम् ॥५४॥

arjuna uvāca
sthita-prajñāsya kā bhāṣā / samādhi-sthasya keśava
sthita-dhīḥ kiṁ prabhāṣeta / kim āsīta vrajeta kim

54. Arjuna said: What are the signs of a man whose intellect is steady, who is absorbed in the Self, O Keshava? How does the man of steady intellect speak, how does he sit, how does he walk?

श्रीभगवानुवाच ।
प्रजहाति यदा कामान्सर्वान्पार्थ मनोगतान् ।
आत्मन्येवात्मना तुष्टः स्थितप्रज्ञस्तदोच्यते ॥५५॥

śrī bhagavān uvāca
prajahāti yadā kāmān sarvān pārtha mano-gatān

ātmany evātmanā tuṣṭaḥ sthita-prajñas tadocyate

55. The Blessed Lord said: When a man completely casts off all desires that have gone (deep) into the mind, O Partha, when he is satisfied in the Self through the Self alone, then is he said to be of steady intellect.

दुःखेष्वनुद्विग्नमनाः, सुखेषु विगतस्पृहः ।
वीतरागभयक्रोधः, स्थितधीर्मुनिरुच्यते ॥५६॥

duḥkheṣv anudvigna-manāḥ / sukheṣu vigata-spṛhaḥ
vīta-rāga-bhaya-krodhaḥ / sthita-dhīr munir ucyate

56. He whose mind is unshaken in the midst of sorrows, who amongst pleasures is free from longing, from whom attachment, fear and anger have departed, he is said to be a sage of steady intellect.

यः सर्वत्रानभिस्नेहस्तत्तत्प्राप्य शुभाशुभम् ।
नाभिनन्दति न द्वेष्टि तस्य प्रज्ञा प्रतिष्ठिता ॥५७॥

yaḥ sarvatrānabhisnehas tat tat prāpya śubhāśubham
nābhinandati na dveṣṭi tasya prajñā pratiṣṭhitā

57. He who has no undue fondness towards anything, who neither exults nor recoils on gaining what is good or bad, his intellect is established.

यदा संहरते चायं कूर्मोऽङ्गानीव सर्वशः ।
इन्द्रियाणीन्द्रियार्थेभ्यस्तस्य प्रज्ञा प्रतिष्ठिता ॥५८॥

yadā saṁharate cāyaṁ kūrmo 'ṅgānīva sarvaśaḥ
indriyāṇīndriyārthebhyas tasya prajñā pratiṣṭhitā

58. And when such a man withdraws his senses from their objects, as a tortoise draws in its limbs from all sides, his intellect is established.

विषया विनिवर्तन्ते, निराहारस्य देहिनः ।
रसवर्जं रसोऽप्यस्य, परं दृष्ट्वा निवर्तते ॥५९॥

viṣayā vinivarttante / nirāhārasya dehinaḥ
rasa-varjaṁ raso 'py asya / paraṁ dṛṣṭvā nivarttate

59. The objects of sense turn away from him who does not feed upon them, but the taste for them persists. On seeing the Supreme even this taste ceases.

यततो ह्यपि कौन्तेय, पुरुषस्य विपश्चितः ।
इन्द्रियाणि प्रमाथीनि, हरन्ति प्रसभं मनः ॥६०॥

yatato hy api kaunteya / puruṣasya vipaścitaḥ
indriyāṇi pramāthīni / haranti prasabhaṁ manaḥ

60. The turbulent senses, O son of Kunti, forcibly carry away the mind even of a discerning man who endeavours (to control them).

तानि सर्वाणि संयम्य, युक्त आसीत मत्परः ।
वशे हि यस्येन्द्रियाणि, तस्य प्रज्ञा प्रतिष्ठिता ॥६१॥

tāni sarvāṇi saṁyamya / yukta āsīta mat-paraḥ
vaśe hi yasyendriyāṇi / tasya prajñā pratiṣṭhitā

61. Having brought them all under control, let him sit united, looking to Me as Supreme; for his intellect is established whose senses are subdued.

ध्यायतो विषयान्पुंसः, सङ्गस्तेषूपजायते ।
सङ्गात्संजायते कामः, कामात्क्रोधोऽभिजायते ॥६२॥

dhyāyato viṣayān puṁsaḥ / saṅgas teṣūpajāyate
saṅgāt sañjāyate kāmaḥ / kāmāt krodho 'bhijāyate

62. Pondering on objects of the senses, a man develops attachment for them; from attachment springs up desire, and desire gives rise to anger.

क्रोधाद्भवति संमोहः, संमोहात्स्मृतिविभ्रमः ।
स्मृतिभ्रंशाद्बुद्धिनाशो, बुद्धिनाशात्प्रणश्यति ॥६३॥

krodhād bhavati sammohaḥ / sammohāt smṛti-vibhramaḥ
smṛti-bhraṁśād buddhi-nāśo / buddhi-nāśāt praṇaśyati

63. From anger arises delusion; from delusion unsteadiness of memory; from unsteadiness of memory destruction of intellect; through the destruction of the intellect he perishes.

रागद्वेषवियुक्तैस्तु, विषयानिन्द्रियैश्चरन् ।
आत्मवश्यैर्विधेयात्मा, प्रसादमधिगच्छति ॥६४॥

rāga-dveṣa-vimuktais tu / viṣayān indriyaiś caran
ātma-vaśyair vidheyātmā / prasādam adhigacchati

64. A man of controlled senses, however, who is free from attachment and aversion, attains happiness of mind even while enjoying various objects through his senses.

प्रसादे सर्वदुःखानां, हानिरस्योपजायते ।
प्रसन्नचेतसो ह्याशु, बुद्धिः पर्यवतिष्ठते ॥६५॥

prasāde sarva-duḥkhānāṁ / hānir asyopajāyate
prasanna-cetaso hy āśu / buddhiḥ paryavatiṣṭhate

65. In 'grace' is born an end to all his sorrows. Indeed the intellect of the man of exalted consciousness soon becomes firmly established.

नास्ति बुद्धिरयुक्तस्य न चायुक्तस्य भावना ।
न चाभावयतः शान्तिरशान्तस्य कुतः सुखम् ॥६६॥

nāsti buddhir ayuktasya na cāyuktasya bhāvanā
na cābhāvayataḥ śāntir aśāntasya kutaḥ sukham

66. He who is not established has no intellect, nor has he any steady thought. The man without steady thought has no peace; for one without peace how can there be happiness?

इन्द्रियाणां हि चरतां, यन्मनोऽनुविधीयते ।
तदस्य हरति प्रज्ञां, वायुर्नावमिवाम्भसि ॥६७॥

indriyāṇāṁ hi caratāṁ / yan mano 'nuvidhīyate
tad asya harati prajñāṁ / vāyur nāvam ivāmbhasi

67. When a man's mind is governed by any of the wandering senses, his intellect is carried away by it as a ship by the wind on water.

तस्माद्यस्य महाबाहो निगृहीतानि सर्वशः ।
इन्द्रियाणीन्द्रियार्थेभ्यस्तस्य प्रज्ञा प्रतिष्ठिता ॥६८॥

tasmād yasya mahā-bāho nigṛhītāni sarvaśaḥ
indriyāṇīndriyārthebhyas tasya prajñā pratiṣhitā

68. Therefore he whose senses are all withdrawn from their objects, O mighty-armed, his intellect is established.

या निशा सर्वभूतानां, तस्यां जागर्ति संयमी ।
यस्यां जाग्रति भूतानि, सा निशा पश्यतो मुनेः ॥६६॥

yā niśā sarva-bhūtānāṁ / tasyāṁ jāgartti saṁyamī
yasyāṁ jāgrati bhūtāni / sā niśā paśyato muneḥ

69. That which is night for all beings, therein the self-controlled is awake. That wherein beings are awake is night for the sage who sees.

आपूर्यमाणमचलप्रतिष्ठं समुद्रमापः प्रविशन्ति यद्वत् ।
तद्वत्कामा यं प्रविशन्ति सर्वे स शान्तिमाप्नोति न
कामकामी ॥७०॥

āpūryamāṇam acala-pratiṣṭhaṁ
samudram āpaḥ praviśanti yadvat
tadvat kāmā yaṁ praviśanti sarve
sa śāntim āpnoti na kāma-kāmī

70. He in whom desires enter ceaselessly like water from rivers enter the sea, but though continuously filled, remains still and undisturbed like the ever-full sea, - he attains peace and not he who cherishes desires.

विहाय कामान्यः सर्वान्पुमांश्चरति निःस्पृहः ।
निर्ममो निरहंकारः स शान्तिमधिगच्छति ॥७१॥

vihāya kāmān yaḥ sarvān pumāṁś carati niḥspṛhaḥ
nirmamo nirahaṅkāraḥ sa śāntim adhigacchati

71. When a man acts without longing, having relinquished all desires, free from the sense of 'I' and 'mine', he attains to peace.

एषा ब्राह्मी स्थितिः पार्थ, नैनां प्राप्य विमुह्यति ।
स्थित्वास्यामन्तकालेऽपि, ब्रह्मनिर्वाणमृच्छति ॥७२॥

eṣā brāhmī sthitiḥ pārtha / naināṁ prāpya vimuhyati
sthitvāsyām anta-kāle 'pi / brahma-nirvāṇam ṛcchati

72. O Partha, attaining brahma in this way is called brahma sthitih. After attaining this state, one is no longer deluded. If, at the time of death, one is situated in this consciousness even for a moment, he attains brahma-nirvana.

ॐ तत् सत् । इति श्रीमद्भगवद्गीतासु उपनिषत्सु ब्रह्मविद्यायां योगशास्त्रे श्रीकृष्णार्जुन संवादे सांख्ययोगो नाम द्वितीयोऽध्यायः ॥

Om Tat Sat. Iti Śrimad Bhagavat Gitasu Upanishatsu Brahmavidyayām yogaśastre Sri Krishnarjuna samvade Sāṅkhyayogo nama dvithiyodhyayaḥ

Thus ends the second chapter named "Sankhya-Yoga" (The Yoga of Knowledge) of the Upanishad of the Bhagavad Gita, the scripture of yoga, dealing with the science of the Absolute in the form of the dialogue between Krishna and Arjuna.

अथ तृतीयोऽध्यायः - कर्मयोगः

Chapter Three: Karma-Yoga

अर्जुन उवाच ।
ज्यायसी चेत्कर्मणस्ते, मता बुद्धिर्जनार्दन ।
तत्किं कर्मणि घोरे मां, नियोजयसि केशव ॥१॥

arjuna uvāca
jyāyasī cet karmaṇas te / matā buddhir janārdana
tat kiṁ karmaṇi ghore māṁ / niyojayasi keśava

1. Arjuna said: If Thou consider knowledge superior to action, O Janardana, why does Thou spur me to this terrible deed, O Keshava?

व्यामिश्रेणेव वाक्येन, बुद्धिं मोहयसीव मे ।
तदेकं वद निश्चित्य, येन श्रेयोऽहमाप्नुयाम् ॥२॥

vyāmiśreṇeva vākyena / buddhiṁ mohayasīva me
tad ekaṁ vada niścitya / yena śreyo 'ham āpnuyām

2. With these apparently opposed statements Thou dost, as it were, bewilder my intelligence. So, having made Thy decision, tell me the one by which I may reach the highest good.

श्रीभगवानुवाच ।
लोकेऽस्मिन्द्विविधा निष्ठा, पुरा प्रोक्ता मयाऽनघ ।
ज्ञानयोगेन सांख्यानां, कर्मयोगेन योगिनाम् ॥३॥

śrī bhagavān uvāca
loke'smin dvi-vidhā niṣṭhā / purā proktā mayānagha
jñāna-yogena sāṅkhyānāṁ / karma-yogena yoginām

3. The Blessed Lord said: As expounded by Me of old, O blameless one, there are in this world two paths: the Yoga of knowledge for men of contemplation and the Yoga of action for men of action.

न कर्मणामनारम्भान्नैष्कर्म्यं पुरुषोऽश्नुते ।
न च संन्यसनादेव सिद्धिं समधिगच्छति ॥४॥

na karmaṇām anārambhān naiṣkarmyaṁ puruṣo'śnute
na ca sannyasanād eva siddhiṁ samadhigacchati

4. Not by abstaining from action does a man achieve non-action; nor by mere renunciation does he attain to perfection.

न हि कश्चित्क्षणमपि, जातु तिष्ठत्यकर्मकृत् ।
कार्यते ह्यवशः कर्म, सर्वः प्रकृतिजैर्गुणैः ॥५॥

na hi kaścit kṣaṇam api / jātu tiṣṭhaty akarmakṛt
kāryate hy avaśaḥ karma / sarvaḥ prakṛti-jair guṇaiḥ

5. No one, indeed, can exist even for an instant without performing action; for everyone is helplessly driven to activity by the gunas born of Nature.

कर्मेन्द्रियाणि संयम्य, य आस्ते मनसा स्मरन् ।
इन्द्रियार्थान्विमूढात्मा, मिथ्याचारः स उच्यते ॥६॥

karmendriyāṇi saṁyamya / ya āste manasā smaran
indriyārthān vimūḍhātmā / mithyācāraḥ sa ucyate

6. He who sits, restraining the organs of action, and dwelling in his mind on the objects of sense, self-deluded, he is said to be a hypocrite.

यस्त्विन्द्रियाणि मनसा, नियम्यारभतेऽर्जुन ।
कर्मेन्द्रियैः कर्मयोगमसक्तः स विशिष्यते ॥७॥

yas tv indriyāṇi manasā / niyamyārabhate'rjuna
karmendriyaiḥ karma-yogam / asaktaḥ sa viśiṣyate

7. But he who, controlling the senses by the mind, without attachment engages the organs of action in the Yoga of action, he excels, O Arjuna.

नियतं कुरु कर्म त्वं, कर्म ज्यायो ह्यकर्मणः ।
शरीरयात्रापि च ते, न प्रसिद्ध्येदकर्मणः ॥८॥

niyataṁ kuru karma tvaṁ / karma jyāyo hy akarmaṇaḥ
śarīra-yātrāpi ca te / na prasidhyed akarmaṇaḥ

8. Do your allotted duty. Action is indeed superior to inaction. Even the survival of your body would not be possible without action.

यज्ञार्थात्कर्मणोऽन्यत्र, लोकोऽयं कर्मबन्धनः ।
तदर्थं कर्म कौन्तेय, मुक्तसङ्गः समाचर ॥९॥

yajñārthāt karmaṇo'nyatra / loko'yaṁ karma-bandhanaḥ
tad-arthaṁ karma kaunteya / mukta-saṅgaḥ samācara

9. Excepting actions performed for yajna, this world is in bondage to action. For the sake of yajna engage in action free from attachment.

सहयज्ञाः प्रजाः सृष्ट्वा, पुरोवाच प्रजापतिः ।
अनेन प्रसविष्यध्वमेष वोऽस्त्विष्टकामधुक् ॥१०॥

saha-yajñāḥ prajāḥ sṛṣṭvā / purovāca prajāpatiḥ
anena prasaviṣyadhvam / eṣa vo 'stv iṣṭa-kāma-dhuk

10. In the beginning, having created men along with yajna, the Lord of Creation said: By this yajna shall you prosper and this shall bring forth the fulfilment of desires.

देवान्भावयतानेन, ते देवा भावयन्तु वः ।
परस्परं भावयन्तः, श्रेयः परमवाप्स्यथ ॥११॥

devān bhāvayatānena / te devā bhāvayantu vaḥ
parasparaṁ bhāvayantaḥ / śreyaḥ param avāpsyatha

11. Through yajna you sustain the gods and those gods will sustain you. By sustaining one another, you will attain the highest good.

इष्टान्भोगान्हि वो देवा, दास्यन्ते यज्ञभाविताः ।
तैर्दत्तानप्रदायैभ्यो, यो भुङ्क्ते स्तेन एव सः ॥१२॥

iṣṭān bhogān hi vo devā / dāsyante yajña-bhāvitāḥ
tair dattān apradāyaibhyo / yo bhuṅkte stena eva saḥ

12. Satisfied by the yajna, the gods will certainly bestow the enjoyments you desire. But he who enjoys their gifts without offering to them is merely a thief.

यज्ञशिष्टाशिनः सन्तो, मुच्यन्ते सर्वकिल्बिषैः ।
भुञ्जते ते त्वघं पापाः, ये पचन्त्यात्मकारणात् ॥१३॥

yajña-śiṣṭāśinaḥ santo / mucyante sarva-kilbiṣaiḥ
bhuñjate te tvaghaṁ pāpā / ye pacantyātma-kāraṇāt

13. The righteous, who eat the remains of the yajna, are freed from all sins. But the unrighteous, who prepare food for themselves alone, truly, they eat sin.

अन्नाद्भवन्ति भूतानि, पर्जन्यादन्नसंभवः ।
यज्ञाद्भवति पर्जन्यो, यज्ञः कर्मसमुद्भवः ॥१४॥

annād bhavanti bhūtāni / parjanyād anna-sambhavaḥ
yajñād bhavati parjanyo / yajñaḥ karma-samudbhavaḥ

14. From food creatures come into being; from rain is produced food; from yajna comes forth rain and yagna is born of action.

कर्म ब्रह्मोद्भवं विद्धि, ब्रह्माक्षरसमुद्भवम् ।
तस्मात्सर्वगतं ब्रह्म, नित्यं यज्ञे प्रतिष्ठितम् ॥१५॥

karma brahmodbhavaṁ viddhi / brahmākṣara-samudbhavam
tasmāt sarva-gataṁ brahma / nityaṁ yajñe pratiṣṭhitam

15. Know that action is born from the Veda, that which springs from the Supreme Consciousness. Therefore the all pervading Brahman is ever established in yajna.

एवं प्रवर्तितं चक्रं, नानुवर्तयतीह यः ।
अघायुरिन्द्रियारामो, मोघं पार्थ स जीवति ॥१६॥

evaṁ pravarttitaṁ cakraṁ / nānuvartayatīha yaḥ
aghāyur indriyārāmo / moghaṁ pārtha sa jīvati

16. He who in this life does not follow the wheel thus set revolving, whose life is sinful, whose contentment lies in the senses, he lives in vain, O Partha.

यस्त्वात्मरतिरेव स्यादात्मतृप्तश्च मानवः ।
आत्मन्येव च संतुष्टस्तस्य कार्यं न विद्यते ॥१७॥

yas tvātma-ratir eva syād / ātma-tṛptaś ca mānavaḥ
ātmany eva ca santuṣṭas / tasya kāryaṁ na vidyate

17. But the man whose delight is in the Self alone, who is content in the Self, who rejoices only in the Self, for him there is no action that he needs to do.

नैव तस्य कृतेनार्थो, नाकृतेनेह कश्चन ।
न चास्य सर्वभूतेषु, कश्चिदर्थव्यपाश्रयः ॥१८॥

naiva tasya kṛtenārtho / nākṛteneha kaścana
na cāsya sarva-bhūteṣu / kaścid artha-vyapāśrayaḥ

18. Neither has he any profit to gain in this life from the actions he has done nor has any loss from the actions he has not done; nor is there any living creature on whom he needs to rely for any purpose.

तस्मादसक्तः सततं, कार्यं कर्म समाचर ।
असक्तो ह्याचरन्कर्म, परमाप्नोति पूरुषः ॥१९॥

tasmād asaktaḥ satataṁ / kāryaṁ karma samācara
asakto hyācaran karma / param āpnoti pūruṣaḥ

19. Therefore, remaining unattached, always do the action worthy of performance. Engaging in action truly unattached, man attains to the Supreme.

कर्मणैव हि संसिद्धिमास्थिता जनकादयः ।
लोकसंग्रहमेवापि संपश्यन्कर्तुमर्हसि ॥२०॥

karmaṇaiva hi saṁsiddhim āsthitā janakādayaḥ
loka-saṅgraham evāpi sampaśyan kartum arhasi

20. By action alone, indeed, Janaka and others gained perfection. Moreover, even looking to the welfare of the world, you should perform action.

यद्यदाचरति श्रेष्ठस्तत्तदेवेतरो जनः ।

स यत्प्रमाणं कुरुते लोकस्तदनुवर्तते ॥२१॥

yad yad ācarati śreṣṭhas tat tad evetaro janaḥ
sa yat pramāṇaṁ kurute lokas tad anuvarttate

21. Whatsoever a great man does, the very same is also done by other men. Whatever the standard he sets, the world follows it.

न मे पार्थास्ति कर्तव्यं, त्रिषु लोकेषु किंचन ।
नानवाप्तमवाप्तव्यं, वर्त एव च कर्मणि ॥२२॥

na me pārthāsti karttavyaṁ / triṣu lokeṣu kiñcana
nānavāptam avāptavyaṁ / varta eva ca karmaṇi

22. In the three worlds there is no action which I need to do, O Partha; nor is there for Me anything worth achieving unattained; even so I am engaged in action.

यदि ह्यहं न वर्तेयं, जातु कर्मण्यतन्द्रितः ।
मम वर्त्मानुवर्तन्ते, मनुष्याः पार्थ सर्वशः ॥२३॥

yadi hyahaṁ na vartteyaṁ / jātu karmaṇyatandritaḥ
mama vartmānuvarttante / manuṣyāḥ pārtha sarvaśaḥ

23. What if I did not continue unweariedly in activity, O Partha? Men in every way follow My example.

उत्सीदेयुरिमे लोकाः न कुर्यां कर्म चेदहम् ।
संकरस्य च कर्ता स्यामुपहन्यामिमाः प्रजाः ॥२४॥

utsīdeyur ime lokā na kuryāṁ karma ced aham
saṅkarasya ca karttā syām upahanyām imāḥ prajāḥ

24. If I did not engage in action, these worlds would perish and I would be the cause of confusion and of the destruction of these people.

सक्ताः कर्मण्यविद्वांसो यथा कुर्वन्ति भारत ।
कुर्याद्विद्वांस्तथासक्तश्चिकीर्षुर्लोकसंग्रहम् ॥२५॥

saktāḥ karmaṇy avidvāṁso yathā kurvanti bhārata
kuryād vidvāṁs tathāsaktaś cikīrṣur loka-saṅgraham

25. As the unwise act out of their attachment to action, O Bharata, so should the wise act, but without any attachment, desiring the welfare of the world.

न बुद्धिभेदं जनयेदज्ञानां कर्मसङ्गिनाम् ।
जोषयेत्सर्वकर्माणि विद्वान्युक्तः समाचरन् ॥२६॥

na buddhi-bhedaṁ janayed ajñānāṁ karma-saṅginām
joshayet sarva-karmāṇi vidvān yuktaḥ samācaran

26. Let not the wise man create a division in the minds of the ignorant, who are attached to action. Established in Being, he should direct them to perform all actions, duly engaging in them himself.

प्रकृतेः क्रियमाणानि, गुणैः कर्माणि सर्वशः ।
अहंकारविमूढात्मा, कर्ताहमिति मन्यते ॥२७॥

prakṛteḥ kriyamāṇāni / guṇaiḥ karmāṇi sarvaśaḥ
ahaṅkāra-vimūḍhātmā / karttāham iti manyate

27. Actions are in every case performed by the gunas of Nature. He whose mind is deluded by the sense of 'I' holds 'I am the doer'.

तत्त्ववित्तु महाबाहो, गुणकर्मविभागयोः ।
गुणा गुणेषु वर्तन्त, इति मत्वा न सज्जते ॥२८॥

tattvavit tu mahā-bāho / guṇa-karma-vibhāgayoḥ
guṇā guṇeṣu varttanta / iti matvā na sajjate

28. But he who knows the truth about the divisions of the gunas and their actions, O mighty-armed, knowing that it is the gunas which act upon the gunas, remains unattached.

प्रकृतेर्गुणसंमूढाः, सज्जन्ते गुणकर्मसु ।
तानकृत्स्नविदो मन्दान्कृत्स्नविन्न विचालयेत् ॥२९॥

prakṛter guṇa-saṁmūḍhāḥ / sajjante guṇa-karmasu
tān akṛtsna-vido mandān / kṛtsna-vin na vicālayet

29. Those deluded by the gunas of Nature are attached to the actions of the gunas. Let not him who knows the whole disturb the ignorant who know only the part.

मयि सर्वाणि कर्माणि, संन्यस्याध्यात्मचेतसा ।
निराशीर्निर्ममो भूत्वा, युध्यस्व विगतज्वरः ॥३०॥

mayi sarvāṇi karmāṇi / sannyasyādhyātma-cetasā
nirāśīr nirmamo bhūtvā / yudhyasva vigata-jvaraḥ

30. Surrendering all actions to Me by maintaining your consciousness in the Self, freed from longing and the sense of 'mine', fight, delivered from the fever (of delusion).

ये मे मतमिदं नित्यमनुतिष्ठन्ति मानवाः ।
श्रद्धावन्तोऽनसूयन्तो, मुच्यन्ते तेऽपि कर्मभिः ॥३१॥

ye me matam idaṁ nityam anutiṣṭhanti mānavāḥ
śraddhāvanto 'nasūyanto mucyante te 'pi karmabhiḥ

31. Those men who are possessed of faith, who do not find fault and always follow this teaching of Mine, they too are liberated from action.

ये त्वेतदभ्यसूयन्तो, नानुतिष्ठन्ति मे मतम् ।
सर्वज्ञानविमूढांस्तान्विद्धि नष्टानचेतसः ॥३२॥

ye tv etad abhyasūyanto / nānutiṣṭhanti me matam
sarva-jñāna-vimūḍhāṁs tān / viddhi naṣṭān acetasaḥ

32. But those who find fault and do not follow My teaching: know them to be deluded about all knowledge, doomed and senseless.

सदृशं चेष्टते स्वस्याः, प्रकृतेर्ज्ञानवानपि ।
प्रकृतिं यान्ति भूतानि, निग्रहः किं करिष्यति ॥३३॥

sadṛśaṁ ceṣṭate svasyāḥ / prakṛter jñānavān api
prakṛtiṁ yānti bhūtāni / nigrahaḥ kiṁ kariṣyati

33. Creatures follow their own nature. Even the enlightened man acts according to his own nature. What can restraint accomplish?

इन्द्रियस्येन्द्रियस्यार्थे रागद्वेषौ व्यवस्थितौ ।
तयोर्न वशमागच्छेत्तौ ह्यस्य परिपन्थिनौ ॥३४॥

indriyasyendriyasyārthe / rāga-dveṣau vyavasthitau
tayor na vaśam āgacchet / tau hyasya paripanthinau

34. The attachment and aversion of each sense are located in the object of that sense; let no man come under their sway, for both indeed are enemies besetting his path.

श्रेयान्स्वधर्मो विगुणः, परधर्मात्स्वनुष्ठितात् ।
स्वधर्मे निधनं श्रेयः, परधर्मो भयावहः ॥३५॥

śreyān sva-dharmo viguṇaḥ / para-dharmāt svanuṣṭhitāt
sva-dharme nidhanaṁ śreyaḥ / para-dharmo bhayāvahaḥ

35. Because one can perform it, one's own dharma (though) lesser in merit, is better than the dharma of another. Better is death in one's own dharma: the dharma of another brings danger.

अर्जुन उवाच ।
अथ केन प्रयुक्तोऽयं, पापं चरति पूरुषः ।
अनिच्छन्नपि वार्ष्णेय, बलादिव नियोजितः ॥३६॥

arjuna uvāca
atha kena prayukto 'yaṁ / pāpam carati pūruṣaḥ
anicchann api vārṣṇeya / balād iva niyojitaḥ

36. Arjuna said: What is it that impels a man to commit sin, even involuntarily, as if driven by force, O Varshneya?

श्रीभगवानुवाच ।
काम एष क्रोध एष, रजोगुणसमुद्भवः ।
महाशनो महापाप्मा, विद्ध्येनमिह वैरिणम् ॥३७॥

śrī bhagavān uvāca
kāma eṣa krodha eṣa / rajo-guṇa-samudbhavaḥ
mahā-śano mahā-pāpmā / viddhy enam iha vairiṇam

37. The Blessed Lord said: It is desire, it is anger, born of rajoguna, all-consuming and most evil. Know this to be the enemy here on earth.

धूमेनाव्रियते वह्निर् यथाऽदर्शो मलेन च ।
यथोल्बेनावृतो गर्भस्तथा तेनेदमावृतम् ॥३८॥

dhūmenāvriyate vahnir / yathādarśo malena ca
yatholbenāvṛto garbhas / tathā tenedam āvṛtam

38. As fire is covered by smoke, as a mirror by dust, as an embryo is covered by the amnion, so is This covered by that.

आवृतं ज्ञानमेतेन, ज्ञानिनो नित्यवैरिणा ।
कामरूपेण कौन्तेय, दुष्पूरेणानलेन च ॥३९॥

āvṛtaṁ jñānam etena / jñānino nitya-vairiṇā
kāma-rūpeṇa kaunteya / duṣpūreṇānalena ca

39. Wisdom is veiled by this insatiable flame of desire which is the constant enemy of the wise, O son of Kunti.

इन्द्रियाणि मनो बुद्धिरस्याधिष्ठानमुच्यते ।
एतैर्विमोहयत्येष, ज्ञानमावृत्य देहिनम् ॥४०॥

indriyāṇi mano buddhir / asyādhiṣṭhānam ucyate
etair vimohayaty eṣa / jñānam āvṛtya dehinam

40. The senses, the mind and the intellect are said to be wisdom's seat. Overshadowing wisdom by means of these, it deludes the dweller in the body.

तस्मात्त्वमिन्द्रियाण्यादौ, नियम्य भरतर्षभ ।
पाप्मानं प्रजहि ह्येनं, ज्ञानविज्ञाननाशनम् ॥४१॥

tasmāt tvam indriyāṇyādau / niyamya bharatarṣabha
pāpmānaṁ prajahi hyenaṁ / jñāna-vijñāna-nāśanam

41. Therefore, having first organized the senses, O best of Bharatas, shake off this evil, the destroyer of knowledge and realization.

इन्द्रियाणि पराण्याहुरिन्द्रियेभ्यः परं मनः ।
मनसस्तु परा बुद्धिर्यो बुद्धेः परतस्तु सः ॥४२॥

indriyāṇi parāṇy āhur / indriyebhyaḥ paraṁ manaḥ
manasas tu parā buddhir /yobuddher paratas tu saḥ

42. The senses, they say, are subtle; more subtle than the senses is mind; yet finer than mind is intellect; that which is beyond even the intellect is he.

एवं बुद्धेः परं बुद्ध्वा, संस्तभ्यात्मानमात्मना ।
जहि शत्रुं महाबाहो, कामरूपं दुरासदम् ॥४३॥

evaṁ buddheḥ paraṁ buddhvā / saṁstabhyātmānam ātmanā
jahi śatruṁ mahā-bāho / kāma-rūpaṁ durāsadam

43. Thus, having known him who is beyond the intellect, having stilled the self by the Self, O mighty-armed, slay the enemy in the form of desire, difficult to subdue.

ॐ तत् सत् । इति श्रीमद्भगवद्गीतासु उपनिषत्सु ब्रह्मविद्यायां योगशास्त्रे श्रीकृष्णार्जुन संवादे कर्मयोगो नाम तृतीयोऽध्यायः ॥

Om Tat Sat. Iti Śrimad Bhagavat Gitasu Upanishatsu Brahmavidyayām yogaśastre Sri Krishnarjuna samvade Kārmayogo nama tṛtiyodhyayaḥ

Thus ends the third chapter named "Karma-Yoga" (Yoga of Action) of the Upanishad of the Bhagavad Gita, the scripture of yoga, dealing with the science of the Absolute in the form of the dialogue between Sri Krishna and Arjuna.

अथ चतुर्थोऽध्यायः - ज्ञानकर्मसंन्यासयोगः

Chapter Four: Jñāna-Karma-Sañyasa-Yoga

श्रीभगवानुवाच ।
इमं विवस्वते योगं, प्रोक्तवानहमव्ययम् ।
विवस्वान्मनवे प्राह, मनुरिक्ष्वाकवेऽब्रवीत् ॥१॥

śrī bhagavān uvāca
imaṁ vivasvate yogaṁ / proktavān aham avyayam
vivasvān manave prāha / manur ikṣvākave 'bravīt

1. The Blessed Lord said: I proclaimed this imperishable Yoga to the Sun God ; He declared it to Manu and Manu told it to Ikshvaku.

एवं परम्पराप्राप्तमिमं राजर्षयो विदुः ।
स कालेनेह महता, योगो नष्टः परंतप ॥२॥

evaṁ paramparā-prāptam / imaṁ rājarṣayo viduḥ
sa kāleneha mahatā / yogo naṣṭaḥ parantapa

2. Thus having received it one from another, the royal sages knew it. With the long lapse of time, O scorcher of enemies, this Yoga has been lost to the world.

स एवायं मया तेऽद्य, योगः प्रोक्तः पुरातनः ।
भक्तोऽसि मे सखा चेति, रहस्यं ह्येतदुत्तमम् ॥३॥

sa evāyaṁ mayā te 'dya / yogaḥ proktaḥ purātanaḥ
bhakto 'si me sakhā ceti / rahasyaṁ hy etad uttamam

3. This same age-old Yoga, which is indeed the supreme secret, I have today declared to you because you are my devotee and friend.

अर्जुन उवाच ।
अपरं भवतो जन्म, परं जन्म विवस्वतः ।
कथमेतद्विजानीयां, त्वमादौ प्रोक्तवानिति ॥४॥

arjuna uvāca
aparaṁ bhavato janma / paraṁ janma vivasvataḥ
katham etad vijānīyāṁ / tvam ādau proktavān iti

4. Arjuna said: Later was Thy birth and earlier the birth of the Sun God. How am I to understand this saying that Thou didst proclaim it in the beginning ?

श्रीभगवानुवाच ।
बहूनि मे व्यतीतानि, जन्मानि तव चार्जुन ।
तान्यहं वेद सर्वाणि, न त्वं वेत्थ परंतप ॥५॥

śrī bhagavān uvāca
bahūni me vyatītāni / janmāni tava cārjuna
tānyahaṁ veda sarvāṇi / na tvaṁ vettha parantapa

5. The Blessed Lord said: Many births have passed for Me and for you also, O Arjuna. I know them all but you know them not, O scorcher of enemies.

अजोऽपि सन्नव्ययात्मा, भूतानामीश्वरोऽपि सन् ।
प्रकृतिं स्वामधिष्ठाय, संभवाम्यात्ममायया ॥६॥

ajo 'pi sann avyayātmā / bhūtānām īśvaro 'pi san
prakṛtiṁ svām adhiṣṭhāya / sambhavāmy ātma-māyayā

6. Though I am unborn and of imperishable nature, though Lord of all beings, yet remaining in My own nature I take birth through My own power of creation.

यदा यदा हि धर्मस्य, ग्लानिर्भवति भारत ।
अभ्युत्थानमधर्मस्य, तदात्मानं सृजाम्यहम् ॥७॥

yadā yadā hi dharmasya / glānir bhavati bhārata
abhyutthānam adharmasya / tadātmānaṁ sṛjāmy aham

7. Whenever dharma is in decay and adharma flourishes, O Bharata I create Myself.

परित्राणाय साधूनां, विनाशाय च दुष्कृताम् ।
धर्मसंस्थापनार्थाय, संभवामि युगे युगे ॥८॥

paritrāṇāya sādhūnāṁ / vināśāya ca duṣkṛtām
dharma-saṁsthāpanārthāya / sambhavāmi yuge yuge

8. To protect the righteous and destroy the wicked, to establish dharma firmly, I take birth age after age.

जन्म कर्म च मे दिव्यमेवं यो वेत्ति तत्त्वतः ।
त्यक्त्वा देहं पुनर्जन्म, नैति मामेति सोऽर्जुन ॥९॥

janma karma ca me divyam / evaṁ yo vetti tattvataḥ
tyaktvā dehaṁ punar janma / naiti mām eti so 'rjuna

9. My birth and My activity are divine. He who knows this in very essence, on leaving the body is not reborn. He comes to Me, O Arjuna.

वीतरागभयक्रोधा, मन्मया मामुपाश्रिताः ।
बहवो ज्ञानतपसा, पूता मद्भावमागताः ॥१०॥

vīta-rāga-bhaya-krodhā / man-mayā mām upāśritāḥ
bahavo jñāna-tapasā / pūtā mad-bhāvam āgatāḥ

10. Freed from attachment, fear and anger, absorbed in Me, taking refuge in Me, purified by the austerity of wisdom, many have come to My Being.

ये यथा मां प्रपद्यन्ते, तांस्तथैव भजाम्यहम् ।
मम वर्त्मानुवर्तन्ते, मनुष्याः पार्थ सर्वशः ॥११॥

ye yathā māṁ prapadyante / tāṁstathaiva bhajāmyaham
mama vartmānuvarttante / manuṣyāḥ pārtha sarvaśaḥ

11. As men approach Me, so do I favour them; in all ways, O Partha, men follow My path.

काङ्क्षन्तः कर्मणां सिद्धिं, यजन्त इह देवताः ।
क्षिप्रं हि मानुषे लोके, सिद्धिर्भवति कर्मजा ॥१२॥

kāṅkṣantaḥ karmaṇāṁ siddhiṁ / yajanta iha devatāḥ
kṣipraṁ hi mānuṣe loke / siddhir bhavati karmajā

12. Those who desire fulfilment of actions here on earth make offerings to the gods, for success born of action comes quickly in the world of men.

चातुर्वर्ण्यं मया सृष्टं, गुणकर्मविभागशः ।
तस्य कर्तारमपि मां, विद्ध्यकर्तारमव्ययम् ॥१३॥

cātur-varṇyaṁ mayā sṛṣṭaṁ / guṇa-karma-vibhāgaśaḥ
tasya karttāram api māṁ / viddhyakarttāram avyayam

13. The fourfold order was created by Me according to the division of gunas and actions. Though I am its author, know Me to be the non doer, immutable.

न मां कर्माणि लिम्पन्ति, न मे कर्मफले स्पृहा ।
इति मां योऽभिजानाति, कर्मभिर्न स बध्यते ॥१४॥

na māṁ karmāṇi limpanti / na me karma-phale spṛhā
iti māṁ yo 'bhijānāti / karmabhir na sa badhyate

14. Actions do not involve Me, nor have I any longing for the fruit of action. He who truly knows Me thus is not bound by actions.

एवं ज्ञात्वा कृतं कर्म, पूर्वैरपि मुमुक्षुभिः ।
कुरु कर्मैव तस्मात्त्वं, पूर्वैः पूर्वतरं कृतम् ॥१५॥

evaṁ jñātvā kṛtaṁ karma / pūrvair api mumukṣubhiḥ
kuru karmaiva tasmāt tvaṁ / pūrvaiḥ pūrvataraṁ kṛtam

15. Having known this, even the ancient seekers of liberation performed action; therefore, do you perform action as did the ancients in olden days.

किं कर्म किमकर्मेति, कवयोऽप्यत्र मोहिताः ।
तत्ते कर्म प्रवक्ष्यामि, यज्ज्ञात्वा मोक्ष्यसेऽशुभात् ॥१६॥

kiṁ karma kim akarmeti / kavayo 'py atra mohitāḥ
tat te karma pravakṣyāmi / yaj jñātvā mokṣyase 'śubhāt

16. What is action, what is inaction? Even the wise are bewildered here. I shall expound to you that action, knowing which you will be freed from evil.

कर्मणो ह्यपि बोद्धव्यं, बोद्धव्यं च विकर्मणः ।
अकर्मणश्च बोद्धव्यं, गहना कर्मणो गतिः ॥१७॥

karmaṇo hyapi boddhavyaṁ / boddhavyaṁ ca vikarmaṇaḥ
akarmaṇaś ca boddhavyaṁ / gahanā karmaṇo gatiḥ

17. Action, indeed, should be understood, wrong action should also be understood and inaction should be understood as well. Unfathomable is the course of action.

कर्मण्यकर्म यः पश्येदकर्मणि च कर्म यः ।
स बुद्धिमान्मनुष्येषु, स युक्तः कृत्स्नकर्मकृत् ॥१८॥

karmaṇy akarma yaḥ paśyed / akarmaṇi ca karma yaḥ
sa buddhimān manuṣyeṣu / sa yuktaḥ kṛtsna-karma-kṛt

18. He who in action sees inaction and in inaction sees action is wise among men. He is unified, he has accomplished all action.

यस्य सर्वे समारम्भाः, कामसंकल्पवर्जिताः ।
ज्ञानाग्निदग्धकर्माणं, तमाहुः पण्डितं बुधाः ॥१६॥

yasya sarve samārambhāḥ / kāma-saṅkalpa-varjitāḥ
jñānāgni-dagdha-karmāṇaṁ / tam āhuḥ paṇḍitaṁ budhāḥ

19. He whose every undertaking is free from desire and the incentive thereof, whose action is burnt up in the fire of knowledge, him the knowers of Reality call wise.

त्यक्त्वा कर्मफलासङ्गं, नित्यतृप्तो निराश्रयः ।
कर्मण्यभिप्रवृत्तोऽपि, नैव किञ्चित्करोति सः ॥२०॥

tyaktvā karma-phalāsaṅgaṁ / nitya-tṛpto nirāśrayaḥ
karmaṇyabhipravṛtto 'pi / naiva kiñcit karoti saḥ

20. Having cast off attachment to the fruit of action, ever contented, depending on nothing, even though fully engaged in action he does not act at all.

निराशीर्यतचित्तात्मा, त्यक्तसर्वपरिग्रहः ।
शारीरं केवलं कर्म, कुर्वन्नाप्नोति किल्बिषम् ॥२१॥

nirāśīr yata-cittātmā / tyakta-sarva-parigrahaḥ
śārīraṁ kevalaṁ karma / kurvan nāpnoti kilbiṣam

21. Expecting nothing, his heart and mind disciplined, having relinquished all possessions, performing action by the body alone, he incurs no sin.

यदृच्छालाभसंतुष्टो, द्वन्द्वातीतो विमत्सरः ।
समः सिद्धावसिद्धौ च, कृत्वापि न निबध्यते ॥२२॥

yadṛcchā-lābha-santuṣṭo / dvandvātīto vimatsaraḥ
samaḥ siddhāv asiddhau ca / kṛtvāpi na nibadhyate

22. Satisfied with whatever comes unasked, beyond the pairs of opposites, free from envy, balanced in success and failure, even though acting, he is not bound.

गतसङ्गस्य मुक्तस्य, ज्ञानावस्थितचेतसः ।
यज्ञायाचरतः कर्म, समग्रं प्रविलीयते ॥२३॥

gata-saṅgasya muktasya / jñānāvasthita-cetasaḥ
yajñāyācarataḥ karma / samagraṁ pravilīyate

23. He who is freed from attachment, liberated, whose mind is established in wisdom, who acts for the sake of yagna, his action is entirely dissolved.

ब्रह्मार्पणं ब्रह्म हविर्ब्रह्माग्नौ ब्रह्मणा हुतम् ।
ब्रह्मैव तेन गन्तव्यं, ब्रह्मकर्मसमाधिना ॥२४॥

brahmārpaṇaṁ brahma havir / brahmāgnau brahmaṇā hutam
brahmaiva tena gantavyaṁ / brahma-karma-samādhinā

24. Brahman is the act of offering. Brahman the oblation, poured by Brahman into fire that is Brahman. To Brahman alone must he go who is fixed in Brahman through action.

दैवमेवापरे यज्ञं, योगिनः पर्युपासते ।
ब्रह्माग्नावपरे यज्ञं, यज्ञेनैवोपजुह्वति ॥२५॥

daivam evāpare yajñaṁ / yoginaḥ paryupāsate
brahmāgnāv apare yajñaṁ / yajñenaivopajuhvati

25. Some yogis perform yagna merely by worshipping the gods, others by offering the yagna itself into the fire that is Brahman.

श्रोत्रादीनीन्द्रियाण्यन्ये, संयमाग्निषु जुह्वति ।
शब्दादीन् विषयानन्य, इन्द्रियाग्निषु जुह्वति ॥२६॥

śrotrādīnīndriyāṇyanye / saṁyamāgniṣu juhvati
śabdādīn viṣayānanya / indriyāgniṣu juhvati

26. Some offer hearing and other senses in the fires of control; some offer sound and other objects of the senses in the fires of the senses.

सर्वाणीन्द्रियकर्माणि, प्राणकर्माणि चापरे ।
आत्मसंयमयोगाग्नौ, जुह्वति ज्ञानदीपिते ॥२७॥

sarvāṇīndriya-karmāṇi / prāṇa-karmāṇi cāpare
ātma-saṁyama-yogāgnau / juhvati jñāna-dīpite

27. Others offer all the activities of the senses and of the life-breath in the fire of Yoga, which is self-control kindled by enlightenment.

द्रव्ययज्ञास्तपोयज्ञाः, योगयज्ञास्तथाऽपरे ।
स्वाध्यायज्ञानयज्ञाश्च, यतयः संशितव्रताः ॥२८॥

dravya-yajñās tapo-yajñā / yoga-yajñās tathāpare
svādhyāya-jñāna-yajñāś ca / yatayaḥ saṁśita-vratāḥ

28. Some likewise perform yagna by means of material possessions, by austerity and by the practice of Yoga; while other aspirants of rigid vows offer as yagna their scriptural learning and knowledge.

अपाने जुह्वति प्राणं, प्राणेऽपानं तथापरे ।
प्राणापानगती रुद्ध्वा, प्राणायामपरायणाः ॥२६॥

apāne juhvati prāṇaṁ / prāṇe 'pānaṁ tathāpare
prāṇāpāna-gatī ruddhvā / prāṇāyāma-parāyaṇāḥ

29. Others again, who are devoted to breathing exercises, pour the inward into the outward breath and the outward into the inward, having restrained the course of inhalation and exhalation.

अपरे नियताहाराः, प्राणान्प्राणेषु जुह्वति ।
सर्वेऽप्येते यज्ञविदो, यज्ञक्षपितकल्मषाः ॥३०॥

apare niyatāhārāḥ / prāṇān prāṇeṣu juhvati
sarve 'py ete yajña-vido / yajña-kṣapita-kalmaṣāḥ

30. Yet others, restricting their food, offer breaths into breaths. All these indeed are knowers of yagna, and through yagna their sins are cast away.

यज्ञशिष्टामृतभुजो, यान्ति ब्रह्म सनातनम् ।
नायं लोकोऽस्त्ययज्ञस्य, कुतोऽन्यः कुरुसत्तम ॥३१॥

yajña-śiṣṭāmṛta-bhujo / yānti brahma sanātanam
nāyaṁ loko 'styayajñasya / kuto 'nyaḥ kuru-sattama

31. Eating the remains of the yagna, which is nectar, they reach the eternal Brahman. This world, O best of Kurus, is not for him who offers no yagna, much less the world hereafter.

एवं बहुविधा यज्ञाः, वितता ब्रह्मणो मुखे ।
कर्मजान्विद्धि तान्सर्वानेवं ज्ञात्वा विमोक्ष्यसे ॥३२॥

evaṁ bahu-vidhā yajñā / vitatā brahmaṇo mukhe
karma-jān viddhi tān sarvān / evaṁ jñātvā vimokṣyase

32. In this way, yagnas of many kinds are set forth in the words of the Veda. Know them all as born of action. Thus knowing you will find release.

श्रेयान्द्रव्यमयाद्यज्ञाज्ज्ञानयज्ञः परंतप ।
सर्वं कर्माखिलं पार्थ ज्ञाने परिसमाप्यते ॥३३॥

śreyān dravyamayād yajñāj jñāna-yajñaḥ parantapa
sarvaṁ karmākhilaṁ pārtha jñāne parisamāpyate

33. Better than the yagna through material means is the yagna of knowledge, O scorcher of enemies. All action without exception, O Partha, culminates in knowledge.

तद्विद्धि प्रणिपातेन, परिप्रश्नेन सेवया ।
उपदेक्ष्यन्ति ते ज्ञानं, ज्ञानिनस्तत्त्वदर्शिनः ॥३४॥

tad viddhi praṇipātena / paripraśnena sevayā
upadekṣyanti te jñānaṁ / jñāninas tattva-darśinaḥ

34. Know this: through homage, repeated inquiry and service, the men of knowledge who have experienced Reality will teach you knowledge.

यज्ज्ञात्वा न पुनर्मोहमेवं यास्यसि पाण्डव ।
येन भूतान्यशेषेण, द्रक्ष्यस्यात्मन्यथो मयि ॥३५॥

yaj jñātvā na punar moham / evaṁ yāsyasi pāṇḍava
yena bhūtāny aśeṣāṇi / drakṣyasy ātmany atho mayi

35. Knowing this, O son of Pandu, you will no more fall into such delusion; for through this you will see all beings in your Self and also in Me.

अपि चेदसि पापेभ्यः, सर्वेभ्यः पापकृत्तमः ।
सर्वं ज्ञानप्लवेनैव, वृजिनं संतरिष्यसि ॥३६॥

api ced asi pāpebhyaḥ / sarvebhyaḥ pāpa-kṛttamaḥ
sarvaṁ jñāna-plavenaiva / vṛjinaṁ santariṣyasi

36. Even if you were the most sinful of all sinners, you would cross over all evil by the raft of knowledge alone.

यथैधांसि समिद्धोऽग्निर्भस्मसात्कुरुतेऽर्जुन ।
ज्ञानाग्निः सर्वकर्माणि भस्मसात्कुरुते तथा ॥३७॥

yathaidhāṁsi samiddho 'gnir bhasmasāt kurute 'rjuna
jñānāgniḥ sarva-karmāṇi bhasmasāt kurute tathā

37. As a blazing fire turns fuel to ashes, so does the fire of knowledge turn all actions into ashes.

न हि ज्ञानेन सदृशं, पवित्रमिह विद्यते ।
तत्स्वयं योगसंसिद्धः, कालेनात्मनि विन्दति ॥३८॥

na hi jñānena sadṛśaṁ / pavitram iha vidyate
tat svayaṁ yoga-saṁsiddhaḥ / kālenātmani vindati

38. Truly there is in this world nothing so purifying as knowledge; he who is perfected in Yoga, of himself in time finds this within himself.

श्रद्धावाँल्लभते ज्ञानं तत्परः संयतेन्द्रियः ।
ज्ञानं लब्ध्वा परां शान्तिमचिरेणाधिगच्छति ॥३९॥

śraddhāvān labhate jñānaṁ tat-paraḥ saṁyatendriyaḥ
jñānaṁ labdhvā parāṁ śāntim acireṇādhigacchati

39. He gains knowledge who is possessed of faith, is active of purpose and has subdued the senses. Having gained knowledge, he comes to supreme peace fast.

अज्ञश्चाश्रद्दधानश्च, संशयात्मा विनश्यति ।
नायं लोकोऽस्ति न परो, न सुखं संशयात्मनः ॥४०॥

ajñaś cāśraddadhānaś ca / saṁśayātmā vinaśyati
nāyaṁ loko 'sti na paro / na sukhaṁ saṁśayātmanaḥ

40. But the man who is without knowledge, without faith and of a doubting nature perishes. For the doubting mind there is neither this world nor another nor any happiness.

योगसंन्यस्तकर्माणं, ज्ञानसंछिन्नसंशयम् ।
आत्मवन्तं न कर्माणि, निबध्नन्ति धनञ्जय ॥४१॥

yoga-sannyasta-karmāṇaṁ / jñāna-sañchinna-saṁśayam
ātma vantaṁ na karmāṇi / nibadhnanti dhanañjaya

41. He who has renounced action by virtue of Yoga, O winner of wealth, whose doubts are rent asunder by knowledge, who is possessed of the Self, him actions do not bind.

तस्मादज्ञानसंभूतं, हृत्स्थं ज्ञानासिनात्मनः ।
छित्त्वैनं संशयं योगमातिष्ठोत्तिष्ठ भारत ॥४२॥

tasmād ajñāna-saṁbhūtaṁ / hṛt-sthaṁ jñānāsinātmanaḥ
chittvainaṁ saṁśayaṁ yogam / ātiṣṭhottiṣṭha bhārata

42. Therefore, having cut asunder with the sword of knowledge this doubt of yours born of ignorance and rooted in the heart, resort to Yoga. Stand up, O Bharata!

ॐ तत् सत् । इति श्रीमद्भगवद्गीतासु उपनिषत्सु ब्रह्मविद्यायां योगशास्त्रे श्रीकृष्णार्जुन संवादे ज्ञानकर्मसंन्यासयोगो नाम चतुर्थोऽध्यायः

Om Tat Sat. Iti Śrimad Bhagavat Gitasu Upanishatsu Brahmavidyayām yogaśastre Sri Krishnarjuna samvade Jñāna Kārma Sanyāsa yogo nama chaturthodhyayaḥ

Thus ends the fourth chapter named "Jnana-Karma-Sanyasa-Yoga" (Path of Renunciation with Knowledge) of the Upanishad of the Bhagavad Gita, the scripture of yoga, dealing with the science of the Absolute in the form of the dialogue between Sri Krishna and Arjuna.

अथ पञ्चमोऽध्यायः - कर्मसंन्यासयोगः

Chapter Five: Karma-Sannyāsa-Yoga

अर्जुन उवाच ।
संन्यासं कर्मणां कृष्ण, पुनर्योगं च शंससि ।
यच्छ्रेय एतयोरेकं, तन्मे ब्रूहि सुनिश्चितम् ॥१॥

arjuna uvāca
sannyāsaṁ karmaṇāṁ kṛṣṇa / punar yogañ ca śaṁsasi
yac chreya etayor ekaṁ / tan me brūhi su-niścitam

1. Arjuna said: Thou praisest, O Krishna, renunciation of action and Yoga (of action) at the same time. Tell me decisively which is the better of these two.

श्रीभगवानुवाच ।
संन्यासः कर्मयोगश्च, निःश्रेयसकरावुभौ ।
तयोस्तु कर्मसंन्यासात्कर्मयोगो विशिष्यते ॥२॥

śrī bhagavān uvāca
sannyāsaḥ karma-yogaś ca / niḥśreyasa-karāv ubhau
tayos tu karma-sannyāsāt / karma-yogo viśiṣyate

2. The Blessed Lord said: Both renunciation and the Yoga of action lead to the supreme good. But of the two, the Yoga of action is superior to the renunciation of action.

ज्ञेयः स नित्यसंन्यासी, यो न द्वेष्टि न काङ्क्षति ।
निर्द्वन्द्वो हि महाबाहो, सुखं बन्धात्प्रमुच्यते ॥३॥

jñeyaḥ sa nitya-sannyāsī / yo na dveṣṭi na kāṅkṣati
nirdvandvo hi mahā-bāho / sukhaṁ bandhāt pramucyate

3. Know him to be ever a man of renunciation who neither hates nor desires; free from the pairs of opposites, he is easily released from bondage, O mighty-armed.

सांख्ययोगौ पृथग्बालाः, प्रवदन्ति न पण्डिताः ।
एकमप्यास्थितः सम्यगुभयोर्विन्दते फलम् ॥४॥

sāṅkhya-yogau pṛthag bālāḥ / pravadanti na paṇḍitāḥ
ekam apyāsthitaḥ samyag / ubhayor vindate phalam

4. The ignorant, and not the wise, speak of the path of knowledge (Sankhya) and the path of action (Yoga) as different. He who is properly established even in one gains the fruit of both.

यत्सांख्यैः प्राप्यते स्थानं, तद्योगैरपि गम्यते ।
एकं सांख्यं च योगं च, यः पश्यति स पश्यति ॥५॥

yat sāṅkhyaiḥ prāpyate sthānaṁ / tad yogair api gamyate
ekaṁ sāṅkhyaṁ ca yogañ ca / yaḥ paśyati sa paśyati

5. The state attained by men on the path of knowledge is also reached by those on the path of action. He who sees Sankhya and Yoga to be one, verily he sees.

संन्यासस्तु महाबाहो, दुःखमाप्तुमयोगतः ।
योगयुक्तो मुनिर्ब्रह्म, नचिरेणाधिगच्छति ॥६॥

sannyāsas tu mahā-bāho / duḥkham āptum ayogataḥ
yoga-yukto munir brahma / na cireṇādhigacchati

6. Renunciation is indeed hard to attain without Yoga, O mighty-armed. The sage who is intent on Yoga comes to Brahman without long delay.

योगयुक्तो विशुद्धात्मा, विजितात्मा जितेन्द्रियः ।
सर्वभूतात्मभूतात्मा, कुर्वन्नपि न लिप्यते ॥७॥

yoga-yukto viśuddhātmā / vijitātmā jitendriyaḥ
sarva-bhūtātma-bhūtātmā / kurvann api na lipyate

7. Intent on Yoga, pure of spirit, he who has fully mastered himself and has conquered the senses, whose self has become the Self of all beings, he is not involved even while he acts.

नैव किंचित्करोमीति युक्तो मन्येत तत्त्ववित् ।
पश्यञ्छृण्वन्स्पृशञ्जिघ्रन्नश्नन्गच्छन्स्वपन्श्वसन् ॥८॥
प्रलपन्विसृजन्गृह्णन्नुन्मिषन्निमिषन्नपि ।
इन्द्रियाणीन्द्रियार्थेषु वर्तन्त इति धारयन् ॥९॥

naiva kiñcit karomīti / yukto manyeta tattva-vit
paśyan śṛṇvan spṛśan jighrann / aśnan gacchan svapan śvasan
pralapan visṛjan gṛhṇann / unmiṣan nimiṣann api
indriyāṇīndriyārtheṣu / varttanta iti dhārayan

8 & 9. One who is in Union with the Divine and who knows the Truth will maintain 'I do not act at all'. In seeing, hearing, touching, smelling, eating, walking, sleeping, breathing, speaking, letting go, seizing and even in opening and closing the eyes, he holds simply that the senses act among the objects of sense.

ब्रह्मण्याधाय कर्माणि, सङ्गं त्यक्त्वा करोति यः ।
लिप्यते न स पापेन, पद्मपत्रमिवाम्भसा ॥१०॥

brahmaṇy ādhāya karmāṇi / saṅgaṁ tyaktvā karoti yaḥ
lipyate na sa pāpena / padma-patram ivāmbhasā

10. He who acts giving over all actions to the universal Being, abandoning attachment, is untouched by sin as a lotus leaf by water.

कायेन मनसा बुद्ध्या, केवलैरिन्द्रियैरपि ।
योगिनः कर्म कुर्वन्ति, सङ्गं त्यक्त्वात्मशुद्धये ॥११॥

kāyena manasā buddhyā / kevalair indriyair api
yoginaḥ karma kurvanti / saṅgaṁ tyaktvātma-śuddhaye

11. By means of the body, by the mind, by the intellect and even by the senses alone, yogis, abandoning attachment, perform action for self purification.

युक्तः कर्मफलं त्यक्त्वा, शान्तिमाप्नोति नैष्ठिकीम् ।
अयुक्तः कामकारेण, फले सक्तो निबध्यते ॥१२॥

yuktaḥ karma-phalaṁ tyaktvā / śāntim āpnoti naiṣṭhikīm
ayuktaḥ kāma-kāreṇa / phale sakto nibadhyate

12. He who is united with the Divine, having abandoned the fruit of action, attains to lasting peace. He who is not united with the Divine, who is spurred by desire, being attached to the fruit of action, is firmly bound.

सर्वकर्माणि मनसा, संन्यस्यास्ते सुखं वशी ।
नवद्वारे पुरे देही, नैव कुर्वन्नकारयन् ॥१३॥

sarva-karmāṇi manasā / sannyasyāste sukhaṁ vaśī
nava-dvāre pure dehī / naiva kurvan na kārayan

13. Having renounced all action by the mind, the dweller in the body rests in happiness, in the city of nine gates, neither acting nor causing action to be done.

न कर्तृत्वं न कर्माणि, लोकस्य सृजति प्रभुः ।
न कर्मफलसंयोगं, स्वभावस्तु प्रवर्तते ॥१४॥

na karttṛtvaṁ na karmāṇi / lokasya sṛjati prabhuḥ
na karma-phala-saṁyogaṁ / svabhāvas tu pravarttate

14. The Lord creates neither the authorship of action nor the action of beings; nor does He create the link between them-the action and its fruit. Nature does this.

नादत्ते कस्यचित्पापं, न चैव सुकृतं विभुः ।
अज्ञानेनावृतं ज्ञानं, तेन मुह्यन्ति जन्तवः ॥१५॥

nādatte kasyacit pāpaṁ / na caiva sukṛtaṁ vibhuḥ
ajñānenāvṛtaṁ jñānaṁ / tena muhyanti jantavaḥ

15. The all-pervading Intelligence does not accept the sin or even the merit of anyone. Wisdom is veiled by ignorance. Thereby creatures are deluded.

ज्ञानेन तु तदज्ञानं, येषां नाशितमात्मनः ।
तेषामादित्यवज्ज्ञानं, प्रकाशयति तत्परम् ॥१६॥

jñānena tu tad ajñānaṁ / yeṣāṁ nāśitam ātmanaḥ
teṣām ādityavaj jñānaṁ / prakāśayati tat param

16. But for those whose ignorance has been destroyed by knowledge of the Supreme, The knowledge of the Absolute, removes ignorance and reveals everything, just like the shining sun removes darkness and lights up everything.

तद्‍बुद्धयस्तदात्मानस्तन्निष्ठास्तत्परायणाः ।
गच्छन्त्यपुनरावृत्तिं ज्ञाननिर्धूतकल्मषाः ॥१७॥

tad-buddhayas tad-ātmānas tan-niṣṭhās tat-parāyaṇāḥ
gacchantyapunar-āvṛttiṁ jñāna-nirdhūta-kalmaṣāḥ

17. Their intellect rooted in That, their being established in That, intent on That, wholly devoted to That, cleansed of all impurities by wisdom, they attain to a state from which there is no return.

विद्याविनयसंपन्ने, ब्राह्मणे गवि हस्तिनि ।
शुनि चैव श्वपाके च, पण्डिताः समदर्शिनः ॥१८॥

vidyā-vinaya-sampanne / brāhmaṇe gavi hastini
śuni caiva śvapāke ca / paṇḍitāḥ sama-darśinaḥ

18. In a brahmin endowed with learning and humility, in a cow, in an elephant, in a dog and even in a dog eater, the enlightened perceives the Supreme Self.

इहैव तैर्जितः सर्गो, येषां साम्ये स्थितं मनः ।
निर्दोषं हि समं ब्रह्म, तस्माद् ब्रह्मणि ते स्थिताः ॥१९॥

ihaiva tair jitaḥ sargo / yeṣāṁ sāmye sthitaṁ manaḥ
nirdoṣaṁ hi samaṁ brahma / tasmād brahmaṇi te sthitāḥ

19. Even here, in this life, the universe is conquered by those whose mind is established in equanimity. Flawless, indeed, and equally present everywhere is Brahman. Therefore they are established in Brahman.

न प्रहृष्येत्प्रियं प्राप्य, नोद्विजेत्प्राप्य चाप्रियम् ।
स्थिरबुद्धिरसंमूढो, ब्रह्मविद्ब्रह्मणि स्थितः ॥२०॥

na prahṛṣyet priyaṁ prāpya / nodvijet prāpya cāpriyam
sthira-buddhir asaṁmūḍho / brahma-vid brahmaṇi sthitaḥ

20. He who neither greatly rejoices on obtaining what is dear to him, nor grieves much on obtaining what is unpleasant, whose intellect is steady, who is free from delusion, he is a knower of Brahman, established in Brahman.

बाह्यस्पर्शेष्वसक्तात्मा, विन्दत्यात्मनि यत्सुखम् ।
स ब्रह्मयोगयुक्तात्मा, सुखमक्षयमश्नुते ॥२१॥

bāhya-sparśeṣv asaktātmā / vindaty ātmani yat sukham
sa brahma-yoga-yuktātmā / sukham akṣayam aśnute

21. He whose self is untouched by external contacts knows that happiness which is in the Self. His self joined in Union with Brahman, he enjoys eternal happiness.

ये हि संस्पर्शजा भोगा, दुःखयोनय एव ते ।
आद्यन्तवन्तः कौन्तेय, न तेषु रमते बुधः ॥२२॥

ye hi saṁsparśajā bhogā / duḥkha-yonaya eva te
ādy-antavantaḥ kaunteya / na teṣu ramate budhaḥ

22. All pleasures born of contact are only sources of sorrow; they have a beginning and an end, O son of Kunti. The enlightened man does not rejoice in them.

शक्नोतीहैव यः सोढुं, प्राक्शरीरविमोक्षणात् ।
कामक्रोधोद्भवं वेगं, स युक्तः स सुखी नरः ॥२३॥

śaknotīhaiva yaḥ soḍhuṁ / prāk śarīra-vimokṣaṇāt
kāma-krodhodbhavaṁ vegaṁ / sa yuktaḥ sa sukhī naraḥ

23. He who is able, even here, before liberation from the body, to resist the excitement born of desire and anger, is united with the Divine, is a happy man.

योऽन्तःसुखोऽन्तरारामस्तथाऽन्तर्ज्योतिरेव यः ।
स योगी ब्रह्मनिर्वाणं, ब्रह्मभूतोऽधिगच्छति ॥२४॥

yo'ntaḥ-sukho'ntarārāmas / tathāntar-jyotir eva yaḥ
sa yogī brahma-nirvāṇaṁ / brahma-bhūto'dhigacchati

24. He whose happiness and contentment is within, whose sight is all within, that yogi, being one with Brahman, attains eternal freedom in divine consciousness.

लभन्ते ब्रह्मनिर्वाणमृषयः क्षीणकल्मषाः ।
छिन्नद्वैधा यतात्मानः, सर्वभूतहिते रताः ॥२५॥

labhante brahma-nirvāṇam / ṛṣayaḥ kṣīṇa-kalmaṣāḥ
chinna-dvaidhā yatātmānaḥ / sarva-bhūta-hite-ratāḥ

25. The seers, whose sins are destroyed, whose doubts are dispelled, who are self-controlled and take delight in doing good to all creatures, attain eternal freedom in divine consciousness.

कामक्रोधवियुक्तानां, यतीनां यतचेतसाम् ।
अभितो ब्रह्मनिर्वाणं, वर्तते विदितात्मनाम् ॥२६॥

kāma-krodha-vimuktānāṁ / yatīnāṁ yata-cetasām
abhito brahma-nirvāṇaṁ / varttate viditātmanām

26. Disciplined men, free from desire and anger, who have disciplined their thoughts and have realized the Self, find eternal freedom in divine consciousness everywhere.

स्पर्शान्कृत्वा बहिर्बाह्यांश्चक्षुश्चैवान्तरे भ्रुवोः ।
प्राणापानौ समौ कृत्वा, नासाभ्यन्तरचारिणौ ॥२७॥

sparśān kṛtvā bahir bāhyāṁś / cakṣuś caivāntare bhruvoḥ
prāṇāpānau samau kṛtvā / nāsābhyantara-cāriṇau

27. Having left external contacts outside; with the vision within the eyebrows; having balanced the ingoing and outgoing breaths that flow through the nostrils,

यतेन्द्रियमनोबुद्धिर्मुनिर्मोक्षपरायणः ।
विगतेच्छाभयक्रोधो, यः सदा मुक्त एव सः ॥२८॥

yatendriya-mano-buddhir / munir mokṣa-parāyaṇaḥ
vigatecchā-bhaya-krodho / yaḥ sadā mukta eva saḥ

28. The sage, whose senses, mind and intellect are controlled, whose aim is liberation, in whom desire, fear and anger have departed, is indeed forever free.

भोक्तारं यज्ञतपसां, सर्वलोकमहेश्वरम् ।
सुहृदं सर्वभूतानां, ज्ञात्वा मां शान्तिमृच्छति ॥२९॥

bhoktāraṁ yajña-tapasāṁ / sarva-loka-maheśvaram
suhṛdaṁ sarva-bhūtānāṁ / jñātvā māṁ śāntim ṛcchati

29. Having known Me as the enjoyer of yajnas and austerities, as the great Lord of all the world, as the friend of all beings, he attains to peace.

ॐ तत् सत् । इति श्रीमद्भगवद्गीतासु उपनिषत्सु ब्रह्मविद्यायां योगशास्त्रे श्रीकृष्णार्जुन संवादे कर्मसंन्यासयोगो नाम पञ्चमोऽध्यायः ॥

Om Tat Sat. Iti Śrimad Bhagavat Gitasu Upanishatsu Brahmavidyayām yogaśastre Sri Krishnarjuna samvade Kārma Sanyāsa yogo nama panchamodhyayaḥ

Thus ends the fifth chapter named "Karma-Sanyasa-Yoga" (Path of Renunciation of Action) of the Upanishad of the Bhagavad Gita, the scripture of yoga, dealing with the science of the Absolute in the form of the dialogue between Sri Krishna and Arjuna.

अथ षष्ठोऽध्यायः - ध्यानयोगोयोगः

Chapter Six: Dhyana-Yoga

श्रीभगवानुवाच ।
अनाश्रितः कर्मफलं, कार्यं कर्म करोति यः ।
स संन्यासी च योगी च, न निरग्निर्न चाक्रियः ॥१॥

śrī bhagavān uvāca
anāśritaḥ karma-phalaṁ / kāryaṁ karma karoti yaḥ
sa sannyāsī ca yogī ca / na niragnir na cākriyaḥ

1. The Blessed Lord said: Those who perform prescribed duties without desiring the results of their actions are actual sannyasis and yogis. Those who cease performing yajnas, such as the agni-hotra-yajna, are not sannyasis, and those who merely abandon all bodily activities are not yogis.

यं संन्यासमिति प्राहुर्योगं तं विद्धि पाण्डव ।
न ह्यसंन्यस्तसंकल्पो, योगी भवति कश्चन ॥२॥

yaṁ sannyāsam iti prāhur / yogaṁ taṁ viddhi pāṇḍava
na hyasannyasta-saṅkalpo / yogī bhavati kaścana

2. That which they call Sanyasa, know it to be Yoga, O son of Pandu, for no one becomes a yogi who has not relinquished the incentive of desire.

आरुरुक्षोर्मुनेर्योगं, कर्म कारणमुच्यते ।
योगारूढस्य तस्यैव, शमः कारणमुच्यते ॥३॥

āruruksor-muner yogaṁ / karma kāraṇam ucyate
yogārūḍhasya tasyaiva / śamaḥ kāraṇam ucyate

3. Action is said to be the means for the man of thought wishing to ascend to Yoga; for the man who has ascended to Yoga, and for him alone, calmness is said to be the means.

यदा हि नेन्द्रियार्थेषु, न कर्मस्वनुषज्जते ।
सर्वसंकल्पसंन्यासी, योगारूढस्तदोच्यते ॥४॥

yadā hi nendriyārtheṣu / na karmasv anuṣajjate
sarva-saṅkalpa-sannyāsī / yogārūḍhas tadocyate

4. Only when a man does not cling to the objects of the senses or to actions, only when he has relinquished all incentive of desire, is he said to have ascended to Yoga.

उद्धरेदात्मनात्मानं नात्मानमवसादयेत् ।
आत्मैव ह्यात्मनो बन्धुरात्मैव रिपुरात्मनः ॥५॥

uddhared ātmanātmānaṁ nātmānam avasādayet
ātmaiva hy ātmano bandhur ātmaiva ripur ātmanaḥ

5. Let a man raise his self by his Self, let him not debase his Self; he alone, indeed, is his own friend, he alone his own enemy.

बन्धुरात्मात्मनस्तस्य, येनात्मैवात्मना जितः ।
अनात्मनस्तु शत्रुत्वे, वर्तेतात्मैव शत्रुवत् ॥६॥

bandhur ātmātmanas tasya / yenātmaivātmanā jitaḥ
anātmanas tu śatrutve / varttetātmaiva śatru-vat

6. He who has conquered his self by his Self alone is himself his own friend; but the Self of him who has not conquered his self will behave with enmity like a foe.

जितात्मनः प्रशान्तस्य, परमात्मा समाहितः ।
शीतोष्णसुखदुःखेषु, तथा मानापमानयोः ॥७॥

jitātmanaḥ praśāntasya / paramātmā samāhitaḥ
śītoṣṇa-sukha-duḥkheṣu / tathā mānāpamānayoḥ

7. For him who has conquered his self, who is deep in peace, the transcendent Self is steadfast in heat and cold, in pleasure and pain, in honour and disgrace.

ज्ञानविज्ञानतृप्तात्मा, कूटस्थो विजितेन्द्रियः ।
युक्त इत्युच्यते योगी, समलोष्टाश्मकाञ्चनः ॥८॥

jñāna-vijñāna-tṛptātmā / kūṭastho vijitendriyaḥ
yukta ityucyate yogī / sama-loṣṭāśma-kāñcanaḥ

8. That yogi is said to be united who is contented in knowledge and experience, unshakeable, master of the senses, who is balanced in experiencing earth, stone or gold.

सुहृन्मित्रार्युदासीनमध्यस्थद्वेष्यबन्धुषु ।
साधुष्वपि च पापेषु, समबुद्धिर्विशिष्यते ॥६॥

suhṛn-mitrāry-udāsīna / madhyastha-dveṣya-bandhuṣu
sādhuṣv api ca pāpeṣu / sama-buddhir viśiṣyate

9. Distinguished is he who is of even intellect among well-wishers, friends and foes, among the indifferent and the impartial, among hateful persons and among kinsmen, among the saints as well as the sinful.

योगी युञ्जीत सततमात्मानं रहसि स्थितः ।
एकाकी यतचित्तात्मा, निराशीरपरिग्रहः ॥१०॥

yogī yuñjīta satatam / ātmānaṁ rahasi sthitaḥ
ekākī yata-cittātmā / nirāśīr aparigrahaḥ

10. Let the yogi always collect himself remaining in seclusion, alone, his mind and body subdued, expecting nothing, without possessions.

शुचौ देशे प्रतिष्ठाप्य, स्थिरमासनमात्मनः ।
नात्युच्छ्रितं नातिनीचं, चैलाजिनकुशोत्तरम् ॥११॥

śucau deśe pratiṣṭhāpya / sthiram āsanam ātmanaḥ
nāty-ucchritaṁ nāti-nīcaṁ / cailājina-kuśottaram

11. In a clean place, having set his seat firm, neither very high nor very low, having placed sacred kusa grass, deerskin and cloth one upon the other.

तत्रैकाग्रं मनः कृत्वा, यतचित्तेन्द्रियक्रियः ।
उपविश्यासने युञ्ज्या - द्योगमात्मविशुद्धये ॥१२॥

tatraikāgraṁ manaḥ kṛtvā / yata-cittendriya-kriyaḥ
upaviśyāsane yuñjyād / yogam ātma-viśuddhaye

12. Seated there on the seat, having made the mind one-pointed, with the activity of the senses and thought subdued, let him practise Yoga for self-purification.

समं कायशिरोग्रीवं, धारयन्नचलं स्थिरः ।
संप्रेक्ष्य नासिकाग्रं स्वं, दिशश्चानवलोकयन् ॥१३॥

samaṁ kāya-śiro-grīvaṁ / dhārayann acalaṁ sthiraḥ
saṁprekṣya nāsikāgraṁ svaṁ / diśaś cānavalokayan

13. Steady, keeping body, head and neck upright and still, having directed his gaze to the front of his nose, without looking in any direction,

प्रशान्तात्मा विगतभीर्ब्रह्मचारिव्रते स्थितः ।
मनः संयम्य मच्चित्तो युक्त आसीत मत्परः ॥१४॥

praśāntātmā vigata-bhīr brahmacāri-vrate sthitaḥ
manaḥ saṁyamya mac-citto yukta āsīta mat-paraḥ

14. With his being deep in peace, freed from fear, settled in the vow of chastity, with mind subdued and thought given over to Me, let him sit united realizing Me as the Transcendent.

युञ्जन्नेवं सदात्मानं, योगी नियतमानसः ।
शान्तिं निर्वाणपरमां, मत्संस्थामधिगच्छति ॥१५॥

yuñjann evaṁ sadātmānaṁ / yogī niyata mānasaḥ
śāntiṁ nirvāṇa-paramāṁ / mat-saṁsthām adhigacchati

15. Ever thus collecting himself, the yogi of disciplined mind attains to peace, the supreme liberation that abides in Me.

नात्यश्नतस्तु योगोऽस्ति, न चैकान्तमनश्नतः ।
न चातिस्वप्नशीलस्य, जाग्रतो नैव चार्जुन ॥१६॥

nātyaśnatas tu yogo'sti / na caikāntam-anaśnataḥ
na cāti-svapna-śīlasya / jāgrato naiva cārjuna

16. Yoga, indeed, is not for him who eats too much nor for him who does not eat at all, O Arjuna; it is not for him who is too much given to sleep nor yet for him who keeps awake.

युक्ताहारविहारस्य, युक्तचेष्टस्य कर्मसु ।
युक्तस्वप्नावबोधस्य, योगो भवति दुःखहा ॥१७॥

yuktāhāra-vihārasya / yukta-ceṣṭasya karmasu
yukta-svapnāvabodhasya / yogo bhavati duḥkha-hā

17. For him who is moderate in food and recreation, moderate of effort in actions, moderate in sleep and waking, for him is the Yoga which destroys sorrow.

यदा विनियतं चित्तमात्मन्येवावतिष्ठते ।
निःस्पृहः सर्वकामेभ्यो युक्त इत्युच्यते तदा ॥१८॥

yadā viniyataṁ cittam ātmany evāvatiṣṭhate
nispṛhaḥ sarva-kāmebhyo yukta ityucyate tadā

18. When his mind, completely settled, is established in the Self alone, when he is free from craving for any pleasure, then is he said to be united.

यथा दीपो निवातस्थो, नेङ्गते सोपमा स्मृता ।
योगिनो यतचित्तस्य, युञ्जतो योगमात्मनः ॥१९॥

yathā dīpo nivāta-stho / neṅgate sopamā smṛtā
yogino yata-cittasya / yuñjato yogam ātmanaḥ

19. A lamp which does not flicker in a windless place, to such is compared the yogi of subdued thought practising Union with the Self.

यत्रोपरमते चित्तं, निरुद्धं योगसेवया ।
यत्र चैवात्मनात्मानं, पश्यन्नात्मनि तुष्यति ॥२०॥

yatroparamate cittaṁ / niruddhaṁ yoga-sevayā
yatra caivātmanātmānaṁ / paśyann ātmani tuṣyati

20. That (state) in which thought, settled through the practice of Yoga, retires, in which, seeing the Self by the Self alone, he finds contentment in the Self.

सुखमात्यन्तिकं यत्तद्‌बुद्धिग्राह्यमतीन्द्रियम्।
वेत्ति यत्र न चैवायं, स्थितश्चलति तत्त्वतः ॥२१॥

sukham ātyantikaṁ yat tad / buddhi-grāhyam atīndriyam
vetti yatra na caivāyaṁ / sthitaś calati tattvataḥ

21. Knowing that which is infinite joy and which, lying beyond the senses, is gained by the intellect, and wherein established, truly he does not waver.

यं लब्ध्वा चापरं लाभं, मन्यते नाधिकं ततः ।
यस्मिन्स्थितो न दुःखेन, गुरुणापि विचाल्यते ॥२२॥

yaṁ labdhvā cāparaṁ lābhaṁ / manyate nādhikaṁ tataḥ
yasmin sthito na duḥkhena / guruṇāpi vicālyate

22. Having gained which he counts no other gain as higher, established in which he is not moved even by great sorrow.

तं विद्याद् दुःखसंयोगवियोगं योगसंज्ञितम् ।
स निश्चयेन योक्तव्यो, योगोऽनिर्विण्णचेतसा ॥२३॥

taṁ vidyād duḥkha-saṁyoga / viyogaṁ yoga-saṁjñitam
sa niścayena yoktavyo / yogo'nirviṇṇa-cetasā

23. Let that disunion of the union with sorrow be known by the name of Yoga (Union). This Yoga should be practised with firm resolve and heart undismayed.

संकल्पप्रभवान्कामांस्त्यक्त्वा सर्वानशेषतः ।
मनसैवेन्द्रियग्रामं, विनियम्य समन्ततः ॥२४॥

saṅkalpa-prabhavān kāmāṁs / tyaktvā sarvān aśeṣataḥ
manasaivendriya-grāmaṁ / viniyamya samantataḥ

24. Abandoning without reserve all desires from which the incentive (to action) is born, controlling the group of senses on every side by the mind alone.

शनैः शनैरुपरमेद्बुद्ध्या धृतिगृहीतया ।
आत्मसंस्थं मनः कृत्वा न किंचिदपि चिन्तयेत् ॥२५॥

śanaiḥ śanair uparamed buddhyā dhṛti-gṛhītayā
ātma-saṁsthaṁ manaḥ kṛtvā na kiñcid api cintayet

25. Let him gradually retire through the intellect possessed of patience; having established the mind in the Self, let him not think anything at all.

यतो यतो निश्चरति मनश्चञ्चलमस्थिरम् ।
ततस्ततो नियम्यैतदात्मन्येव वशं नयेत् ॥२६॥

yato yato niścalati manaś cañcalam asthiram
tatastato niyamyaitad ātmanyeva vaśaṁ nayet

26. Whatever makes the fickle and unsteady mind wander forth, from that withdrawn, let him bring it under the sway of the Self alone.

प्रशान्तमनसं ह्येनं, योगिनं सुखमुत्तमम् ।
उपैति शान्तरजसं, ब्रह्मभूतमकल्मषम् ॥२७॥

praśānta-manasaṁ hyenaṁ / yoginaṁ sukham uttamam
upaiti śānta-rajasaṁ / brahma-bhūtam akalmaṣam

27. For supreme happiness comes to the yogi whose mind is deep in peace, in whom the spur to activity is stilled, who is without blemish and has become one with Brahman.

युञ्जन्नेवं सदात्मानं योगी विगतकल्मषः ।
सुखेन ब्रह्मसंस्पर्शमत्यन्तं सुखमश्नुते ॥२८॥

yuñjannevaṁ sadātmānaṁ yogī vigata-kalmaṣaḥ
sukhena brahma-saṁsparśam atyantaṁ sukham aśnute

28. Ever thus collecting himself, the yogi, freed from blemish, with ease attains contact with Brahman, which is infinite joy.

सर्वभूतस्थमात्मानं, सर्वभूतानि चात्मनि ।
ईक्षते योगयुक्तात्मा, सर्वत्र समदर्शनः ॥२९॥

sarva-bhūta-stham ātmānaṁ / sarva-bhūtāni cātmani
īkṣate yoga-yuktātmā / sarvatra sama-darśanaḥ

29. He whose self is established in Yoga, whose vision everywhere is even, sees the Self in all beings, and all beings in the Self.

यो मां पश्यति सर्वत्र, सर्वं च मयि पश्यति ।
तस्याहं न प्रणश्यामि, स च मे न प्रणश्यति ॥३०॥

yo māṁ paśyati sarvatra / sarvaṁ ca mayi paśyati
tasyāhaṁ na praṇaśyāmi / sa ca me na praṇaśyati

30. He who sees Me everywhere, and sees everything in Me, I am not lost to him nor is he lost to Me.

सर्वभूतस्थितं यो मां, भजत्येकत्वमास्थितः ।
सर्वथा वर्तमानोऽपि, स योगी मयि वर्तते ॥३१॥

sarva-bhūta-sthitaṁ yo māṁ / bhajatyekatvam āsthitaḥ
sarvathā varttamāno'pi / sa yogī mayi varttate

31. Established in Unity, he who worships Me abiding in all beings, in whatever way he lives, that yogi lives in Me.

आत्मौपम्येन सर्वत्र, समं पश्यति योऽर्जुन ।
सुखं वा यदि वा दुःखं, स योगी परमो मतः ॥३२॥

ātmaupamyena sarvatra / samaṁ paśyati yo'rjuna
sukhaṁ vā yadi vā duḥkhaṁ / sa yogī paramo mataḥ

32. He who sees everything with an even vision by comparison with the Self, be it pleasure or pain, he is deemed the highest yogi, O Arjuna.

अर्जुन उवाच ।
योऽयं योगस्त्वया प्रोक्तः, साम्येन मधुसूदन ।
एतस्याहं न पश्यामि, चञ्चलत्वात्स्थितिं स्थिराम् ॥३३॥

arjuna uvāca
yo 'yaṁ yogastvayā proktaḥ / sāmyena madhusūdana
etasyāhaṁ na paśyāmi / cañcalatvāt sthitiṁ sthirām

33. Arjuna said: This Yoga described by Thee as characterized by evenness, O Madhusudana, I do not see its steady endurance, because of wavering.

चञ्चलं हि मनः कृष्ण, प्रमाथि बलवद्दृढम् ।
तस्याहं निग्रहं मन्ये, वायोरिव सुदुष्करम् ॥३४॥

cañcalaṁ hi manaḥ kṛṣṇa / pramāthi balavad dṛḍham
tasyāhaṁ nigrahaṁ manye / vāyor iva suduṣkaram

34. For wavering is the mind, O Krishna, turbulent, powerful and unyielding; I consider it as difficult to control as the wind.

श्रीभगवानुवाच ।
असंशयं महाबाहो, मनो दुर्निग्रहं चलम् ।
अभ्यासेन तु कौन्तेय, वैराग्येण च गृह्यते ॥३५॥

śrī bhagavān uvāca
asaṁśayaṁ mahā-bāho / mano durnigrahaṁ calam
abhyāsena tu kaunteya / vairāgyeṇa ca gṛhyate

35. The Blessed Lord said: No doubt, O mighty-armed, the mind is hard to control, it is wavering, but by practice and non-attachment it is held, O son of Kunti.

असंयतात्मना योगो, दुष्प्राप इति मे मतिः ।
वश्यात्मना तु यतता, शक्योऽवाप्तुमुपायतः ॥३६॥

asaṁyatātmanā yogo / duṣprāpa iti me matiḥ
vaśyātmanā tu yatatā / śakyo'vāptum upāyataḥ

36. For an indisciplined man, Yoga is hard to achieve, so I consider; but it can be gained through proper means by the man of endeavour who is disciplined.

अर्जुन उवाच ।
अयतिः श्रद्धयोपेतो, योगाच्चलितमानसः ।
अप्राप्य योगसंसिद्धिं, कां गतिं कृष्ण गच्छति ॥३७॥

arjuna uvāca
ayatiḥ śraddhayopeto / yogāc calita-mānasaḥ
aprāpya yoga-saṁsiddhiṁ / kāṁ gatiṁ kṛṣṇa gacchati

37. Arjuna said: What goal does he reach, O Krishna, who is not perfected in Yoga, being endowed with faith, yet lacking effort, his mind strayed from Yoga?

कच्चिन्नोभयविभ्रष्टश्छिन्नाभ्रमिव नश्यति ।
अप्रतिष्ठो महाबाहो, विमूढो ब्रह्मणः पथि ॥३८॥

kaccin nobhaya-vibhraṣṭaś / chinnābhramiva naśyati
apratiṣṭho mahā-bāho / vimūḍho brahmaṇaḥ pathi

38. Deluded on the path to Brahman, O mighty-armed, without foothold and fallen from both, does he not perish like a broken cloud?

एतन्मे संशयं कृष्ण, छेत्तुमर्हस्यशेषतः ।
त्वदन्यः संशयस्यास्य, छेत्ता न ह्युपपद्यते ॥३६॥

etan me saṁśayaṁ kṛṣṇa / chettum arhasy aśeṣataḥ
tvad-anyaḥ saṁśayasyāsya / chettā na hyupapadyate

39. Thou art able to dispel this doubt of mine completely, O Krishna. Truly, there is none save Thee who can dispel this doubt.

श्रीभगवानुवाच ।
पार्थ नैवेह नामुत्र, विनाशस्तस्य विद्यते ।
न हि कल्याणकृत्कश्चिद्दुर्गतिं तात गच्छति ॥४०॥

śrī bhagavān uvāca
pārtha naiveha nāmutra / vināśas tasya vidyate
na hi kalyāṇa-kṛt kaścid / durgatiṁ tāta gacchati

40. The Blessed Lord said: O Partha, there is no destruction for him in this world or hereafter; for none who acts uprightly, My dear, goes the way of misfortune.

प्राप्य पुण्यकृतां लोकानुषित्वा शाश्वतीः समाः ।
शुचीनां श्रीमतां गेहे, योगभ्रष्टोऽभिजायते ॥४१॥

prāpya puṇya-kṛtāṁ lokān / uṣitvā śāśvatīḥ samāḥ
śucīnāṁ śrīmatāṁ gehe / yoga-bhraṣṭo'bhijāyate

41. Having attained the worlds of the righteous and dwelt there for countless years, he that strayed from Yoga is born in the house of the pure and illustrious.

अथवा योगिनामेव, कुले भवति धीमताम् ।
एतद्धि दुर्लभतरं, लोके जन्म यदीदृशम् ॥४२॥

athavā yogināṁ eva / kule bhavati dhīmatām
etad dhi durlabhataraṁ / loke janma yadīdṛśam

42. Or he is born in an actual family of yogis endowed with wisdom, though such a birth as this on earth is more difficult to attain.

तत्र तं बुद्धिसंयोगं, लभते पौर्वदेहिकम् ।
यतते च ततो भूयः, संसिद्धौ कुरुनन्दन ॥४३॥

tatra taṁ buddhi-saṁyogaṁ / labhate paurva-daihikam
yatate ca tato bhūyaḥ / saṁsiddhau kuru-nandana

43. There he regains that level of Union reached by the intellect in his former body, and by virtue of this, O joy of the Kurus, he strives yet more for perfection.

पूर्वाभ्यासेन तेनैव, ह्रियते ह्यवशोऽपि सः ।
जिज्ञासुरपि योगस्य, शब्दब्रह्मातिवर्तते ॥४४॥

pūrvābhyāsena tenaiva / hriyate hyavaśo'pi saḥ
jijñāsur api yogasya / śabda-brahmātivarttate

44. By that former practice itself he is irresistibly borne on. Even the aspirant to Yoga passes beyond the Veda.

प्रयत्नाद्यतमानस्तु योगी संशुद्धकिल्बिषः ।
अनेकजन्मसंसिद्धस्ततो याति परां गतिम् ॥४५॥

prayatnād yatmānas tu yogī saṁśuddha-kilbiṣaḥ
aneka-janma-saṁsiddhas tato yāti parāṁ gatim

45. But the yogi who strives with zeal, purified of all sin and perfected through many births, thereupon reaches the transcendent goal.

तपस्विभ्योऽधिको योगी, ज्ञानिभ्योऽपि मतोऽधिकः ।
कर्मिभ्यश्चाधिको योगी, तस्माद्योगी भवार्जुन ॥४६॥

tapasvibhyo'dhiko yogī / jñānibhyo'pi
mato'dhikaḥ
karmibhyaś cādhiko yogī / tasmād yogī
bhavārjuna

46. A yogi is superior to the austere; he is deemed superior even to men of knowledge. A yogi is superior to men of action. Therefore be a yogi, O Arjuna.

योगिनामपि सर्वेषां, मद्गतेनान्तरात्मना ।
श्रद्धावान्भजते यो मां, स मे युक्ततमो मतः ॥४७॥

yogināṁ api sarveṣāṁ / mad-gatenāntarātmanā
śraddhāvān bhajate yo māṁ / sa me yuktatamo mataḥ

47. And of all yogis, I hold him most fully united who worships Me with faith, his inmost Self absorbed in Me.

ॐ तत् सत् । इति श्रीमद्भगवद्गीतासु उपनिषत्सु ब्रह्मविद्यायां योगशास्त्रे श्रीकृष्णार्जुन संवादे ध्यानयोगो नाम षष्ठोऽध्यायः ॥

Om Tat Sat. Iti Śrimad Bhagavat Gitasu Upanishatsu Brahmavidyayām yogaśastre Sri Krishnarjuna samvade Dhyana yogo nama Shashtodhyayaḥ

Thus ends the sixth chapter named "Dhyana-Yoga" (Path of Meditation) of the Upanishad of the Bhagavad Gita, the scripture of yoga, dealing with the science of the Absolute in the form of the dialogue between Sri Krishna and Arjuna.

अथ सप्तमोऽध्यायः - ज्ञानविज्ञानयोगः

Chapter Seven: Jñāna-Vijñāna-Yoga

श्रीभगवानुवाच ।
मय्यासक्तमनाः पार्थ, योगं युञ्जन्मदाश्रयः ।
असंशयं समग्रं मां, यथा ज्ञास्यसि तच्छृणु ॥१॥

śrī bhagavān uvāca
mayyāsakta-manāḥ pārtha / yogaṁ yuñjan mad-āśrayaḥ
asaṁśayaṁ samagraṁ māṁ / yathā jñāsyasi tac chṛṇu

1. The Blessed Lord said: With the mind fixed on me, O son of Pritha, taking refuge in Me, and practicing yoga, how you shall know Me fully, without doubt, that do you hear.

ज्ञानं तेऽहं सविज्ञानमिदं वक्ष्याम्यशेषतः ।
यज्ज्ञात्वा नेह भूयोऽन्यत्ज्ञातव्यमवशिष्यते ॥२॥

jñānaṁ te'haṁ sa-vijñānam idaṁ vakṣyāmyaśeṣataḥ
yajjñātvā neha bhūyo'nyat jñātavyam avaśiṣyate

2. Of knowledge, speculative and practical, I shall tell you in full, knowing which, nothing more remains to be known.

मनुष्याणां सहस्रेषु, कश्चिद्यतति सिद्धये ।
यततामपि सिद्धानां, कश्चिन्मां वेत्ति तत्त्वतः ॥३॥

manuṣyāṇāṁ sahasreṣu / kaścid yatati siddhaye
yatatām api siddhānāṁ / kaścin māṁ vetti tattvataḥ

3. One, in thousands of men, by chance, strives for perfection; and one per chance, among the blessed ones, striving thus, knows Me in truth.

भूमिरापोऽनलो वायुः, खं मनो बुद्धिरेव च ।
अहंकार इतीयं मे, भिन्ना प्रकृतिरष्टधा ॥४॥

bhūmir āpo'nalo vāyuḥ / khaṁ mano buddhir eva ca
ahaṅkāra itīyaṁ me / bhinnā prakṛtir aṣṭadhā

4. Bhumi (earth), Ap (water), Anala (fire), Vayu (air), Kham (ether), mind, intellect, and egoism: thus is my Nature, divided eightfold.

अपरेयमितस्त्वन्यां, प्रकृतिं विद्धि मे पराम् ।
जीवभूतां महाबाहो, ययेदं धार्यते जगत् ॥५॥

apareyam itastvanyāṁ / prakṛtiṁ viddhi me parām
jīva-bhūtāṁ mahā-bāho / yayedaṁ dhāryate jagat

5. This is the lower material nature. But different from it, know, O mighty-armed, My higher nature–the principle of self-consciousness, by which this creation is sustained.

एतद्योनीनि भूतानि, सर्वाणीत्युपधारय ।
अहं कृत्स्नस्य जगतः, प्रभवः प्रलयस्तथा ॥६॥

etad yonīni bhūtāni / sarvāṇītyupadhāraya
ahaṁ kṛtsnasya jagataḥ / prabhavaḥ pralayas tathā

6. Arjuna, know that these natures are the womb of all beings and I am the source and dissolution of the entire universe.

मत्तः परतरं नान्यत्किंचिदस्ति धनंजय ।
मयि सर्वमिदं प्रोतं, सूत्रे मणिगणा इव ॥७॥

mattaḥ parataraṁ nānyat / kiñcid asti dhanañjaya
mayi sarvam idaṁ protaṁ / sūtre maṇi-gaṇā iva

7. O Dhananjaya, there is nothing beyond Me. All this is threaded and strung in Me, as an array of jewels.

रसोऽहमप्सु कौन्तेय, प्रभाऽस्मि शशिसूर्ययोः ।
प्रणवः सर्ववेदेषु, शब्दः खे पौरुषं नृषु ॥८॥

raso'ham apsu kaunteya / prabhāsmi śaśi-sūryayoḥ
praṇavaḥ sarva-vedeṣu / śabdaḥ khe pauruṣaṁ nṛṣu

8. Arjuna, I am the sapidity in water and I, the light in the moon and the sun; I am the Om in all the Vedas, sound in ether, and manhood in men.

पुण्यो गन्धः पृथिव्यां च, तेजश्चास्मि विभावसौ ।
जीवनं सर्वभूतेषु, तपश्चास्मि तपस्विषु ॥९॥

puṇyo gandhaḥ pṛthivyāñ ca / tejaś cāsmi vibhāvasau
jīvanaṁ sarva-bhūteṣu / tapaś cāsmi tapasviṣu

9. I am the pure odour in earth, and the brilliance in fire am I; the life in all beings, and the austerity am I in ascetics.

बीजं मां सर्वभूतानां, विद्धि पार्थ सनातनम् ।
बुद्धिर्बुद्धिमतामस्मि, तेजस्तेजस्विनामहम् ॥१०॥

bījaṁ māṁ sarva-bhūtānāṁ / viddhi pārtha sanātanam
buddhir buddhimatām asmi / tejas tejasvinām aham

10. Know me Partha, as the eternal seed of all beings. I am the intelligence of the intelligent, and the glory of the glorious.

बलं बलवतामस्मि, कामरागविवर्जितम् ।
धर्माविरुद्धो भूतेषु, कामोऽस्मि भरतर्षभ ॥११॥

balaṁ balavatāmasmi / kāma-rāga-vivarjitam
dharmāviruddho bhūteṣu / kāmo'smi bharatarṣabha

11. Of the mighty, I am the might, free from passion and desire. I am, O Bharata, desire in beings, unopposed to dharma.

ये चैव सात्त्विका भावाः, राजसास्तामसाश्च ये ।
मत्त एवेति तान्विद्धि, न त्वहं तेषु ते मयि ॥१२॥

ye caiva sāttvikā bhāvā / rājasās tāmasāś ca ye
matta eveti tān viddhi / na tv ahaṁ teṣu te mayi

12. Whatever be the quality-sattwa, rajas or tamas, they all are evolved from me alone. Yet I am not in them, but they are in Me.

त्रिभिर्गुणमयैर्भावैरेभिः सर्वमिदं जगत् ।
मोहितं नाभिजानाति, मामेभ्यः परमव्ययम् ॥१३॥

tribhir guṇa-mayair bhāvair / ebhiḥ sarvam idaṁ jagat
mohitaṁ nābhijānāti / mām ebhyaḥ param avyayam

13. The whole of creation is deluded by these three qualities. So all this world does not know Me who is beyond them, and is imperishable.

दैवी ह्येषा गुणमयी, मम माया दुरत्यया ।
मामेव ये प्रपद्यन्ते, मायामेतां तरन्ति ते ॥१४॥

daivī hyeṣā guṇamayī / mama māyā duratyayā
mām eva ye prapadyante / māyām etāṁ taranti te

14. This divine illusion of Mine, made of the three qualities or gunas, is difficult to break through; those who always adore Me alone, cross over this Maya.

न मां दुष्कृतिनो मूढाः, प्रपद्यन्ते नराधमाः ।
माययाऽपहृतज्ञानाः, आसुरं भावमाश्रिताः ॥१५॥

na māṁ duṣkṛtino mūḍhāḥ / prapadyante narādhamāḥ
māyayāpahṛta-jñānā / āsuraṁ bhāvam āśritāḥ

15. They, the evil-doers, the deluded, the lowest of men, deprived of discrimination by Maya, and following the way of the Asuras, they do not adore Me.

चतुर्विधा भजन्ते मां, जनाः सुकृतिनोऽर्जुन ।
आर्तो जिज्ञासुरर्थार्थी, ज्ञानी च भरतर्षभ ॥१६॥

catur-vidhā bhajante māṁ / janāḥ sukṛtino'rjuna
ārtto jijñāsur arthārthī / jñānī ca bharatarṣabha

16. O Arjuna, four types of noble men worship Me, the distressed, the seeker of knowledge, the seeker of enjoyment, and the wise.

तेषां ज्ञानी नित्ययुक्तः, एकभक्तिर्विशिष्यते ।
प्रियो हि ज्ञानिनोऽत्यर्थ महं स च मम प्रियः ॥१७॥

teṣāṁ jñānī nitya-yukta / eka-bhaktir viśiṣyate
priyo hi jñānino'ty-artham / ahaṁ sa ca mama priyaḥ

17. Of them, the wise man, steadfast in his identity with Me and having exclusive devotion to me, excels; for supremely dear am I to him, and he to Me.

उदाराः सर्व एवैते, ज्ञानी त्वात्मैव मे मतम् ।
आस्थितः स हि युक्तात्मा, मामेवानुत्तमां गतिम् ॥१८॥

udārāḥ sarvaḥ evaite / jñānī tvātmaiva me matam
āsthitaḥ sa hi yuktātmā / mām evānuttamāṁ gatim

18. They are all noble, but the wise man I regard as My very self; for with the mind and intellect merged in me, he is established in Me alone, as the highest goal.

बहूनां जन्मनामन्ते, ज्ञानवान्मां प्रपद्यते ।
वासुदेवः सर्वमिति, स महात्मा सुदुर्लभः ॥१९॥

bahūnāṁ janmanām ante / jñānavān māṁ prapadyate
vāsudevaḥ sarvam iti / sa mahātmā sudurlabhaḥ

19. After many births, the wise man worships Me, realizing that all this is God (the innermost self). Such a great soul is very rare.

कामैस्तैस्तैर्हृतज्ञानाः, प्रपद्यन्तेऽन्यदेवताः ।
तं तं नियममास्थाय, प्रकृत्या नियताः स्वया ॥२०॥

kāmais tais tair hṛta-jñānāḥ / prapadyante'nya-devatāḥ
taṁ taṁ niyamam āsthāya / prakṛtyā niyatāḥ svayā

20. Deprived of discrimination by desire, following their respective rites, others again devote themselves to other gods, led by their own natures.

यो यो यां यां तनुं भक्तः, श्रद्धयार्चितुमिच्छति ।
तस्य तस्याचलां श्रद्धां, तामेव विदधाम्यहम् ॥२१॥

yo yo yāṁ yāṁ tanuṁ bhaktaḥ / śraddhayārcitum icchati
tasya tasyācalāṁ śraddhāṁ / tām eva vidadhāmy aham

21. Whatsoever form any devotee seeks to worship with shraddha, I make his shraddha unwavering.

स तया श्रद्धया युक्तस्तस्याराधनमीहते ।
लभते च ततः कामान्मयैव विहितान्हि तान् ॥२२॥

sa tayā śraddhayā yuktastasyārādhanam īhate
labhate ca tataḥ kāmān mayaiva vihitān hi tān

22. With shraddha, he worships that, and from it, gains his desires, being dispensed by Me alone.

अन्तवत्तु फलं तेषां, तद्भवत्यल्पमेधसाम् ।
देवान्देवयजो यान्ति मद्भक्ता यान्ति मामपि ॥२३॥

antavat tu phalaṁ teṣāṁ tad bhavaty alpa-medhasām
devān deva-yajo yānti mad-bhaktā yānti mām api

23. The gains of these men of little understanding is limited. The devotees of the devas go to the devas; My devotees come to me alone.

अव्यक्तं व्यक्तिमापन्नं, मन्यन्ते मामबुद्धयः ।
परं भावमजानन्तो, ममाव्ययमनुत्तमम् ॥२४॥

avyaktaṁ vyaktimāpannaṁ / manyante mām abuddhayaḥ
paraṁ bhāvam ajānanto / mamāvyayam anuttamam

24. The ignorant believe that the infinite has come as finite, not knowing My supreme state – immutable and transcendental.

नाहं प्रकाशः सर्वस्य, योगमायासमावृतः ।
मूढोऽयं नाभिजानाति, लोको मामजमव्ययम् ॥२५॥

nāhaṁ prakāśaḥ sarvasya / yogamāyā-samāvṛtaḥ
mūḍho'yaṁ nābhijānāti / loko mām ajam avyayam

25. Veiled by Maya, I am not manifest to all. This deluded world knows Me as subject to birth and death, not as the Unborn, the Immutable.

वेदाहं समतीतानि, वर्तमानानि चार्जुन ।
भविष्याणि च भूतानि, मां तु वेद न कश्चन ॥२६॥

vedāhaṁ samatītāni / varttamānāni cārjuna
bhaviṣyāṇi ca bhūtāni / māṁ tu veda na kaścana

26. O Arjuna, I know, the beings of the past and the present and even of the future, but without faith none know me.

इच्छाद्वेषसमुत्थेन, द्वन्द्वमोहेन भारत ।
सर्वभूतानि संमोहं, सर्गे यान्ति परंतप ॥२७॥

icchā-dveṣa-samutthena / dvandva-mohena bhārata
sarva-bhūtāni sammohaṁ / sarge yānti parantapa

27. O scorcher of foes, by the delusion of duality of opposites, born of desire and aversion, O descendant of Bharata, all beings fall into delusion at birth.

येषां त्वन्तगतं पापं, जनानां पुण्यकर्मणाम् ।
ते द्वन्द्वमोहनिर्मुक्ताः, भजन्ते मां दृढव्रताः ॥२८॥

yeṣāṁ tvanta-gataṁ pāpaṁ / janānāṁ puṇya-karmaṇām
te dvandva-moha-nirmuktā / bhajante māṁ dṛḍha-vratāḥ

28. Those men whose sin has come to an end by virtuous deeds and freed from the delusion of the pairs of opposites, worship Me with firm resolve, in every way.

जरामरणमोक्षाय मामाश्रित्य यतन्ति ये ।
ते ब्रह्म तद्विदुः कृत्स्नमध्यात्मं कर्म चाखिलम् ॥२९॥

jarā-maraṇa-mokṣāya mām āśritya yatanti ye
te brahma tad viduḥ kṛtsnam adhyātmaṁ karma cākhilam

29. Those who strive for deliverance from old age and death, having taken refuge in Me – they know Brahman, the whole of Adhyatma, and karma in its entirety.

साधिभूताधिदैवं मां, साधियज्ञं च ये विदुः ।
प्रयाणकालेऽपि च मां, ते विदुर्युक्तचेतसः ॥३०॥

sādhibhūtādhidaivaṁ māṁ / sādhiyajñañca ye viduḥ
prayāṇa-kāle'pi ca māṁ / te vidur yukta-cetasaḥ

30. Those who know my integral being composed of the Adhibhuta, the Adhidaiva and the Adhiyajna, (continue to) know Me even at the hour of death with a steadfast mind.

ॐ तत् सत् । इति श्रीमद्भगवद्गीतासु उपनिषत्सु ब्रह्मविद्यायां योगशास्त्रे श्रीकृष्णार्जुन संवादे ज्ञानविज्ञानयोगो नाम सप्तमोऽध्यायः ॥

Om Tat Sat. Iti Śrimad Bhagavat Gitasu Upanishatsu Brahmavidyayām yogaśastre Sri Krishnarjuna samvade Jñāna Vijñāna Yogonama Saptamodhyayaḥ

Thus ends the seventh chapter named "Jnana-Vijnana-Yoga" (Self-knowledge and Enlightenment) of the Upanishad of the Bhagavad Gita, the scripture of yoga, dealing with the science of the Absolute in the form of the dialogue between Sri Krishna and Arjuna.

अथ अष्टमोऽध्यायः - अक्षरब्रह्मयोगः

Chapter Eight: Akshara-Brahma-Yoga

अर्जुन उवाच ।
किं तद्ब्रह्म किमध्यात्मं किं कर्म पुरुषोत्तम ।
अधिभूतं च किं प्रोक्तमधिदैवं किमुच्यते ॥१॥

arjuna uvāca
kiṁ tad brahma kim adhyātmaṁ kiṁ karma puruṣottama
adhibhūtañ ca kiṁ proktam adhidaivaṁ kim ucyate

1. Arjuna said: Krishna, what is the Brahman, what is Adhyatma, what is karma? What is called Adhibhuta, and what is Adhidaiva?

अधियज्ञः कथं कोऽत्र, देहेऽस्मिन्मधुसूदन ।
प्रयाणकाले च कथं, ज्ञेयोऽसि नियतात्मभिः ॥२॥

adhiyajñaḥ kathaṁ ko 'tra / dehe 'smin madhusūdana
prayāṇa-kāle ca kathaṁ / jñeyo 'si niyatātmabhiḥ

2. Who is Adhiyajna here Krishna and how does he dwell in this body? And how are You known at the time of death, by the steadfast in mind?

श्रीभगवानुवाच ।
अक्षरं ब्रह्म परमं, स्वभावोऽध्यात्ममुच्यते ।
भूतभावोद्भवकरो, विसर्गः कर्मसंज्ञितः ॥३॥

śrī-bhagavān uvāca
akṣaraṁ brahma paramaṁ/ svabhāvo 'dhyātmam ucyate
bhūta-bhāvodbhava-karo / visargaḥ karma-saṁjñitaḥ

3. The Blessed Lord said: The supreme imperishable is the Brahman. Its dwelling in each individual body is called Adhyatma; the offering in sacrifice which enables the development and support of the material body, is known as karma.

अधिभूतं क्षरो भावः, पुरुषश्चाधिदैवतम् ।
अधियज्ञोऽहमेवात्र, देहे देहभृतां वर ॥४॥

adhibhūtaṁ kṣaro bhāvaḥ / puruṣaś cādhidaivatam
adhiyajño 'ham evātra / dehe deha-bhṛtāṁ vara

4. O Arjuna, the perishable objects are Adhibhuta, and the shining Indweller is the Adhidaivata; I alone am the Adhiyajna, the inner witness, here in this body.

अन्तकाले च मामेव, स्मरन्मुक्त्वा कलेवरम् ।
यः प्रयाति स मद्भावं, याति नास्त्यत्र संशयः ॥५॥

anta-kāle ca mām eva / smaran muktvā kalevaram
yaḥ prayāti sa mad-bhāvaṁ / yāti nāstyatra saṁśayaḥ

5. And he who departs from the body, meditating on Me alone, while leaving the body, attains My state: there is no doubt about it.

यं यं वापि स्मरन्भावं, त्यजत्यन्ते कलेवरम् ।
तं तमेवैति कौन्तेय, सदा तद्भावभावितः ॥६॥

yaṁ yaṁ vāpi smaran bhāvaṁ / tyajatyante kalevaram
taṁ tam evaiti kaunteya / sadā tad-bhāva-bhāvitaḥ

6. Arjuna, thinking of whatever entity he leaves the body, that and that alone is reached by him, being absorbed in that thought.

तस्मात्सर्वेषु कालेषु, मामनुस्मर युध्य च ।
मय्यर्पितमनोबुद्धिर्मामेवैष्यस्यसंशयः ॥७॥

tasmāt sarveṣu kāleṣu / mām anusmara yudhya ca
mayyarpita-mano-buddhir / mām evaiṣyasy asaṁśayaḥ

7. Therefore Arjuna, think of me at all times and fight. With mind and intellect thus set on Me, you will doubtless come to Me.

अभ्यासयोगयुक्तेन, चेतसा नान्यगामिना ।
परमं पुरुषं दिव्यं, याति पार्थानुचिन्तयन् ॥८॥

abhyāsa-yoga-yuktena / cetasā nānya-gāminā
paramaṁ puruṣaṁ divyaṁ / yāti pārthānucintayan

8. O Partha, with the mind disciplined by Yoga, thinking of nothing else but made steadfast by meditation and dwelling on the Supreme, effulgent Purusha, one attains to Him.

कविं पुराणमनुशासितार मणोरणीयांसमनुस्मरेद्यः ।
सर्वस्य धातारमचिन्त्यरूपम् आदित्यवर्णं तमसः परस्तात् ॥९॥
प्रयाणकाले मनसाऽचलेन भक्त्या युक्तो योगबलेन चैव ।
भ्रुवोर्मध्ये प्राणमावेश्य सम्यक् स तं परं पुरुषमुपैति दिव्यम् ॥१०॥

kaviṁ purāṇam anuśāsitāram
aṇoraṇīyāṁsamanusmared yaḥ
sarvasya dhātāram acintya-rūpam āditya-varṇaṁ tamasaḥ parastāt
prayāṇa-kāle manasā'calena bhaktyā yukto yoga-balena caiva

bhruvor madhye prāṇam āveśya samyak sa taṁ paraṁ puruṣam upaiti divyam

9 & 10. The All knowing, the Ancient, the Over Lord, minuter than an atom, the Universal Sustainer, of inconceivable form, self-effulgent like the sun, and beyond the darkness of Maya – He who contemplates on Him, at the time of death, full of devotion, thus: with the mind steady, and also by the power of yoga, fixing the life breath between the eyebrows, he goes to that Supreme, Divine Purusha.

यदक्षरं वेदविदो वदन्ति विशन्ति यद्यतयो वीतरागाः ।
यदिच्छन्तो ब्रह्मचर्यं चरन्ति तत्ते पदं संग्रहेण प्रवक्ष्ये ॥११॥

yad akṣaraṁ veda-vido vadanti viśanti yad
yatayo vīta-rāgāḥ
yad icchanto brahmacaryaṁ caranti tat te
padaṁ
saṅgraheṇa pravakṣye

11. I shall tell you in brief about that Supreme Goal, what the knowers of the Veda describe as Imperishable, what the selfcontrolled (Sannyasis), free of attachments enter into, and to gain which goal they live the life of a celibate.

सर्वद्वाराणि संयम्य मनो हृदि निरुध्य च ।
मूर्ध्न्याधायात्मनः प्राणमास्थितो योगधारणाम् ॥१२॥

ओमित्येकाक्षरं ब्रह्म, व्याहरन्मामनुस्मरन् ।
यः प्रयाति त्यजन्देहं, स याति परमांगतिम् ॥१३॥

sarva-dvārāṇi saṁyamya mano hṛdi nirudhya ca
mūrdhny ādhāyātmanaḥ prāṇam āsthito yoga-dhāraṇām
om ity ekākṣaraṁ brahma vyāharan mām anusmaran
yaḥ prayāti tyajan dehaṁ sa yāti paramāṁ gatim

12 & 13. Restraining all the senses, the mind having been drawn into the heart, confining the prana in the head, meditating on the one-syllabled "Om", the Brahman, and contemplating on Me – he who so departs, leaving the body, attains the Supreme Goal.

अनन्यचेताः सततं, यो मां स्मरति नित्यशः ।
तस्याहं सुलभः पार्थ, नित्ययुक्तस्य योगिनः ॥१४॥

ananya-cetāḥ satataṁ / yo māṁ smarati nityaśaḥ
tasyāhaṁ sulabhaḥ pārtha / nitya-yuktasya yoginaḥ

14. O Partha, I am easily attainable to that Yogi who is ever-steadfast, who remembers Me constantly with a single mind.

मामुपेत्य पुनर्जन्म, दुःखालयमशाश्वतम् ।
नाप्नुवन्ति महात्मानः, संसिद्धिं परमां गताः ॥१५॥

mām upetya punar janma / duḥkhālayam aśāśvatam
nāpnuvanti mahātmānaḥ / saṁsiddhiṁ paramāṁ gatāḥ

15. After attaining perfection and having reached Me, the great-souled ones are no more subject to rebirth – which is the abode of sorrow and is transient.

आब्रह्मभुवनाल्लोकाः, पुनरावर्तिनोऽर्जुन ।
मामुपेत्य तु कौन्तेय, पुनर्जन्म न विद्यते ॥१६॥

ā-brahma-bhuvanāl lokāḥ / punarāvarttino 'rjuna
mām upetya tu kaunteya / punar janma na vidyate

16. O Arjuna, all the worlds, including the realm of Brahma, are subject to return, but after attaining Me, O son of Kunti, there is no rebirth.

सहस्रयुगपर्यन्तमहर्यद्ब्रह्मणो विदुः ।
रात्रिं युगसहस्रान्तां, तेऽहोरात्रविदो जनाः ॥१७॥

sahasra-yuga-paryantam / ahar yad brahmaṇo viduḥ
rātriṁ yuga-sahasrāntāṁ / te 'ho-rātra-vido janāḥ

17. Those who know the true measure of time, know the day of Brahma, as extending to a thousand Yugas and the night also to be a thousand Yugas.

अव्यक्ताद्व्यक्तयः सर्वाः, प्रभवन्त्यहरागमे ।
रात्र्यागमे प्रलीयन्ते, तत्रैवाव्यक्तसंज्ञके ॥१८॥

avyaktād vyaktayaḥ sarvāḥ / prabhavanty ahar-āgame
rātry-āgame pralīyante / tatraivāvyakta-saṁjñake

18. At the dawn of (Brahma's) day, all embodied beings emanate from the unmanifested state; at the approach of night, they merge verily into that alone, which is called the unmanifested.

भूतग्रामः स एवायं, भूत्वा भूत्वा प्रलीयते ।
रात्र्यागमेऽवशः पार्थ, प्रभवत्यहरागमे ॥१९॥

bhūta-grāmaḥ sa evāyaṁ / bhūtvā bhūtvā pralīyate
rātry-āgame 'vaśaḥ pārtha / prabhavaty ahar-āgame

19. O Partha, the multitude of beings (that existed in the preceding day of Brahma), being born again and under compulsions of its nature, merge into the unmanifested, at the approach of night, and re-manifest at the approach of day.

परस्तस्मात्तु भावोऽन्योऽव्यक्तोऽव्यक्तात्सनातनः ।
यः स सर्वेषु भूतेषु नश्यत्सु न विनश्यति ॥२०॥

paras tasmāt tu bhāvo 'nyo 'vyakto 'vyaktāt sanātanaḥ
yaḥ sa sarveṣu bhūteṣu naśyatsu na vinaśyati

20. But beyond this unmanifested, is that other Unmanifested - the Eternal Existence–That which is not destroyed at the dissolution of all beings.

अव्यक्तोऽक्षर इत्युक्तस्तमाहुः परमां गतिम् ।
यं प्राप्य न निवर्तन्ते तद्धाम परमं मम ॥२१॥

avyakto 'kṣara ity uktas tam āhuḥ paramāṁ gatim
yaṁ prāpya na nivarttante tad dhāma paramaṁ mama

21. The Unmanifested and Imperishable has been described as the Supreme Goal. That is My highest state, having attained which, there is no rebirth.

पुरुषः स परः पार्थ, भक्त्या लभ्यस्त्वनन्यया ।
यस्यान्तःस्थानि भूतानि, येन सर्वमिदं ततम् ॥२२॥

puruṣaḥ sa paraḥ pārtha / bhaktyā labhyas tv ananyayā
yasyāntaḥ-sthāni bhūtāni / yena sarvam idaṁ tatam

22. Arjuna, that Supreme Purusha is attainable by whole-hearted devotion to Him alone, in Whom all beings dwell, and by Whom all this is pervaded.

यत्र काले त्वनावृत्तिमावृत्तिं चैव योगिनः ।
प्रयाता यान्ति तं कालं वक्ष्यामि भरतर्षभ ॥२३॥

yatra kāle tvanāvṛttim āvṛttim caiva yoginaḥ
prayātā yānti taṁ kālaṁ vakṣyāmi bharatarṣabha

23. Arjuna, now I shall tell thee, of the time (path) departing when, the Yogis return, (and again of that, departing when) they do not return.

अग्निर्ज्योतिरहः शुक्लः, षण्मासा उत्तरायणम् ।
तत्र प्रयाता गच्छन्ति, ब्रह्म ब्रह्मविदो जनाः ॥२४॥

agnir jyotir ahaḥ śuklaḥ / ṣaṇ-māsā uttarāyaṇam
tatra prayātā gacchanti / brahma brahma-vido janāḥ

24. The knowers of Brahman go to Brahman by taking the path of fire, light, daytime, the bright fortnight and the six months of the Northern passage of the sun.

धूमो रात्रिस्तथा कृष्णः षण्मासा दक्षिणायनम् ।
तत्र चान्द्रमसं ज्योतिर्योगी प्राप्य निवर्तते ॥२५॥

dhūmo rātristathā kṛṣṇaḥ ṣaṇ-māsā
dakṣiṇāyanam
tatra cāndramasaṁ jyotir yogī prāpya nivarttate

25. The other path is that of smoke, night-time, the dark fortnight and the six months of the Southern passage of the sun. Taking this path the Yogi, attaining the lunar light, returns.

शुक्लकृष्णे गती ह्येते जगतः शाश्वते मते ।
एकया यात्यनावृत्तिमन्ययावर्तते पुनः ॥२६॥

śukla-kṛṣṇe gatī hyete jagataḥ śāśvate mate
ekayā yātyanāvṛttim anyayāvarttate punaḥ

26. Truly are these two bright and dark paths of the world considered perennial: one leads to non-return; by the other, one returns to the mortal world.

नैते सृती पार्थ जानन्योगी मुह्यति कश्चन ।
तस्मात्सर्वेषु कालेषु, योगयुक्तो भवार्जुन ॥२७॥

naite sṛtī pārtha jānan / yogī muhyati kaścana
tasmāt sarveṣu kāleṣu / yoga-yukto bhavārjuna

27. O son of Pritha, no Yogi is deluded after knowing these paths. Therefore, O Arjuna, be steadfast in yoga, at all times.

वेदेषु यज्ञेषु तपस्सु चैव दानेषु यत्पुण्यफलं प्रदिष्टम् ।
अत्येति तत्सर्वमिदं विदित्वा योगी परं स्थानमुपैति चाद्यम्
॥२८॥

vedeṣu yajñeṣu tapaḥsu caiva dāneṣu yat puṇya-phalaṁ pradiṣṭam
atyeti tat sarvamidaṁ viditvā yogī paraṁ sthānamupaiti cādyam

28. Meritorious effect is pronounced (in the Scriptures) to accrue from (the study of) the Vedas, (the performance of) yajnas, (the practice of) austerities and gifts. But the Yogi, having known this, rises above all these and attains to the primeval, Supreme State.

ॐ तत् सत् । इति श्रीमद्भगवद्गीतासु उपनिषत्सु
ब्रह्मविद्यायां योगशास्त्रे श्रीकृष्णार्जुन संवादे
अक्षरब्रह्मयोगो नाम अष्टमोऽध्यायः ॥

Om Tat Sat. Iti Śrimad Bhagavat Gitasu Upanishatsu Brahmavidyayām yogaśastre Sri Krishnarjuna samvade Akshara Brahma yogo nama ashtamodhyayaḥ

Thus ends the eighth chapter named "Akshara-Brahma-Yoga" (The Eternal Brahman) of the Upanishad of the Bhagavad Gita, the scripture of yoga, dealing with the science of the Absolute in the form of the dialogue between Sri Krishna and Arjuna.

अथ नवमोऽध्यायः - राजविद्याराजगुह्ययोगः

Chapter Nine: Rāja-Vidyā-Rāja-Guhya-Yoga

श्रीभगवानुवाच ।
इदं तु ते गुह्यतमं, प्रवक्ष्याम्यनसूयवे ।
ज्ञानं विज्ञानसहितं, यज्ज्ञात्वा मोक्ष्यसेऽशुभात् ॥१॥

śrī-bhagavān uvāca
idaṁ tu te guhyatamaṁ / pravakṣyāmy anasūyave
jñānaṁ vijñāna-sahitaṁ / yaj jñātvā mokṣyase 'śubhāt

1. The Blessed Lord said: To you, who is devoid of the carping spirit, verily shall I now declare this, the most profound knowledge, of both manifest and unmanifest Divinity, having known which, you shall be free from the evil of worldy existense.

राजविद्या राजगुह्यं, पवित्रमिदमुत्तमम् ।
प्रत्यक्षावगमं धर्म्यं, सुसुखं कर्तुमव्ययम् ॥२॥

rāja-vidyā rāja-guhyaṁ / pavitramidamuttamam
pratyakṣāvagamaṁ dharmyaṁ / su-sukhaṁ karttumavyayam

2. The knowledge of the Nirguna and Saguna aspects of the Supreme is the deepest of all sciences and purifiers. It is realizable directly, endowed with merit, easy to perform and is of imperishable nature.

अश्रद्धधानाः पुरुषाः, धर्मस्यास्य परंतप ।
अप्राप्य मां निवर्तन्ते, मृत्युसंसारवर्त्मनि ॥३॥

aśraddadhānāḥ puruṣā / dharmasyāsya parantapa
aprāpya māṁ nivarttante / mṛtyu-saṁsāra-vartmani

3. Those without faith in this dharma, failing to reach Me, revolve in the path of the world of death.

मया ततमिदं सर्वं, जगदव्यक्तमूर्तिना ।
मत्स्थानि सर्वभूतानि, न चाहं तेष्ववस्थितः ॥४॥

mayā tatamidaṁ sarvaṁ / jagad avyakta-mūrttinā
mat-sthāni sarva-bhūtāni / na cāhaṁ teṣvavasthitaḥ

4. The whole of this world is permeated by Me in My unmanifested form: all beings abide in Me, but I do not dwell in them.

न च मत्स्थानि भूतानि, पश्य मे योगमैश्वरम् ।
भूतभृन्न च भूतस्थो, ममात्मा भूतभावनः ॥५॥

na ca mat-sthāni bhūtāni / paśya me yogam aiśvaram
bhūta-bhṛn na ca bhūta-stho / mamātmā bhūta-bhāvanaḥ

5. Nay, all these beings abide not in Me (in reality), behold My wonderful divine Yoga! Though the creator and sustainer of the beings, My Self does not dwell in them.

यथाकाशस्थितो नित्यं, वायुः सर्वत्रगो महान् ।
तथा सर्वाणि भूतानि, मत्स्थानीत्युपधारय ॥६॥

yathākāśa-sthito nityaṁ / vāyuḥ sarvatra-go mahān
tathā sarvāṇi bhūtāni / mat-sthānītyupadhāraya

6. As the wind, moving everywhere, rests ever in the ether, know that even so do all beings rest in Me.

सर्वभूतानि कौन्तेय, प्रकृतिं यान्ति मामिकाम् ।
कल्पक्षये पुनस्तानि, कल्पादौ विसृजाम्यहम् ॥७॥

sarva-bhūtāni kaunteya / prakṛtiṁ yānti māmikām
kalpa-kṣaye punastāni / kalpādau visṛjāmy aham

7. Arjuna, during final dissolution, all beings enter My Prakriti and at the beginning of creation, I send them forth again.

प्रकृतिं स्वामवष्टभ्य विसृजामि पुनः पुनः ।
भूतग्राममिमं कृत्स्नमवशं प्रकृतेर्वशात् ॥८॥

prakṛtiṁ svām avaṣṭabhya visṛjāmi punaḥ punaḥ
bhūta-grāmam imaṁ kṛtsnam avaśaṁ prakṛter vaśāt

8. Weilding My nature, I release again and again, all this multitude of beings, helpless under the sway of their own nature.

न च मां तानि कर्माणि निबध्नन्ति धनंजय ।
उदासीनवदासीनमसक्तं तेषु कर्मसु ॥९॥

na ca māṁ tāni karmāṇi nibadhnanti dhanañjaya
udāsīna-vad āsīnam asaktaṁ teṣu karmasu

9. Unattached to them O Dhananjaya, these actions do not bind Me, standing apart as it were.

मयाऽध्यक्षेण प्रकृतिः, सूयते सचराचरम् ।
हेतुनानेन कौन्तेय, जगद्विपरिवर्तते ॥१०॥

mayādhyakṣeṇa prakṛtiḥ / sūyate sa-carācaram
hetunānena kaunteya / jagad viparivarttate

10. O son of Kunti, by reason of My proximity, nature produces all this, the sentient and the insentient beings and the world wheels go round and round because of this.

अवजानन्ति मां मूढा, मानुषीं तनुमाश्रितम् ।
परं भावमजानन्तो, मम भूतमहेश्वरम् ॥११॥

avajānanti māṁ mūḍhā / mānuṣīṁ tanumāśritam
paraṁ bhāvam ajānanto / mama bhūta-maheśvaram

11. Not aware of My supreme state, as the over Lord of beings, fools disregard Me, dwelling in the human garb.

मोघाशा मोघकर्माणो, मोघज्ञाना विचेतसः ।
राक्षसीमासुरीं चैव, प्रकृतिं मोहिनीं श्रिताः ॥१२॥

moghāśā mogha-karmāṇo / mogha-jñānā vicetasaḥ
rākṣasīm āsurīñ caiva / prakṛtiṁ mohinīṁ śritāḥ

12. Of vain hopes, of futile works, of fruitless knowledge, and senseless, they verily are possessed of the demonic and delusive nature of Rakshasas and Asuras.

महात्मानस्तु मां पार्थ, दैवीं प्रकृतिमाश्रिताः ।
भजन्त्यनन्यमनसो, ज्ञात्वा भूतादिमव्ययम् ॥१३॥

mahātmānas tu māṁ pārtha / daivīṁ prakṛtim āśritāḥ
bhajanty ananya-manaso / jñātvā bhūtādim avyayam

13. But O Arjuna, the great-soul, possessed of the Divine nature, knowing Me to be the origin of beings and imperishable, worship Me single mindedly.

सततं कीर्तयन्तो मां, यतन्तश्च दृढव्रताः ।
नमस्यन्तश्च मां भक्त्या, नित्ययुक्ता उपासते ॥१४॥

satataṁ kīrttayanto māṁ / yatantaś ca dṛḍha-vratāḥ
namasyantaś ca māṁ bhaktyā / nitya-yuktā upāsate

14. Always steadfast, they worship Me, glorifying Me and striving with firm resolve, bow down to Me in devotion.

ज्ञानयज्ञेन चाप्यन्ये, यजन्तो मामुपासते ।
एकत्वेन पृथक्त्वेन, बहुधा विश्वतोमुखम् ॥१५॥

jñāna-yajñena cāpyanye / yajanto mām upāsate
ekatvena pṛthaktvena / bahudhā viśvato-mukham

15. Others, too, sacrificing by the offering of knowledge (i.e., seeing the self in all), worship My Universal Form, as one, as diverse, as manifold.

अहं क्रतुरहं यज्ञः, स्वधाहमहमौषधम् ।
मन्त्रोऽहमहमेवाज्यमहमग्निरहं हुतम् ॥१६॥

ahaṁ kratur ahaṁ yajñaḥ / svadhāham aham auṣadham
mantro 'ham aham evājyam / aham agnir ahaṁ hutam

16. I am the Kratu, I the Yajna, I the Svadha, I the Aushadha, I the Mantra, I the Ajya, I the fire, and I the oblation.

पिताहमस्य जगतो, माता धाता पितामहः ।
वेद्यं पवित्रमोंकारः, ऋक्साम यजुरेव च ॥१७॥

pitāham asya jagato / mātā dhātā pitāmahaḥ
vedyaṁ pavitram oṁkāra / ṛk sāma yajur eva ca

17. I am the sustainer and ruler of this world – its Father, the Mother, the Grandfather, the Purifier and the (one) thing worth knowing, (the syllable) Om and also the Rik, Sama and Yajus.

गतिर्भर्ता प्रभुः साक्षी, निवासः शरणं सुहृत् ।
प्रभवः प्रलयः स्थानं, निधानं बीजमव्ययम् ॥१८॥

gatir bharttā prabhuḥ sākṣī / nivāsaḥ śaraṇaṁ suhṛt
prabhavaḥ pralayaḥ sthānaṁ / nidhānaṁ bījam avyayam

18. I am the Goal, the Supporter, the Lord, the Witness, the Abode, the Refuge, the Friend, the Origin, the Dissolution, the Substratum, the Storehouse, the Seed imperishable.

तपाम्यहमहं वर्षं, निगृह्णाम्युत्सृजामि च ।
अमृतं चैव मृत्युश्च, सदसच्चाहमर्जुन ॥१९॥

tapāmy aham ahaṁ varṣaṁ / nigṛhṇāmy utsṛjāmi ca
amṛtañ caiva mṛtyuś ca / sad asac cāham arjuna

19. O Arjuna, as the sun I give heat; I withhold and send forth rain; I am immortality and also death; being and non-being am I.

त्रैविद्या मां सोमपाः पूतपापा यज्ञैरिष्ट्वा स्वर्गतिं प्रार्थयन्ते ।
ते पुण्यमासाद्य सुरेन्द्रलोकमश्नन्ति दिव्यान्दिवि देवभोगान् ॥२०॥

trai-vidyā māṁ soma-pāḥ pūta-pāpā
yajñair iṣṭvā svar-gatiṁ prārthayante
te puṇyam āsādya surendra-lokam
aśnanti divyān divi deva-bhogān

20. The practitioners of rituals of the three Vedas, worshipping Me by yajna, drinking the Soma, and thus getting purified from sin, pray for access to heaven; reaching the world of the Lord of the devas, they enjoy there, the divine pleasures of the devas.

ते तं भुक्त्वा स्वर्गलोकं विशालं क्षीणे पुण्ये मर्त्यलोकं विशन्ति ।
एवं त्रयीधर्ममनुप्रपन्नाः गतागतं कामकामा लभन्ते ॥२१॥

te taṁ bhuktvā svarga-lokaṁ viśālaṁ
kṣīṇe puṇye martya-lokaṁ viśanti
evaṁ trayī-dharmam anuprapannā
gatāgataṁ kāma-kāmā labhante

21. Having enjoyed the extensive heaven-world, they return to the mortal world, after exhausting their merit. Thus, abiding by the injunctions of the three Vedas, desiring worldly enjoyments, they (constantly) come and go.

अनन्याश्चिन्तयन्तो मां, ये जनाः पर्युपासते ।
तेषां नित्याभियुक्तानां, योगक्षेमं वहाम्यहम् ॥२२॥

ananyāś cintayanto māṁ / ye janāḥ paryupāsate
teṣāṁ nityābhiyuktānāṁ / yoga-kṣemaṁ
vahāmy aham

22. Those who constantly meditate on Me as not separate from beings, worship Me in all beings, to them I give full protection and fulfill their needs.

येऽप्यन्यदेवताभक्ताः, यजन्ते श्रद्धयाऽन्विताः ।
तेऽपि मामेव कौन्तेय, यजन्त्यविधिपूर्वकम् ॥२३॥

ye 'py anya-devatā-bhaktā / yajante śraddhayānvitāḥ
te 'pi mām eva kaunteya / yajanty avidhi-pūrvakam

23. O son of Kunti, even those devotees, who endowed with faith, worship other gods, they too worship Me alone, (but) by the wrong method.

अहं हि सर्वयज्ञानां, भोक्ता च प्रभुरेव च ।
न तु मामभिजानन्ति, तत्त्वेनातश्च्यवन्ति ते ॥२४॥

ahaṁ hi sarva-yajñānāṁ / bhoktā ca prabhur eva ca
na tu mām abhijānanti / tattvenātaś cyavanti te

24. For I am the Enjoyer and also the Lord of all sacrifices; but because they do not know Me in reality, they return, (to the mortal world).

यान्ति देवव्रता देवान्पितॄन्यान्ति पितृव्रताः ।
भूतानि यान्ति भूतेज्याः, यान्ति मद्याजिनोऽपि माम् ॥२५॥

yānti deva-vratā devān / pitṝn yānti pitṛ-vratāḥ
bhūtāni yānti bhūtejyā / yānti mad-yājino 'pi mām

25. Votaries of the gods go to the gods, to the manes, go their votaries; to the spirits, go the spirit worshippers; My votaries come unto Me alone.

पत्रं पुष्पं फलं तोयं यो मे भक्त्या प्रयच्छति ।
तदहं भक्त्युपहृतमश्नामि प्रयतात्मनः ॥२६॥

patraṁ puṣpaṁ phalaṁ toyaṁ yo me bhaktyā prayacchati
tad ahaṁ bhakty-upahṛtam aśnāmi prayatātmanaḥ

26. Whoever offers Me with devotion a leaf, a flower, a fruit, or water, that I partake – the loving gift of the pure-minded.

यत्करोषि यदश्नासि, यज्जुहोषि ददासि यत् ।
यत्तपस्यसि कौन्तेय, तत्कुरुष्व मदर्पणम् ॥२७॥

yat karoṣi yad aśnāsi / yaj juhoṣi dadāsi yat
yat tapasyasi kaunteya / tat kuruṣva mad-arpaṇam

27. Arjuna, whatever you do, whatever you eat, whatever you offer as oblation in sacrifice, whatever you give away, whatever austerity you practice, offer it all unto Me.

शुभाशुभफलैरेवं, मोक्ष्यसे कर्मबन्धनैः ।
संन्यासयोगयुक्तात्मा, विमुक्तो मामुपैष्यसि ॥२८॥

śubhāśubha-phalair evaṁ / mokṣyase karma-bandhanaiḥ
sannyāsa-yoga-yuktātmā / vimukto mām upaiṣyasi

28. With the heart established in the yoga of renunciation, thus, shall you be freed from the bondages of actions, bearing good and evil results. Liberated, you shall attain Me.

समोऽहं सर्वभूतेषु, न मे द्वेष्योऽस्ति न प्रियः ।
ये भजन्ति तु मां भक्त्या, मयि ते तेषु चाप्यहम् ॥२६॥

samo 'haṁ sarva-bhūteṣu / na me dveṣyo 'sti na priyaḥ
ye bhajanti tu māṁ bhaktyā / mayi te teṣu cāpy aham

29. I am equally present in all beings: to Me there is none hateful or dear. But those who devotedly worship Me, abide in Me, and I too stand revealed to them.

अपि चेत्सुदुराचारो, भजते मामनन्यभाक् ।
साधुरेव स मन्तव्यः, सम्यग्व्यवसितो हि सः ॥३०॥

api cet su-durācāro / bhajate mām ananya-bhāk
sādhur eva sa mantavyaḥ / samyag vyavasito hi saḥ

30. If even the worst sinner worships Me, with exclusive devotion to me, he should be regarded as a saint, for he has rightly resolved.

क्षिप्रं भवति धर्मात्मा, शश्वच्छान्तिं निगच्छति ।
कौन्तेय प्रतिजानीहि, न मे भक्तः प्रणश्यति ॥३१॥

kṣipraṁ bhavati dharmātmā / śaśvac chāntiṁ nigacchati

kaunteya pratijānīhi / na me bhaktaḥ praṇaśyati

31. Soon does he become virtuous and secures lasting Peace, O son of Kunti; Know it for certain, that My devotee never falls.

मां हि पार्थ व्यपाश्रित्य, येऽपि स्युः पापयोनयः ।
स्त्रियो वैश्यास्तथा शूद्रास्तेऽपि यान्ति परां गतिम् ॥३२॥

māṁ hi pārtha vyapāśritya / ye 'pi syuḥ pāpa-yonayaḥ

striyo vaiśyās tathā śūdrās / te 'pi yānti parāṁ gatim

32. O son of Pritha, by taking refuge in Me, they also who might be of inferior birth, even they attain the Supreme Goal.

किं पुनर्ब्राह्मणाः पुण्याः भक्ता राजर्षयस्तथा ।
अनित्यमसुखं लोकमिमं प्राप्य भजस्व माम् ॥३३॥

kiṁ punar brāhmaṇāḥ puṇyā bhaktā rājarṣayas tathā

anityam asukhaṁ lokam imaṁ prāpya bhajasva mām

33. How much more are, then, holy Brahmanas and royal sages devoted to Me! Having obtained this transient and joyless human life, worship Me.

मन्मना भव मद्भक्तो मद्याजी मां नमस्कुरु ।
मामेवैष्यसि युक्त्वैवमात्मानं मत्परायणः ॥३४॥

man-manā bhava mad-bhakto mad-yājī māṁ namaskuru
mām evaiṣyasi yuktvaivam ātmānaṁ mat-parāyaṇaḥ

34. Fix your mind on Me, be devoted to Me, make obeisance unto Me, bow down to Me; thus linking yourself with Me and entirely depending on Me, you shall come to Me.

ॐ तत् सत् । इति श्रीमद्भगवद्गीतासु उपनिषत्सु
ब्रह्मविद्यायां योगशास्त्रे श्रीकृष्णार्जुन संवादे
राजविद्याराजगुह्ययोगो नाम नवमोऽध्यायः ॥

Om Tat Sat. Iti Śrimad Bhagavat Gitasu Upanishatsu Brahmavidyayām yogaśastre Sri Krishnarjuna samvade Rāja Vidyā-Rāja-Guhya-Yogonama Navamodhyayaḥ

Thus ends the ninth chapter named "Raja-Vidya-Raja-Guhya-Yoga" (Supreme Knowledge and the Big Mystery) of the Upanishad of the Bhagavad Gita, the scripture of yoga, dealing with the science of the Absolute in the form of the dialogue between Sri Krishna and Arjuna.

अथ दशमोऽध्यायः - विभूतिविस्तरयोगः

Chapter Ten: Vibhūti-Vistara-Yoga

श्रीभगवानुवाच ।
भूय एव महाबाहो, शृणु मे परमं वचः ।
यत्तेऽहं प्रीयमाणाय, वक्ष्यामि हितकाम्यया ॥१॥

śrī-bhagavān uvāca
bhūya eva mahā-bāho / śṛṇu me paramaṁ vacaḥ
yat te 'haṁ prīyamāṇāya / vakṣyāmi hita-kāmyayā

1. The Blessed Lord said: Arjuna, hear once again, My supreme word, which, I, wishing your welfare, will tell you who are so loving.

न मे विदुः सुरगणाः, प्रभवं न महर्षयः ।
अहमादिर्हि देवानां, महर्षीणां च सर्वशः ॥२॥

na me viduḥ sura-gaṇāḥ / prabhavaṁ na maharṣayaḥ
aham ādir hi devānāṁ / maharṣīṇāñ ca sarvaśaḥ

2. Neither the gods, nor the great sages, know the secret of My birth, for I am the cause in all respects of all the gods and the great sages.

यो मामजमनादिं च, वेत्ति लोकमहेश्वरम् ।
असंमूढः स मर्त्येषु, सर्वपापैः प्रमुच्यते ॥३॥

yo mām ajam anādiñ ca / vetti loka-maheśvaram
asammūḍhaḥ sa marttyeṣu / sarva-pāpaiḥ pramucyate

3. He who knows Me as birthless and without beginning and as the Supreme Lord of the Universe, he, among mortals, is undeluded, he is purged of all sins.

बुद्धिर्ज्ञानमसंमोहः, क्षमा सत्यं दमः शमः ।
सुखं दुःखं भवोऽभावो, भयं चाभयमेव च ॥४॥
अहिंसा समता तुष्टिस्तपो दानं यशोऽयशः ।
भवन्ति भावा भूतानां, मत्तेव पृथग्विधाः ॥५॥

buddhir jñānam asammohaḥ kṣamā satyaṁ damaḥ śamaḥ
sukhaṁ duḥkhaṁ bhavo 'bhāvo bhayaṁ cābhayam eva ca
ahiṁsā samatā tuṣṭistapo dānaṁ yaśo 'yaśaḥ
bhavanti bhāvā bhūtānāṁ matta eva pṛthag-vidhāḥ

4 & 5. Reason, right knowledge, unclouded understanding, forbearance, truth, restraint of senses, calmness of heart, joy, sorrow, birth, death, fear and fearlessness, non-violence, equanimity, contentment, austerity, charity, fame, (as well as) ill-fame – (these) diverse traits of beings emanate from Me alone.

महर्षयः सप्त पूर्वे, चत्वारो मनवस्तथा ।
मद्भावा मानसा जाताः, येषां लोक इमाः प्रजाः ॥६॥

maharṣayaḥ sapta pūrve / catvāro manavas tathā
mad-bhāvā mānasā jātā / yeṣāṁ loka imāḥ prajāḥ

6. The seven great Seers and the four ancient Manus, were born of my will, (due to their thoughts having fixed on Me) and from them descended these creatures in the world.

एतां विभूतिं योगं च, मम यो वेत्ति तत्त्वतः ।
सोऽविकम्पेन योगेन, युज्यते नात्र संशयः ॥७॥

etāṁ vibhūtiṁ yogaṁ ca / mama yo vetti tattvataḥ
so 'vikaṁpena yogena / yujyate nātra saṁśayaḥ

7. He who knows in reality these manifold manifestations of My being and (this) supernatural power of Mine, gets established in the unfaltering yoga. About this, there is no doubt.

अहं सर्वस्य प्रभवो, मत्तः सर्वं प्रवर्तते ।
इति मत्वा भजन्ते मां, बुधा भावसमन्विताः ॥८॥
aham sarvasya prabhavo / mattaḥ sarvaṁ pravarttate
iti matvā bhajante māṁ / budhā bhāva-samanvitāḥ

8. I am the source of all, creation and everything in the world moves because of Me. The wise worship Me with loving devotion.

मच्चित्ता मद्‌गतप्राणाः, बोधयन्तः परस्परम् ।,
कथयन्तश्च मां नित्यं, तुष्यन्ति च रमन्ति च ॥९॥
mac-cittā mad-gata-prāṇā / bodhayantaḥ parasparam
kathayantaś ca māṁ nityaṁ / tuṣyanti ca ramanti ca

9. With their minds set on Me, with their senses absorbed in Me, enlightening one another, and always speaking of Me, My devotees remain contented and delighted.

तेषां सततयुक्तानां, भजतां प्रीतिपूर्वकम् ।
ददामि बुद्धियोगं तं, येन मामुपयान्ति ते ॥१०॥
teṣāṁ satata-yuktānāṁ / bhajatāṁ prīti-pūrvakam
dadāmi buddhi-yogaṁ taṁ / yena mām upayānti te

10. To them, ever steadfast in meditation and worshipping Me with affection, I give that yoga of wisdom, by which they come to Me.

तेषामेवानुकम्पार्थमहमज्ञानजं तमः ।
नाशयाम्यात्मभावस्थो, ज्ञानदीपेन भास्वता ॥११॥

teṣām evānukampārtham / aham ajñāna-jaṁ tamaḥ
nāśayāmy ātma-bhāva-stho / jñāna-dīpena bhāsvatā

11. To shower grace on them, I, dwelling in their hearts, destroy the darkness (in them) born of ignorance, by the shining light of wisdom.

अर्जुन उवाच ।
परं ब्रह्म परं धाम, पवित्रं परमं भवान् ।
पुरुषं शाश्वतं दिव्यमादिदेवमजं विभुम् ॥१२॥
आहुस्त्वामृषयः सर्वे, देवर्षिर्नारदस्तथा ।
असितो देवलो व्यासः, स्वयं चैव ब्रवीषि मे ॥१३॥

arjuna uvāca
paraṁ brahma paraṁ dhāma / pavitraṁ paramaṁ bhavān
puruṣaṁ śāśvataṁ divyam / ādi-devam ajaṁ vibhum
āhus tvām ṛṣayaḥ sarve / devarṣir nāradas tathā
asito devalo vyāsaḥ / svayaṁ caiva bravīṣi me

12 & 13. Arjuna said: You are the Supreme eternal Brahman, the supreme Abode, the greatest purifier. All the Rishis, the deva-Rishi Narada as well as Asita, Devala, and Vyasa have declared You as the unborn and the self-luminous all pervading Purusha, the first Diety. You yourself also proclaims this to me.

सर्वमेतदृतं मन्ये, यन्मां वदसि केशव ।
न हि ते भगवन्व्यक्तिं, विदुर्देवा न दानवाः ॥१४॥
sarvam etad ṛtaṁ manye / yan māṁ vadasi keśava
na hi te bhagavan vyaktiṁ / vidur devā na dānavāḥ

14. Krishna, I regard all this that you tell me as true. Verily, O Lord, neither the gods nor the demons know Your manifestation.

स्वयमेवात्मनात्मानं, वेत्थ त्वं पुरुषोत्तम ।
भूतभावन भूतेश, देवदेव जगत्पते ॥१५॥
svayam evātmanātmānaṁ / vettha tvaṁ puruṣottama
bhūta-bhāvana bhūteśa / deva-deva jagat-pate

15. Verily, You alone know what you are, by Yourself, O Supreme Purusha, O creator of beings, O Lord of beings, O God of gods, O Ruler of the Universe.

वक्तुमर्हस्यशेषेण, दिव्या ह्यात्मविभूतयः ।
याभिर्विभूतिभिर्लोकानिमांस्त्वं व्याप्य तिष्ठसि ॥१६॥

vaktum arhasy aśeṣeṇa / divyā hyātma-vibhūtayaḥ
yābhir vibhūtibhir lokān / imāṁs tvaṁ vyāpya tiṣṭhasi

16. Therefore, you alone can describe in full Your divine glories, by which You pervade and reside in all of these worlds.

कथं विद्यामहं योगिंस्त्वां सदा परिचिन्तयन् ।
केषु केषु च भावेषु चिन्त्योऽसि भगवन्मया ॥१७॥
kathaṁ vidyām ahaṁ yogiṁs tvāṁ sadā paricintayan
keṣu keṣu ca bhāveṣu cintyo 'si bhagavan mayā

17. How shall I, O Yogi, meditate to know You? In what particular forms, O Bhagavan, are You to be meditated by me?

विस्तरेणात्मनो योगं, विभूतिं च जनार्दन ।
भूयः कथय तृप्तिर्हि, शृण्वतो नास्ति मेऽमृतम् ॥१८॥
vistareṇātmano yogaṁ / vibhūtiṁ ca janārdana
bhūyaḥ kathaya tṛptir hi / śṛṇvato nāsti me 'mṛtam

18. Krishna, tell to me again in detail, your yoga-powers and glories; for I am not satiated in hearing your nectar like words.

श्रीभगवानुवाच
हन्त ते कथयिष्यामि, दिव्या ह्यात्मविभूतयः ।
प्राधान्यतः कुरुश्रेष्ठ, नास्त्यन्तो विस्तरस्य मे ॥१९॥

śrī-bhagavān uvāca
hanta te kathayiṣyāmi / divyā hyātma-vibhūtayaḥ
prādhānyataḥ kuru-śreṣṭha / nāsty anto vistarasya me

19. The Blessed Lord said: I shall speak to thee now, O best of the Kurus, of my divine glories, according to their prominence. For there is no limit to the magnitude of My manifestation.

अहमात्मा गुडाकेश, सर्वभूताशयस्थितः ।
अहमादिश्च मध्यं च, भूतानामन्त एव च ॥२०॥
aham ātmā guḍākeśa / sarva-bhūtāśaya-sthitaḥ
aham ādiś ca madhyaṁ ca / bhūtānām anta eva ca

20. I am the Universal Self, O Arjuna, seated in the heart of all beings; So, I alone am the beginning, the middle and also the end of all beings.

आदित्यानामहं विष्णुर्ज्योतिषां रविरंशुमान् ।
मरीचिर्मरुतामस्मि नक्षत्राणामहं शशी ॥२१॥
ādityānām ahaṁ viṣṇur jyotiṣāṁ ravir aṁśumān

marīcir marutām asmi nakṣatrāṇām ahaṁ śaśī

21. Of the twelve Adityas, I am Vishnu; the radiant Sun among the luminaries; of the forty nine winds, I am Marichi and of the stars, the Moon.

वेदानां सामवेदोऽस्मि, देवानामस्मि वासवः ।
इन्द्रियाणां मनश्चास्मि भूतानामस्मि चेतना ॥२२॥
vedānāṁ sāma-vedo 'smi devānām asmi vāsavaḥ
indriyāṇāṁ manaś cāsmi bhūtānām asmi cetanā'

22. Of the Vedas, I am the Sama-Veda and Vasava (Indra) among the gods; of the senses I am the mind and consciousness (life energy) in living beings am I.

रुद्राणां शंकरश्चास्मि, वित्तेशो यक्षरक्षसाम् ।
वसूनां पावकश्चास्मि, मेरुः शिखरिणामहम् ॥२३॥
rudrāṇāṁ śaṅkaraś cāsmi / vitteśo yakṣa-rakṣasām
vasūnāṁ pāvakaś cāsmi / meruḥ śikhariṇām aham

23. Among the eleven Rudras, I am Shankara; among the Yakshas and Rakshasas, the lord of wealth (Kubera); Among the eight Vasus I am the fire god; and among the mountains, Meru am I.

पुरोधसां च मुख्यं मां, विद्धि पार्थ बृहस्पतिम् ।

सेनानीनामहं स्कन्दः, सरसामस्मि सागरः ॥२४॥

purodhasāñ ca mukhyaṁ māṁ / viddhi pārtha bṛhaspatim

senānīnām ahaṁ skandaḥ / sarasām asmi sāgaraḥ

24. Among the priests, O son of Pritha, know Me to be their chief, Brihaspati; among warrior chiefs, I am Skanda; and among the bodies of water, I am the ocean.

महर्षीणां भृगुरहं, गिरामस्म्येकमक्षरम् ।
यज्ञानां जपयज्ञोऽस्मि, स्थावराणां हिमालयः ॥२५॥

maharṣīṇāṁ bhṛgur ahaṁ / girām asmy ekam akṣaram

yajñānāṁ japa-yajño 'smi / sthāvarāṇāṁ himālayaḥ

25. Among the great Seers, I am Bhrigu; among words I am the sacred syllable Om; among the yajnas I am the yajna of japa (silent repetition of sacred formulas); among the immovable things, I am the Himalaya.

अश्वत्थः सर्ववृक्षाणां, देवर्षीणां च नारदः ।
गन्धर्वाणां चित्ररथः, सिद्धानां कपिलो मुनिः ॥२६॥

aśvatthaḥ sarva-vṛkṣāṇāṁ / devarṣīṇāṁ ca nāradaḥ

gandharvāṇāṁ citrarathaḥ / siddhānāṁ kapilo muniḥ

26. Among all trees (I am) the Ashvattha and Narada among celestial sages ; Chitraratha, among celestial musicians am I and sage Kapila among the perfected ones.

उच्चैःश्रवसमश्वानां, विद्धि माममृतोद्भवम् ।
ऐरावतं गजेन्द्राणां, नराणां च नराधिपम् ॥२७॥

uccaiḥśravasam aśvānāṁ / viddhi mām amṛtodbhavam
airāvataṁ gajendrāṇāṁ / narāṇāṁ ca narādhipam

27. Know me among horses as Uchchaisshravas, among mighty elephants, Airavata and among men, the king.

आयुधानामहं वज्रं, धेनूनामस्मि कामधुक् ।
प्रजनश्चास्मि कन्दर्पः, सर्पाणामस्मि वासुकिः ॥२८॥

āyudhānām ahaṁ vajraṁ / dhenūnām asmi kāmadhuk
prajanaś cāsmi kandarpaḥ / sarpāṇām asmi vāsukiḥ

28. Among weapons I am the thunderbolt; Among cows I am Kamadhenu; I am the Kandarpa, the cause of offspring; among serpents I am Vasuki.

अनन्तश्चास्मि नागानां, वरुणो यादसामहम् ।
पितॄणामर्यमा चास्मि, यमः संयमतामहम् ॥२९॥
anantaś cāsmi nāgānāṁ / varuṇo yādasām aham
pitṝṇām aryamā cāsmi / yamaḥ saṁyamatām aham

29. Among snakes, I am Ananta ; I am Varuna, the Lord of aquatic beings; and Aryaman of Pitris I am and among rulers I am Yama.

प्रह्लादश्चास्मि दैत्यानां, कालः कलयतामहम् ।
मृगाणां च मृगेन्द्रोऽहं, वैनतेयश्च पक्षिणाम् ॥३०॥
prahlādaś cāsmi daityānāṁ / kālaḥ kalayatām aham
mṛgāṇāṁ ca mṛgendro 'haṁ / vainateyaś ca pakṣiṇām

30. And Prahlada am I among Diti's progeny, among reckoners I am Time; and among beasts I am the King of beasts [lion] and Garuda among birds.

पवनः पवतामस्मि, रामः शस्त्रभृतामहम् ।
झषाणां मकरश्चास्मि, स्रोतसामस्मि जाह्नवी ॥३१॥
pavanaḥ pavatām asmi / rāmaḥ śastra-bhṛtām aham
jhaṣāṇāṁ makaraś cāsmi / srotasām asmi jāhnavī

31. Among purifiers I am the wind, Rama among warriors am I; among fishes I am the shark and among streams I am Jahnavi (the Ganga).

सर्गाणामादिरन्तश्च, मध्यं चैवाहमर्जुन ।
अध्यात्मविद्या विद्यानां, वादः प्रवदतामहम् ॥३२॥
sargāṇām ādir antaś ca / madhyaṁ caivāham arjuna
adhyātma-vidyā vidyānāṁ / vādaḥ pravadatām aham

32. I am the beginning, the middle and also the end of all creations ; of all knowledges I am the knowledge of the Self and Vada (right reasoning) among disputants.

अक्षराणामकारोऽस्मि, द्वन्द्वः सामासिकस्य च ।
अहमेवाक्षयः कालो, धाताहं विश्वतोमुखः ॥३३॥
akṣarāṇām a-kāro 'smi / dvandvaḥ sāmāsikasya ca
aham evākṣayaḥ kālo / dhātāhaṁ viśvato-mukhaḥ

33. Among letters the letter 'A' am I, and Dvandva of all compounds (in grammar); I alone am the endless Time and I am the Sustainer (by dispensing fruits of actions).

मृत्युः सर्वहरश्चाहमुद्भवश्च भविष्यताम् ।
कीर्तिः श्रीर्वाक्च नारीणां स्मृतिर्मेधा धृतिः क्षमा ॥३४॥

mṛtyuḥ sarva-haraś cāham udbhavaś ca bhaviṣyatām
kīrttiḥ śrīr vāk ca nārīṇāṁ smṛtir medhā dhṛtiḥ kṣamā

34. I am the all-devouring death and the source of all that shall be born. Among feminine qualities I am fame, beauty, fine speech, memory, intelligence, forbearance and forgiveness.

बृहत्साम तथा साम्नां गायत्री छन्दसामहम् ।
मासानां मार्गशीर्षोऽहमृतूनां कुसुमाकरः ॥३५॥
bṛhat-sāma tathā sāmnāṁ gāyatrī chandasām aham
māsānāṁ mārga-śīrṣo 'ham ṛtūnāṁ kusumākaraḥ

35. Among Sruthis, I am the Brihat-Sama; among metres Gayatri am I; among months I am Margashirsha and among seasons, the flowery season.

द्यूतं छलयतामस्मि, तेजस्तेजस्विनामहम् ।
जयोऽस्मि व्यवसायोऽस्मि, सत्त्वं सत्त्ववतामहम् ॥३६॥
dyūtaṁ chalayatām asmi / tejas tejasvinām aham
jayo 'smi vyavasāyo 'smi / sattvaṁ sattvavatām aham

36. I am the gambling among the fraudulent practices, I am the power of the powerful; I am the victory of the victorious, I am the resolve of the resolute and the sattwa of the sattwic.

वृष्णीनां वासुदेवोऽस्मि, पाण्डवानां धनंजयः ।
मुनीनामप्यहं व्यासः, कवीनामुशना कविः ॥३७॥
vṛṣṇīnāṁ vāsudevo 'smi / pāṇḍavānāṁ dhanañjayaḥ
munīnām apy ahaṁ vyāsaḥ / kavīnām uśanā kaviḥ

37. I am Vasudeva among the Vrishnis ; among the Pandavas, I am Arjuna and also of the sages I am Vyasa; among the wise, I am sage Shukracharya.

दण्डो दमयतामस्मि, नीतिरस्मि जिगीषताम् ।
मौनं चैवास्मि गुह्यानां, ज्ञानं ज्ञानवतामहम् ॥३८॥
daṇḍo damayatām asmi / nītir asmi jigīṣatām
maunaṁ caivāsmi guhyānāṁ / jñānaṁ jñānavatām aham

38. Among those who dispense justice, I am the subduing power; among those who seek to conquer, I am righteousness; and also of things secret I am silence and the wisdom of the wise am I.

यच्चापि सर्वभूतानां बीजं तदहमर्जुन ।
न तदस्ति विना यत्स्यान्मया भूतं चराचरम् ॥३९।

yac cāpi sarva-bhūtānāṁ bījaṁ tad aham arjuna
na tad asti vinā yat syān mayā bhūtaṁ carācaram

39. O Arjuna, I am also the seed of all beings. There is no being, whether moving or inert, existing without Me.

नान्तोऽस्ति मम दिव्यानां, विभूतीनां परंतप ।
एष तूदेदशतः प्रोक्तो, विभूतेर्विस्तरो मया ॥४०॥
nānto 'sti mama divyānāṁ / vibhūtīnāṁ parantapa
eṣa tūddeśataḥ prokto / vibhūter vistaro mayā

40. Arjuna, there is no limit to My divine manifestations; even this is only a brief statement by Me of the extent of My divine glory.

यद्यद्विभूतिमत्सत्त्वं, श्रीमदूर्जितमेव वा ।
तत्तदेवावगच्छ त्वं, मम तेजोंऽशसंभवम् ॥४१॥
yad yad vibhūtimat sattvaṁ / śrīmad ūrjitam eva vā
tat tad evāvagaccha tvaṁ / mama tejo 'ṁśa-sambhavam

41. Whatever being is there, great, prosperous, or powerful, know that to be a manifestation of a part of My glory.

अथवा बहुनैतेन किं ज्ञातेन तवार्जुन ।
विष्टभ्याहमिदं कृत्स्नमेकांशेन स्थितो जगत् ॥४२॥

atha vā bahunaitena kiṁ jñātena tavārjuna
viṣṭabhyāham idaṁ kṛtsnam ekāṁśena sthito jagat

42. Or what will you gain by knowing all this in detail, O Arjuna? (Know this that) I stand, holding this whole world by a fraction of My Yogic power.

ॐ तत् सत् । इति श्रीमद्भगवद्गीतासु उपनिषत्सु ब्रह्मविद्यायां योगशास्त्रे श्रीकृष्णार्जुन संवादे विभूतियोगो नाम दशमोऽध्यायः ॥

Om Tat Sat. Iti Śrimad Bhagavat Gitasu Upanishatsu Brahmavidyayām yogaśastre Sri Krishnarjuna samvade Vibhūti-Yogonama Daśamodhyayaḥ

Thus ends the tenth chapter named "Vibhuti-Vistara-Yoga" (Manifestation of the Absolute) of the Upanishad of the Bhagavad Gita, the scripture of yoga, dealing with the science of the Absolute in the form of the dialogue between Sri Krishna and Arjuna.

अथ एकादशोऽध्यायः - विश्वरूपदर्शनयोगः

Chapter Eleven: Viśvarūpa-Darśana-Yoga

अर्जुन उवाच ।
मदनुग्रहाय परमं, गुह्यमध्यात्मसंज्ञितम् ।
यत्त्वयोक्तं वचस्तेन, मोहोऽयं विगतो मम ॥१॥

arjuna uvāca
mad-anugrahāya paramaṁ / guhyam adhyātma-saṁjñitam
yat tvayoktaṁ vacas tena / moho 'yaṁ vigato mama

1. Arjuna said: By the most profound words of supreme spiritual wisdom that you spoke out of compassion towards me, this delusion of mine has disappeared.

भवाप्ययौ हि भूतानां, श्रुतौ विस्तरशो मया ।
त्वत्तः कमलपत्राक्ष, माहात्म्यमपि चाव्ययम् ॥२॥

bhavāpyayau hi bhūtānāṁ / śrutau vistaraśo mayā
tvattaḥ kamala-patrākṣa / māhātmyam api cāvyayam

2. About you, O lotus-eyed Krishna, I have heard in detail, of the evolution and dissolution of beings and also Your immortal glory.

एवमेतद्यथात्थ त्वमात्मानं परमेश्वर ।
द्रष्टुमिच्छामि ते रूपमैश्वरं पुरुषोत्तम ॥३॥

evam etad yathāttha tvam / ātmānaṁ parameśvara
draṣṭum icchāmi te rūpam / aiśvaraṁ puruṣottama

3. You are indeed the Supreme Lord as You have declared Yourself. But I long to see Your Divine-Form, O Supreme Purusha.

मन्यसे यदि तच्छक्यं, मया द्रष्टुमिति प्रभो ।
योगेश्वर ततो मे त्वं, दर्शयात्मानमव्ययम् ॥४॥

manyase yadi tac chakyaṁ / mayā draṣṭum iti prabho
yogeśvara tato me tvaṁ / darśayātmānam avyayam

4. If You think I am capable of seeing it, O Lord of Yoga, reveal me Your imperishable form.

श्रीभगवानुवाच
पश्य मे पार्थ रूपाणि, शतशोऽथ सहस्रशः ।
नानाविधानि दिव्यानि, नानावर्णाकृतीनि च ॥५॥

śrī-bhagavān uvāca
paśya me pārtha rūpāṇi / śataśo 'tha sahasraśaḥ
nānā-vidhāni divyāni / nānā-varṇākṛtīni ca

5. The Blessed Lord said: Behold, Arjuna now in hundreds and thousands, My multifarouis celestial forms, of various colours and shapes.

पश्यादित्यान्वसून्रुद्रानश्विनौ मरुतस्तथा ।
बहून्यदृष्टपूर्वाणि पश्याश्चर्याणि भारत ॥६॥

paśyādityān vasūn rudrān aśvinau marutas tathā
bahūny adṛṣṭa-pūrvāṇi paśyāścaryāṇi bhārata

6. Behold in me Arjuna, the Adityas, the Vasus, the Rudras, the twin Ashvins, and the Maruts; behold many wonders never seen before.

इहैकस्थं जगत्कृत्स्नं, पश्याद्य सचराचरम् ।
मम देहे गुडाकेश, यच्चान्यद्द्रष्टुमिच्छसि ॥७॥

ihaika-sthaṁ jagat kṛtsnaṁ / paśyādya sa-carācaram
mama dehe guḍākeśa / yac cānyad draṣṭum icchasi

7. O Gudakesha, see now in this body of mine, the whole creation centred in, including the animate and the inanimate and whatever else that you desire to see.

न तु मां शक्यसे द्रष्टुमनेनैव स्वचक्षुषा ।
दिव्यं ददामि ते चक्षुः पश्य मे योगमैश्वरम् ॥८॥

na tu māṁ śakyase draṣṭum anenaiva sva-cakṣuṣā
divyaṁ dadāmi te cakṣuḥ paśya me yogam aiśvaram

8. But you surely cannot see Me with these human eyes of yours. Therefore, I give you the divine eye and with this you behold My supreme power of yoga.

संजय उवाच
एवमुक्त्वा ततो राजन्महायोगेश्वरो हरिः ।
दर्शयामास पार्थाय परमं रूपमैश्वरम् ॥६॥

sañjaya uvāca
evam uktvā tato rājan mahā-yogeśvaro hariḥ
darśayāmāsa pārthāya paramaṁ rūpam aiśvaram

9. Sanjaya said: O King, having thus spoken, Hari, the Supreme Master of Yoga, revealed to Arjuna, His supremely glorious Ishvara-Form.

अनेकवक्त्रनयनमनेकाद्भुतदर्शनम् ।
अनेकदिव्याभरणं, दिव्यानेकोद्यतायुधम् ॥१०॥
aneka-vaktra-nayanam anekādbhuta-darśanam
aneka-divyābharaṇaṁ divyānekodyatāyudham

10. With numberless mouths and eyes, with innumerable wonderful sights, with numerous celestial ornaments, with numerous heavenly weapons uplifted.

दिव्यमाल्याम्बरधरं दिव्यगन्धानुलेपनम् ।
सर्वाश्चर्यमयं देवमनन्तं विश्वतोमुखम् ॥११॥

divya-mālyāmbara-dharaṁ divya-gandhānulepanam
sarvāścarya-mayaṁ devam anantaṁ viśvato-mukham

11. Wearing divine garlands and apparel, anointed with celestial-perfumed oil, the All-wonderful Resplendent, Infinite and having faces on all sides.

दिवि सूर्यसहस्रस्य भवेद्युगपदुत्थिता ।
यदि भाः सदृशी सा स्याद्भासस्तस्य महात्मनः ॥१२॥

divi sūrya-sahasrasya bhaved yugapad utthitā
yadi bhāḥ sadṛśī sā syād bhāsas tasya mahātmanaḥ

12. If the effulgence of a thousand suns were to burst forth all at once in the sky, that would hardly approach the splendour of that Mighty Being.

तत्रैकस्थं जगत्कृत्स्नं, प्रविभक्तमनेकधा ।
अपश्यद्देवदेवस्य, शरीरे पाण्डवस्तदा ॥१३॥

tatraika-sthaṁ jagat kṛtsnaṁ pravibhaktam anekadhā
apaśyad deva-devasya śarīre pāṇḍavas tadā

13. Contained in the body of that Supreme Person, Arjuna, saw the whole universe at one place, with its manifold divisions.

ततः स विस्मयाविष्टो, हृष्टरोमा धनंजयः ।
प्रणम्य शिरसा देवं, कृताञ्जलिरभाषत ॥१४॥

tataḥ sa vismayāviṣṭo / hṛṣṭa-romā dhanañjayaḥ
praṇamya śirasā devaṁ / kṛtāñjalir abhāṣata

14. Then Dhananjaya, full of wonder, with his hairs standing on end, reverentially bowed his head to the divine Lord in adoration and with joined palms addressed him thus:

अर्जुन उवाच ।
पश्यामि देवांस्तव देव देहे सर्वांस्तथा भूतविशेषसंघान् ।
ब्रह्माणमीशं कमलासनस्थमृषींश्च सर्वानुरगांश्च दिव्यान्
॥१५॥

arjuna uvāca
paśyāmi devāṁs tava deva dehe sarvāṁs tathā bhūta-viśeṣa-saṅghān
brahmāṇam īśaṁ kamalāsana-stham ṛṣīṁś ca sarvān uragāṁś ca divyān

15. Arjuna said: O Lord I see all the gods in your body and the whole host of different beings; Brahma seated on the lotus and all the Rishis and celestial serpents.

अनेकबाहूदरवक्त्रनेत्रं पश्यामि त्वां सर्वतोऽनन्तरूपम् ।
नान्तं न मध्यं न पुनस्तवादिं पश्यामि विश्वेश्वर विश्वरूप
॥१६॥

aneka-bāhūdara-vaktra-netraṁ paśyāmi tvāṁ
sarvato 'nanta-rūpam
nāntaṁ na madhyaṁ na punas tavādiṁ
paśyāmi viśveśvara viśva-rūpa

16. O Lord of the universe, I see You of limitless forms on all sides with numerous arms, stomachs, mouths, and eyes. Neither the end nor the middle nor the beginning of You do I see, manifested as You are in this Universal Form.

किरीटिनं गदिनं चक्रिणं च तेजोराशिं सर्वतो दीप्तिमन्तम् ।
पश्यामि त्वां दुर्निरीक्ष्यं समन्ताद् दीप्तानलार्कद्युतिमप्रमेयम्
॥१७॥

kirīṭinaṁ gadinaṁ cakriṇañ ca tejo-rāśiṁ
sarvato dīptimantam
paśyāmi tvāṁ durnirīkṣyaṁ samantād
dīptānalārka-dyutim aprameyam

17. I see You endowed with diadems, clubs, and discuses; a mass of splendour flaming everywhere, very hard to look at; all around blazing like burning fire and sun and limitless, on all sides.

त्वमक्षरं परमं वेदितव्यं त्वमस्य विश्वस्य परं निधानम् ।
त्वमव्ययः शाश्वतधर्मगोप्ता सनातनस्त्वं पुरुषो मतो मे
॥१८॥

tvam akṣaraṁ paramaṁ veditavyaṁ tvam asya viśvasya paraṁ nidhānam
tvam avyayaḥ śāśvata-dharma-goptā sanātanas tvaṁ puruṣo mato me

18. You are the Imperishable, the Supreme Being, worthy of being known; You are the ultimate salvation of this universe; You are the protector of the ageless Dharma and I consider You as the Eternal Imperishable being.

अनादिमध्यान्तमनन्तवीर्यमनन्तबाहुं शशिसूर्यनेत्रम् ।
पश्यामि त्वां दीप्तहुताशवक्त्रं स्वतेजसा विश्वमिदं तपन्तम्
॥१९॥

anādi-madhyāntam ananta-vīryam ananta-bāhuṁ
śaśi-sūrya-netram
paśyāmi tvāṁ dīpta-hutāśa-vaktraṁ sva-tejasā viśvamidaṁ tapantam

19. I see You without beginning, middle, or end; possessing unlimited prowess and of numberless arms; having the sun and the moon for Your eyes; burning fire for Your mouth and scorching this universe with Your radiance.

द्यावापृथिव्योरिदमन्तरं हि व्याप्तं त्वयैकेन दिशश्च सर्वाः ।
दृष्ट्वाऽद्भुतं रूपमुग्रं तवेदं लोकत्रयं प्रव्यथितं महात्मन्
॥२०॥

dyāv ā-pṛthivyor idam antaraṁ hi vyāptaṁ
tvayaikena diśaś ca sarvāḥ
dṛṣṭvādbhutaṁ rūpam idaṁ tavograṁ loka-
trayaṁ pravyathitaṁ mahātman

20. This space between heaven and earth and all the quarters are entirely filled by You alone. Seeing this transcendent and dreadful form of Yours, O soul of the Universe, all the three worlds are greatly alarmed.

अमी हि त्वां सुरसंघा विशन्ति केचिद्भीताः प्राञ्जलयो
गृणन्ति ।
स्वस्तीत्युक्त्वा महर्षिसिद्धसंघाः स्तुवन्ति त्वां स्तुतिभिः
पुष्कलाभिः ॥२१॥

amī hi tvāṁ sura-saṅghā viśanti kecid bhītāḥ
prāñjalayo gṛṇanti
svastītyuktvā maharṣi-siddha-saṅghāḥ stuvanti
tvāṁ stutibhiḥ puṣkalābhiḥ

21. Verily, into You enter these crowds of gods; some extol You in fear with joined palms; "Let there be Peace", thus saying, multitudes of great Rishis and Siddhas extoll You with splendid hymns.

रुद्रादित्या वसवो ये च साध्याः विश्वेऽश्विनौ
मरुतश्चोष्मपाश्च ।
गन्धर्वयक्षासुरसिद्धसंघाः वीक्षन्ते त्वां विस्मिताश्चैव सर्वे
॥२२॥

rudrādityā vasavo ye ca sādhyā viśve 'śvinau
marutaś
coṣmapāś ca
gandharva-yakṣāsura-siddha-saṅghā vīkṣante
tvāṁ
vismitāś caiva sarve

22. The Rudras, Adityas, Vasus, Sadhyas, Vishvadevas, the two Ashvins, Maruts, Ushmapas and multitudes of Gandharvas, Yakshas, Asuras, and Siddhas – all these gaze upon You, all quite astounded.

रूपं महत्ते बहुवक्त्रनेत्रं महाबाहो बहुबाहूरुपादम् ।
बहूदरं बहुदंष्ट्राकरालं दृष्ट्वा लोकाः प्रव्यथितास्तथाहम्
॥२३॥

rūpaṁ mahat te bahu-vaktra-netraṁ mahā-
bāho bahu-bāhūru-pādam
bahūdaraṁ bahu-daṁṣṭrā-karālaṁ dṛṣṭvā lokāḥ
pravyathitās tathāham

23. Lord, seeing this stupendous and dreadful Form of Yours, with numerous mouths and eyes, armed with many arms, thighs, and feet, with many stomachs, and fearful with many tusks – the worlds are terrified, and so am I.

नभःस्पृशं दीप्तमनेकवर्णं व्यात्ताननं दीप्तविशालनेत्रम् ।
दृष्ट्वा हि त्वां प्रव्यथितान्तरात्मा धृतिं न विन्दामि शमं च विष्णो ॥२४॥

nabhaḥ-spṛśaṁ dīptam aneka-varṇaṁ
vyāttānanaṁ dīpta-viśāla-netram
dṛṣṭvā hi tvāṁ pravyathitāntar-ātmā dhṛtiṁ na vindāmi śamañ ca viṣṇo

24. Lord, seeing Your from reaching the heavens, shining multi-coloured, with mouths wide open, with large fiery eyes, I am frightened at heart and I have lost control and find no peace.

दंष्ट्राकरालानि च ते मुखानि दृष्ट्वैव कालानलसन्निभानि ।
दिशो न जाने न लभे च शर्म प्रसीद देवेश जगन्निवास ॥२५॥

daṁṣṭrā-karālāni ca te mukhāni dṛṣṭvaiva kālānala-sannibhāni
diśo na jāne na labhe ca śarma prasīda deveśa jagan-nivāsa

25. Having seen Your mouths, frightful with tusks, (blazing) like Pralaya-fires, I am utterly bewildered and nor do I find happiness; therefore be kind to me, O Lord of the celestials, O Abode of the universe.

अमी च त्वां धृतराष्ट्रस्य पुत्राः सर्वे सहैवावनिपालसंघैः ।
भीष्मो द्रोणः सूतपुत्रस्तथासौ सहास्मदीयैरपि योधमुख्यैः
॥२६॥
वक्त्राणि ते त्वरमाणा विशन्ति दंष्ट्राकरालानि भयानकानि ।
केचिद्विलग्ना दशनान्तरेषु संदृश्यन्ते चूर्णितैरुत्तमाङ्गैः
॥२७॥

amī ca tvāṁ dhṛtarāṣṭrasya putrāḥ sarve
sahaivāvani-pāla-saṅghaiḥ
bhīṣmo droṇaḥ sūta-putras tathāsau
sahāsmadīyair api yodha-mukhyaiḥ
vaktrāṇi te tvaramāṇā viśanti daṁṣṭrā-karālāni bhayānakāni
kecid vilagnā daśanāntareṣu sandṛśyante cūrṇitair uttamāṅgaiḥ

26 & 27. All those sons of Dhritarashtra, with host of Kings, Bhishma, Drona and Karna, with the principal warriors of our side, are rushing headlong into Your mouth, terrible with tusks and fearful to behold. Some are seen sticking in the interstices of Your teeth, with their heads crushed.

यथा नदीनां बहवोऽम्बुवेगाः समुद्रमेवाभिमुखा द्रवन्ति ।
तथा तवामी नरलोकवीराः विशन्ति वक्त्राण्यभिविज्वलन्ति
॥२८॥

yathā nadīnāṁ bahavo'mbu-vegāḥ samudram evābhimukhā dravanti
tathā tavāmī nara-loka-vīrā viśanti vaktrāṇy abhivijvalanti

28. Verily, as the myriad streams of rivers rush towards the sea alone, so do those heroes in the mortal world enter Your flaming mouths.

यथा प्रदीप्तं ज्वलनं पतङ्गाः विशन्ति नाशाय समृद्धवेगाः ।
तथैव नाशाय विशन्ति लोकास्तवापि वक्त्राणि समृद्धवेगाः
॥२९॥

yathā pradīptaṁ jvalanaṁ pataṅgā viśanti nāśāya samṛddha-vegāḥ
tathaiva nāśāya viśanti lokāstavāpi vaktrāṇi samṛddha-vegāḥ

29. As moths rush with great speed into a blazing fire only to perish, even so do those warriors precipitately rush into Your flaming mouths.

लेलिह्यसे ग्रसमानः समन्तात् लोकान्समग्रान्वदनैर्ज्वलद्भिः ।
तेजोभिरापूर्य जगत्समग्रं भासस्तवोग्राः प्रतपन्ति विष्णो
॥३०॥

lelihyase grasamānaḥ samantāt lokān samagrān vadanair jvaladbhiḥ
tejobhir āpūrya jagat samagraṁ bhāsas tavogrāḥ pratapanti viṣṇo

30. Swallowing with your blazing mouths, You are licking all those people on all sides. O Vishnu, Your fierce rays, filling the whole world with radiance, are burning the entire Universe.

आख्याहि मे को भवानुग्ररूपो नमोऽस्तुते देववर प्रसीद ।
विज्ञातुमिच्छामि भवन्तमाद्यं न हि प्रजानामि तव प्रवृत्तिम् ॥३१॥

ākhyāhi me ko bhavān ugra-rūpo namo 'stu te deva-vara prasīda
vijñātum icchāmi bhavantam ādyaṁ na hi prajānāmi tava pravṛttim

31. Tell me who You are with a form so terrible? My obeisance to You, O Supreme Deva! Have mercy. I wish to know You, the Primal Being, in particular, for, I know not Your purpose.

श्रीभगवानुवाच
कालोऽस्मि लोकक्षयकृत्प्रवृद्धो लोकान्समाहर्तुमिह प्रवृत्तः ।
ऋतेऽपि त्वां न भविष्यन्ति सर्वे येऽवस्थिताः प्रत्यनीकेषु योधाः ॥३२॥

śrī-bhagavān uvāca
kālo 'smi loka-kṣaya-kṛt pravṛddho lokān
samāhartum iha pravṛttaḥ
ṛte 'pi tvāṁ na bhaviṣyanti sarve ye 'vasthitāḥ
pratyanīkeṣu yodhāḥ

32. The Blessed Lord said: I am the mighty all-devouring Time, manifested here for the purpose of annihilating these people. Even without you, all those warriors arrayed in the enemy camp must die.

तस्मात्त्वमुत्तिष्ठ यशो लभस्व जित्वा शत्रून्भुङ्क्ष्व राज्यं
समृद्धम् ।
मयैवैते निहताः पूर्वमेव निमित्तमात्रं भव सव्यसाचिन् ॥३३॥

tasmāt tvam uttiṣṭha yaśo labhasva jitvā śatrūn
bhuṅkṣva rājyaṁ samṛddham
mayaivaite nihatāḥ pūrvam eva nimitta-mātraṁ
bhava savya-sācin

33. Therefore do you arise and acquire glory, conquer the foes and enjoy the affluent Kingdom. Verily by Myself have they already been slain; be merely an instrument, O Savyasachin (Arjuna).

द्रोणं च भीष्मं च जयद्रथं च कर्णं तथान्यानपि योधवीरान् ।
मया हतांस्त्वं जहि मा व्यथिष्ठाः युध्यस्व जेतासि रणे
सपत्नान् ॥३४॥

droṇam ca bhīṣmam ca jayadratham ca karṇaṁ
tathānyān api yodha-vīrān
mayā hatāṁs tvaṁ jahi mā vyathiṣṭhā
yudhyasva jetāsi raṇe sapatnān

34. Drona, Bhishma, Jayadratha, Karna and other brave warriors have already been killed by Me. So fear not; fight and you shall conquer the enemies in this war.

संजय उवाच
एतच्छ्रुत्वा वचनं केशवस्य कृताञ्जलिर्वेपमानः किरीटी।
नमस्कृत्वा भूय एवाह कृष्णं सगद्गदं भीतभीतः प्रणम्य
॥३५॥

sañjaya uvāca
etac chrutvā vacanaṁ keśavasya kṛtāñjalir
vepamānaḥ kirīṭī
namaskṛtvā bhūya evāha kṛṣṇaṁ sa-gadgadaṁ
bhīta-bhītaḥ praṇamya

35. Sanjaya said: Having heard these words of Bhagavan Keshava, Arjuna, with joined palms, trembling, bowed to him and overwhelmed with fear, again addressed Krishna in a faltering tone.

अर्जुन उवाच ।
स्थाने हृषीकेश तव प्रकीर्त्या जगत्प्रहृष्यत्यनुरज्यते च ।
रक्षांसि भीतानि दिशो द्रवन्ति सर्वे नमस्यन्ति च सिद्धसं
घाः ॥३६॥

arjuna uvāca
sthāne hṛṣīkeśa tava prakīrtyā jagat prahṛṣyaty anurajyate ca
rakṣāṁsi bhītāni diśo dravanti sarve namasyanti ca siddha-saṅghāḥ

36. Arjuna said: Lord, well it is, the Universe exults and rejoices in Your praise by chanting your names, that rakshasas flee with fear in all directions and the whole host of Siddhas bow down to You in adoration.

कस्माच्च ते न नमेरन्महात्मन् गरीयसे ब्रह्मणोऽप्यादिकर्त्रे ।
अनन्त देवेश जगन्निवास त्वमक्षरं सदसत्तत्परं यत् ॥३७॥

kasmāc ca te na nameran mahātman garīyase brahmaṇo 'py ādi-kartre
ananta deveśa jagan-nivāsa tvam akṣaraṁ sad-asat tat paraṁ yat

37. O Great soul, and why should they not bow to You, who are greater than the greatest and the progenitor of even Brahma? O Infinite Lord of celestials, O Abode of the universe, You are the Imperishable, the Being and the non-Being and That which is beyond them.

त्वमादिदेवः पुरुषः पुराणस्त्वमस्य विश्वस्य परं निधानम् ।
वेत्तासि वेद्यं च परं च धाम त्वया ततं विश्वमनन्तरूप
॥३८॥

tvam ādi-devaḥ puruṣaḥ purāṇas tvam asya
viśvasya paraṁ nidhānam
vettāsi vedyam ca param ca dhāma tvayā tataṁ
viśvam ananta-rūpa

38. You are the Primal Deity, the ancient Person; You are the ultimate Refuge of this universe; You are the Knower and the knowable and You are the Supreme goal. By You is the universe pervaded assuming endless forms.

वायुर्यमोऽग्निर्वरुणः शशाङ्कः प्रजापतिस्त्वं प्रपितामहश्च ।
नमो नमस्तेऽस्तु सहस्रकृत्वः पुनश्च भूयोऽपि नमो नमस्ते
॥३९॥

vāyur yamo 'gnir varuṇaḥ śaśāṅkaḥ prajāpatis
tvaṁ prapitāmahaś ca
namo namas te 'stu sahasra-kṛtvaḥ punaś ca
bhūyo 'pi namo namas te

39. You are Vayu, Yama, Agni, Varuna, the Moon, Brahma, nay the father of Brahma himself. Hail, hail to you a thousand times, repeated salutations to you, once again.

नमः पुरस्तादथ पृष्ठतस्ते नमोऽस्तुते सर्वत एव सर्व ।
अनन्तवीर्यामितविक्रमस्त्वं सर्वं समाप्नोषि ततोऽसि सर्वः ॥४०॥

namaḥ purastād atha pṛṣṭhatas te namo 'stu te sarvata eva sarva
ananta-vīryāmita-vikramas tvaṁ sarvaṁ samāpnoṣi tato 'si sarvaḥ

40. O Lord of infinite powers, my salutation to You from before and from behind. O soul of all, my obeisance to You from all sides. You, infinite in power pervades all; therefore, You are all.

सखेति मत्वा प्रसभं यदुक्तं हे कृष्ण हे यादव हे सखेति ।
अजानता महिमानं तवेदं मया प्रमादात्प्रणयेन वापि ॥४१॥
यच्चावहासार्थमसत्कृतोऽसि विहारशय्यासनभोजनेषु ।
एकोऽथवाप्यच्युत तत्समक्षं तत्क्षामये त्वामहमप्रमेयम् ॥४२॥

sakheti matvā prasabhaṁ yad uktaṁ he kṛṣṇa he yādava he sakheti
ajānatā mahimānaṁ tavedaṁ mayā pramādāt praṇayena vāpi

yac cāvahāsārtham asat-kṛto 'si vihāra-śayyāsana-bhojaneṣu
eko 'tha vāpy acyuta tat-samakṣaṁ tat kṣāmaye tvām aham aprameyam

41 & 42. The way I have presumptuously called out to you either because of carelessness or love, as "O Krishna, O Yadava, O friend," considering You merely as a friend, not knowing this greatness of yours – in whatever way I may have been disrespectful to You in fun, while walking, reposing, sitting, or at meals, either alone (with You), O Achyuta, or in the company of others – I implore You, the Infinite One, to forgive me.

पितासि लोकस्य चराचरस्य त्वमस्य पूज्यश्च गुरुर्गरीयान् ।
न त्वत्समोऽस्त्यभ्यधिकः कुतोऽन्यो लोकत्रयेऽप्यप्रतिमप्रभाव ॥४३॥

pitāsi lokasya carācarasya tvam asya pūjyaś ca gurur garīyān
na tvat-samo 'sty abhyadhikaḥ kuto 'nyo loka-traye 'py apratima-prabhāva

43. You are the Father, nay the greatest teacher of this moving and unmoving creation; the object of adoration. None exists who is equal to You in the three worlds; who then can surpass You, O You of power incomparable?

तस्मात्प्रणम्य प्रणिधाय कायं प्रसादये त्वामहमीशमीड्यम् ।
पितेव पुत्रस्य सखेव सख्युः प्रियः प्रियायार्हसि देव सोढुम् ॥४४॥

tasmāt praṇamya praṇidhāya kāyaṁ prasādaye tvām aham īśam īḍyam
piteva putrasya sakheva sakhyuḥ priyaḥ priyāyārhasi deva soḍhum

44. So, prostrating my body at your feet and bowing low, I crave Your forgiveness, Lord adorable! As a father forgives his son, a friend a dear friend; a lover his beloved, even so should You forgive me, O Lord.

अदृष्टपूर्वं हृषितोऽस्मि दृष्ट्वा भयेन च प्रव्यथितं मनो मे ।
तदेव मे दर्शय देव रूपं प्रसीद देवेश जगन्निवास ॥४५॥

adṛṣṭa-pūrvaṁ hṛṣito 'smi dṛṣṭvā bhayena ca pravyathitaṁ mano me
tad eva me darśaya deva rūpaṁ prasīda deveśa jagan-nivāsa

45. Overjoyed am I to have seen what I saw never before; yet my mind is tormented by fear. Show me, O Lord, only that benevolent Divine form of Yours. O Lord of celestials, O Abode of the universe, be gracious.

किरीटिनं गदिनं चक्रहस्तमिच्छामि त्वां द्रष्टुमहं तथैव ।
तेनैव रूपेण चतुर्भुजेन सहस्रबाहो भव विश्वमूर्ते ॥४६॥

kirīṭinaṁ gadinaṁ cakra-hastam icchāmi tvāṁ draṣṭum ahaṁ tathaiva
tenaiva rūpeṇa catur-bhujena sahasra-bāho bhava viśva-mūrtte

46. I wish to see you as before, diademed, bearing a mace and a discus. Assume that same four-armed Form, O You the Universal form of thousand arms.

श्रीभगवानुवाच ।
मया प्रसन्नेन तवार्जुनेदं रूपं परं दर्शितमात्मयोगात् ।
तेजोमयं विश्वमनन्तमाद्यं यन्मे त्वदन्येन न दृष्टपूर्वम्
॥४७॥

śrī-bhagavān uvāca
mayā prasannena tavārjunedaṁ rūpaṁ paraṁ darśitam ātma-yogāt
tejo-mayaṁ viśvam anantam ādyaṁ yan me tvad anyena na dṛṣṭa-pūrvam

47. The Blessed Lord said: Pleased with you I have shown to you, O Arjuna, this Form supreme, by My own power of yoga, this resplendent, primeval, infinite, universal Form of Mine, which has never been seen before by anyone else.

न वेदयज्ञाध्ययनैर्न दानै र्न च क्रियाभिर्न तपोभिरुग्रैः ।
एवंरूपः शक्य अहं नृलोके द्रष्टुं त्वदन्येन कुरुप्रवीर ॥४८॥

na veda-yajñādhyayanair na dānair
na ca kriyābhir na tapobhir ugraiḥ
evaṁ-rūpaḥ śakya ahaṁ nṛ-loke
drasṭuṁ tvad anyena kuru-pravīra

48. O Arjuna, I cannot be seen in this form, neither by the study of the Veda nor by doing yajna, nor by gifts, nor by rituals, nor by severe austerities by anyone else other than you.

मा ते व्यथा मा च विमूढभावो दृष्ट्वा रूपं
घोरमीदृङ्ममेदम् ।
व्यपेतभीः प्रीतमनाः पुनस्त्वं तदेव मे रूपमिदं प्रपश्य ॥४६॥

mā te vyathā mā ca vimūḍha-bhāvo dṛṣṭvā
rūpaṁ ghoram īdṛṅ mamedam
vyapeta-bhīḥ prīta-manāḥ punas tvaṁ tad eva
me rūpam idaṁ prapaśya

49. Having seen this Form of Mine, so terrific, be not afraid nor bewildered. With your fears dispelled and with gladdened heart, now behold again the former Form of Mine.

संजय उवाच ।
इत्यर्जुनं वासुदेवस्तथोक्त्वा स्वकं रूपं दर्शयामास भूयः ।
आश्वासयामास च भीतमेनं भूत्वा पुनः सौम्यवपुर्महात्मा
॥५०॥

sañjaya uvāca
ity arjunaṁ vāsudevas tathoktvā svakaṁ rūpaṁ darśayām āsa bhūyaḥ
āśvāsayām āsa ca bhītam enaṁ bhūtvā punaḥ saumya-vapur mahātmā

50. Sanjaya said: Having thus spoken to Arjuna, Krishna revealed again His own Form; and the Great-souled One, assuming His gentle Form, pacified Arjuna who was terrified.

अर्जुन उवाच।
दृष्ट्वेदं मानुषं रूपं, तव सौम्यं जनार्दन।
इदानीमस्मि संवृत्तः, सचेताः प्रकृतिं गतः ॥५१॥

arjuna uvāca
dṛṣṭvedaṁ mānuṣaṁ rūpaṁ / tava saumyaṁ janārdana
idānīm asmi saṁvṛttaḥ / sa-cetāḥ prakṛtiṁ gataḥ

51. Arjuna said: Having seen this gentle human Form of Yours, O Janardana, I have regained my composure and I am myself again.

श्रीभगवानुवाच
सुदुर्दर्शमिदं रूपं, दृष्टवानसि यन्मम।
देवा अप्यस्य रूपस्य, नित्यं दर्शनकाङ्क्षिणः ॥५२॥

śrī-bhagavān uvāca
su-durdarśam idaṁ rūpaṁ / dṛṣṭavān asi yan mama
devā apy asya rūpasya / nityaṁ darśana-kāṅkṣiṇaḥ

52. The Blessed Lord said: To see this form of Mine, which you have seen is very hard indeed. Even the gods are always eager to behold this Form.

नाहं वेदैर्न तपसा, न दानेन न चेज्यया ।
शक्य एवं विधो द्रष्टुं, दृष्टवानसि मां यथा ॥५३॥

nāhaṁ vedair na tapasā / na dānena na cejyayā
śakya evaṁ-vidho draṣṭuṁ / dṛṣṭavān asi yan mama

53. Neither by the study of Vedas, nor by austerity, nor by charity, nor by ritual can I be seen as you have seen Me.

भक्त्या त्वनन्यया शक्य, अहमेवंविधोऽर्जुन ।
ज्ञातुं द्रष्टुं च तत्त्वेन, प्रवेष्टुं च परंतप ॥५४॥

bhaktyā tv ananyayā śakya / aham evaṁ-vidho 'rjuna
jñātuṁ draṣṭuñ ca tattvena / praveṣṭuñ ca parantapa

54. Through single-minded devotion I may be known in this form O Arjuna, and known, and also entered into.

मत्कर्मकृन्मत्परमो, मद्भक्तः सङ्गवर्जितः ।
निर्वैरः सर्वभूतेषु, यः स मामेति पाण्डव ॥५५॥

mat-karma-kṛn mat-paramo / mad-bhaktaḥ saṅga-varjitaḥ
nirvairaḥ sarva-bhūteṣu / yaḥ sa mām eti pāṇḍava

55. Arjuna, he who performs all his duties for my sake and depends on Me alone and has Me as his goal, is devoted to Me, is freed from attachment and free from malice towards all, reaches Me.

ॐ तत् सत् । इति श्रीमद्भगवद्गीतासु उपनिषत्सु ब्रह्मविद्यायां योगशास्त्रे श्रीकृष्णार्जुन संवादे विश्वरूपदर्शनयोगो नाम एकादशोऽध्यायः ॥

Om Tat Sat. Iti Śrimad Bhagavad Gitasu Upanishatsu Brahmavidyayām yogaśastre Sri Krishnarjuna samvade Viśvarūpa Darśana yogonama ekādaśodhyayaḥ

Thus ends the eleventh chapter named "Visvarupa-Darshana-Yoga" (Vision of the Cosmic Form) of the Upanishad of the Bhagavad Gita, the scripture of yoga, dealing with the science of the Absolute in the form of the dialogue between Sri Krishna and Arjuna.

अथ द्वादशोऽध्यायः - भक्तियोगः

Chapter Twelve: Bhakti-Yoga

अर्जुन उवाच ।
एवं सततयुक्ता ये, भक्तास्त्वां पर्युपासते ।
ये चाप्यक्षरमव्यक्तं, तेषां के योगवित्तमाः ॥१॥

arjuna uvāca
evaṁ satata-yuktā ye / bhaktās tvāṁ paryupāsate
ye cāpy akṣaram avyaktaṁ / teṣāṁ ke yoga-vittamāḥ

1. Arjuna said: Those devotees who are exclusively and constantly devoted to You and those who worship the Unmanifested Brahman, which of them are the best knowers of Yoga?

श्रीभगवानुवाच ।
मय्यावेश्य मनो ये मां नित्ययुक्ता उपासते ।
श्रद्धया परयोपेतास्ते मे युक्ततमा मताः ॥२॥

śrī bhagavān uvāca
mayy āveśya mano ye māṁ nitya-yuktā upāsate
śraddhayā parayopetās te me yuktatamā matāḥ

2. The Blessed Lord said: I consider them to be the best yogis, who, fixing their mind on Me, worship Me, ever-steadfast, and are endowed with supreme shraddha.

ये त्वक्षरमनिर्देश्यमव्यक्तं पर्युपासते ।
सर्वत्रगमचिन्त्यं च कूटस्थमचलं ध्रुवम् ॥३॥
संनियम्येन्द्रियग्रामं सर्वत्र समबुद्धयः ।
ते प्राप्नुवन्ति मामेव सर्वभूतहिते रताः ॥४॥

ye tv akṣaram anirdeśyam avyaktaṁ paryupāsate
sarvatra-gam acintyañ ca kūṭastham acalaṁ dhruvam
sanniyamyendriya-grāmaṁ sarvatra sama-buddhayaḥ
te prāpnuvanti mām eva sarva-bhūta-hite ratāḥ

3 & 4. But those also, who worship the Imperishable, the Indefinable, the Unmanifested, the Omnipresent, the Unthinkable, the Unchange-able, the Immovable, the Eternal – having controlled all their senses, even-minded towards all and engaged in the welfare of all beings – verily they reach only Me.

क्लेशोऽधिकतरस्तेषामव्यक्तासक्तचेतसाम् ।
अव्यक्ता हि गतिर्दुःखं देहवद्भिरवाप्यते ॥५॥

kleśo'dhikataras teṣām avyaktāsakta-cetasām
avyaktā hi gatir duḥkhaṁ dehavadbhir avāpyate

5. Of course, the striving is greater for those whose minds are set on the Unmanifested; for the goal of the Unmanifested is very hard for the embodied to reach.

ये तु सर्वाणि कर्माणि, मयि संन्यस्य मत्पराः ।
अनन्येनैव योगेन, मां ध्यायन्त उपासते ॥६॥
तेषामहं समुद्धर्ता, मृत्युसंसारसागरात् ।
भवामि नचिरात्पार्थ, मय्यावेशितचेतसाम् ॥७॥

ye tu sarvāṇi karmāṇi / mayi sannyasya mat-parāḥ
ananyenaiva yogena / māṁ dhyāyanta upāsate
teṣām ahaṁ samuddhartā / mṛtyu-saṁsāra-sāgarāt
bhavāmi na cirāt pārtha / mayy āveśita-cetasām

6 & 7. But those who depending exclusivey on Me and surrendering all actions to Me, regarding me as the Supreme Goal, meditating on Me with single-minded devotion and whose mind is set on Me, verily, I become, before long, O Arjuna, their deliverer from the ocean of the mortal Samsara.

मय्येव मन आधत्स्व, मयि बुद्धिं निवेशय ।
निवसिष्यसि मय्येव, अत ऊर्ध्वं न संशयः ॥८॥

mayy eva mana ādhatsva / mayi buddhiṁ niveśaya
nivasiṣyasi mayy eva / ata ūrddhvaṁ na saṁśayaḥ

8. Fix your mind on Me and establish your intellect in Me: thereafter you shall, no doubt, abide in Me.

अथ चित्तं समाधातुं, न शक्नोषि मयि स्थिरम् ।
अभ्यासयोगेन ततो, मामिच्छाप्तुं धनंजय ॥६॥

atha cittaṁ samādhātuṁ / na śaknoṣi mayi sthiram
abhyāsa-yogena tato / mām icchāptuṁ dhanañjaya

9. If you cannot fix your mind steadily on Me, then seek to reach Me through abhyasa-yoga (repeated practice), O Dhananjaya.

अभ्यासेऽप्यसमर्थोऽसि, मत्कर्मपरमो भव ।
मदर्थमपि कर्माणि, कुर्वन्सिद्धिमवाप्स्यसि ॥१०॥

abhyāse 'py asamartho'si / mat-karma-paramo bhava
mad-artham api karmāṇi / kurvan siddhim avāpsyasi

10. If also you are unable to practice Abhyasa, be intent to work for Me. Even by doing actions for My sake, you shall attain perfection.

अथैतदप्यशक्तोऽसि, कर्तुं मद्योगमाश्रितः।
सर्वकर्मफलत्यागं, ततः कुरु यतात्मवान् ॥११॥

athaitad apy aśakto 'si / karttuṁ mad-yogam āśritaḥ
sarva-karma-phala-tyāgaṁ / tataḥ kuru yatātmavān

11. If you cannot do even this, then taking refuge in Me and subduing your mind and intellect, abandon the fruit of all actions.

श्रेयो हि ज्ञानमभ्यासाज्ज्ञानाद्ध्यानं विशिष्यते ।
ध्यानात्कर्मफलत्यागस्त्यागाच्छान्तिरनन्तरम् ॥१२॥

śreyo hi jñānam abhyāsāj jñānād dhyānaṁ viśiṣyate
dhyānāt karma-phala-tyāgas tyāgāc chāntir anantaram

12. Better indeed is knowledge than mere Abhyasa. Meditation (with knowledge) is more esteemed than (mere) knowledge. Even superior, the renunciation of the fruit of action, for peace immediately follows renunciation.

अद्वेष्टा सर्वभूतानां मैत्रः करुण एव च ।
निर्ममो निरहंकारः समदुःखसुखः क्षमी ॥१३॥
संतुष्टः सततं योगी यतात्मा दृढनिश्चयः ।
मय्यर्पितमनोबुद्धिर्यो मद्भक्तः स मे प्रियः ॥१४॥

adveṣṭā sarva-bhūtānāṁ maitraḥ karuṇa eva ca
nirmamo nirahaṅkāraḥ sama-duḥkha-sukhaḥ kṣamī

santuṣṭaḥ satataṁ yogī yatātmā dṛḍha-niścayaḥ
mayy arpita-mano-buddhir yo mad-bhaktaḥ sa me priyaḥ

13 & 14. He who is free from malice towards all, is friendly and compassionate towards all beings, free from the feelings of "I" and "mine," even-minded in pain and pleasure, forgiving, ever content, steady in meditation, self-controlled and possessed of firm conviction, with mind and intellect fixed on Me– that devotee of Mine, is dear to Me.

यस्मान्नोद्विजते लोको, लोकान्नोद्विजते च यः ।
हर्षामर्षभयोद्वेगैर्मुक्तो यः स च मे प्रियः ॥१५॥

yasmān nodvijate loko lokān nodvijate ca yaḥ
harṣāmarṣa-bhayodvegair mukto yaḥ sa ca me priyaḥ

15. He by whom others are not annoyed and who cannot be annoyed by the others, who is freed from delight, envy, fear and anxiety–that devotee of Mine is dear to Me.

अनपेक्षः शुचिर्दक्षः, उदासीनो गतव्यथः ।
सर्वारम्भपरित्यागी, यो मद्भक्तः स मे प्रियः ॥१६॥

anapekṣaḥ śucir dakṣa / udāsīno gata-vyathaḥ
sarvārambha-parityāgī / yo mad-bhaktaḥ sa me priyaḥ

16. He who wants nothing, who is both internally and externally pure, prompt, unconcerned, untroubled, renouncing the sense of doership in all undertakings – that devotee of Mine, is dear to Me.

यो न हृष्यति न द्वेष्टि, न शोचति न काङ्क्षति ।
शुभाशुभपरित्यागी, भक्तिमान्यः स मे प्रियः ॥१७॥

yo na hṛṣyati na dveṣṭi / na śocati na kāṅkṣati
śubhāśubha-parityāgī / bhaktimān yaḥ sa me priyaḥ

17. He who neither rejoices, nor hates, nor grieves, nor desires and who renounces both good and evil actions and is full of devotion, he is dear to Me.

समः शत्रौ च मित्रे च तथा मानापमानयोः ।
शीतोष्णसुखदुःखेषु समः सङ्गविवर्जितः ॥१८॥
तुल्यनिन्दास्तुतिर्मौनी संतुष्टो येन केनचित् ।
अनिकेतः स्थिरमतिर्भक्तिमान्मे प्रियो नरः ॥१९॥

samaḥ śatrau ca mitre ca tathā mānāpamānayoḥ
śītoṣṇa-sukha-duḥkheṣu samaḥ saṅga-vivarjitaḥ

tulya-nindā-stutir maunī santuṣṭo yena kenacit
aniketaḥ sthira-matir bhaktimān me priyo naraḥ

18 & 19. He who is alike to friend and foe and also in honor and ignominy; who remains balanced in heat and cold, in pleasure and pain and other such contrary experiences and is free from attachment. To whom censure and praise are equal; who is contemplative, content with any means of living, steady-minded, full of devotion – that man is dear to Me.

ये तु धर्म्यामृतमिदं, यथोक्तं पर्युपासते ।
श्रद्दधाना मत्परमाः, भक्तास्तेऽतीव मे प्रियाः ॥२०॥

ye tu dharmāmṛtam idaṁ / yathoktaṁ paryupāsate
śraddadhānā mat-paramā / bhaktās te'tīva me priyāḥ

20. And they who follow this Immortal Dharma, as set forth above, endowed with faith in Me as the Supreme Goal, and devoted – they are exceedingly dear to Me.

ॐ तत् सत् । इति श्रीमद्भगवद्गीतासु उपनिषत्सु ब्रह्मविद्यायां योगशास्त्रे श्रीकृष्णार्जुन संवादे भक्तियोगो नाम द्वादशोऽध्यायः ॥

Om Tat Sat. Iti Śrimad Bhagavat Gitasu Upanishatsu Brahmavidyayām yogaśastre Sri Krishnarjuna samvade Bhakti-Yogonama dhvadhaśodhyayaḥ

Thus ends the twelfth chapter named "Bhakti-Yoga" (Path of Devotion) of the Upanishad of the Bhagavad Gita, the scripture of yoga, dealing with the science of the Absolute in the form of the dialogue between Sri Krishna and Arjuna.

अथ त्रयोदशोऽध्यायः - क्षेत्रक्षेत्रज्ञविभागयोगः

Chapter Thirteen: Kṣetra-Kṣetrañja-Vibhā-ga-Yoga

अर्जुन उवाच
प्रकृतिं पुरुषं चैव क्षेत्रं क्षेत्रज्ञमेव च ।
एतद्वेदितुमिच्छामी ज्ञानं ज्ञेयं च केशव ॥१॥

arjuna uvāca
prakritimpurusham chaiva kshetram kshetrajnameva cha
edadveditumicchami jnaanam jneyam cha kesava

1. Arjuna said: I wish to learn about Nature (matter) and the Spirit (soul), the Field and the Knower of the Field, Knowledge and that which ought to be known.

श्रीभगवानुवाच ।
इदं शरीरं कौन्तेय, क्षेत्रमित्यभिधीयते ।
एतद्यो वेत्ति तं प्राहुः, क्षेत्रज्ञ इति तद्विदः ॥२॥

śrī bhagavān uvāca
idaṁ śarīraṁ kaunteya / kṣetram ity abhidhīyate
etadyo vetti taṁ prāhuḥ / kṣetrajña iti tad-vidaḥ

2. The Blessed Lord said: This body, O son of Kunti, is called kshetra and he who knows it is called kshetrajna by those who know the truth of both kshetra and kshetrajna.

क्षेत्रज्ञं चापि मां विद्धि, सर्वक्षेत्रेषु भारत ।
क्षेत्रक्षेत्रज्ञयोर्ज्ञानं, यत्तज्ज्ञानं मतं मम ॥३॥

kṣetrajñaṁ cāpi māṁ viddhi / sarva-kṣetreṣu bhārata
kṣetra-kṣetrajñayor jñānaṁ / yat taj jñānaṁ matam mama

3. Know myself to be the kshetrajna in all kshetras, Arjuna. The knowledge of kshetra and kshetrajna is considered by Me to be wisdom.

तत्क्षेत्रं यच्च यादृक्च, यद्विकारि यतश्च यत् ।
स च यो यत्प्रभावश्च, तत्समासेन मे शृणु ॥४॥

tat kṣetraṁ yac ca yādṛk ca / yad-vikāri yataś ca yat
sa ca yo yat prabhāvaś ca / tat samāsena me śṛṇu

4. What the kshetra is, what its properties are, what its modifications are, what effects arise from what causes, and also who He is and what His powers are, all this hear from Me in a nutshell.

ऋषिभिर्बहुधा गीतं, छन्दोभिर्विविधैः पृथक् ।
ब्रह्मसूत्रपदैश्चैव, हेतुमद्भिर्विनिश्चितैः ॥५॥

ṛṣibhir bahudhā gītaṁ / chandobhir vividhaiḥ pṛthak
brahma-sūtra-padaiś caiva / hetumadbhir viniścitaiḥ

5. The truth about Kshetra and Kshetrajna has been sung by Rishis in many ways, in various distinctive vedic chants, in the reasoning and convincing passages of the Brahma sutras.

महाभूतान्यहंकारो, बुद्धिरव्यक्तमेव च ।
इन्द्रियाणि दशैकं च, पञ्च चेन्द्रियगोचराः ॥६॥
इच्छा द्वेषः सुखं दुःखं, संघातश्चेतना धृतिः ।
एतत्क्षेत्रं समासेन, सविकारमुदाहृतम् ॥७॥

mahā-bhūtāny ahaṅkāro / buddhir avyaktam eva ca
indriyāṇi daśaikañ ca / pañca cendriya-gocarāḥ

icchā dveṣaḥ sukhaṁ duḥkhaṁ / sanghātaś cetanā dhṛtiḥ
etat kṣetraṁ samāsena / sa-vikāram udāhṛtam

6 & 7. The five great Elements, Egoism, Intellect, as also the unmanifested Moola Prakriti, the ten senses and the one mind and the five objects of the senses; desire, aversion, pleasure, pain, the physical body, sentience, fortitude–this is the kshetra with its evolutes briefly stated.

अमानित्वमदम्भित्वमहिंसा क्षान्तिरार्जवम् ।
आचार्योपासनं शौचं स्थैर्यमात्मविनिग्रहः ॥८॥

amānitvam adambhitvam ahiṁsā kṣāntir ārjavam
ācāryopāsanaṁ śaucaṁ sthairyam ātma-vinigrahaḥ

8. Absence of pride, freedom from hypocrisy, non-violence, forbearance, uprightness, service to the teacher, purity, steadfastness, self-control.

इन्द्रियार्थेषु वैराग्यमनहंकार एव च ।
जन्ममृत्युजराव्याधिदुःखदोषानुदर्शनम् ॥९॥

indriyārtheṣu vairāgyam / anahaṅkāra eva ca
janma-mṛtyu-jarā-vyādhi- / duḥkha-doṣānudarśanam

9. Dispassion towards sense objects and also absence of egoism; reflection on the pain and evils of birth, death, old age, sickness and disease.

असक्तिरनभिष्वङ्गः, पुत्रदारगृहादिषु ।
नित्यं च समचित्तत्वमिष्टानिष्टोपपत्तिषु ॥१०॥

asaktir anabhiṣvaṅgaḥ / putra-dāra-gṛhādiṣu
nityañ ca sama-cittatvam / iṣṭāniṣṭopapattiṣu

10. Absence of attachment and the feeling of mine-ness in respect of son, wife, home, and the rest, and constant equipose of mind in both the desirable and the undesirable circumstances.

मयि चानन्ययोगेन भक्तिरव्यभिचारिणी ।
विविक्तदेशसेवित्वमरतिर्जनसंसदि ॥११॥

mayi cānanya-yogena / bhaktir avyabhicāriṇī
vivikta-deśa-sevitvam / aratir jana-saṁsadi

11. Unflinching devotion to Me through exclusive attachment, living in holy and lonely places, distaste for the company of men.

अध्यात्मज्ञाननित्यत्वं तत्त्वज्ञानार्थदर्शनम् ।
एतज्ज्ञानमिति प्रोक्तमज्ञानं यदतोऽन्यथा ॥१२॥

adhyātma-jñāna-nityatvaṁ tattva-jñānārtha-darśanam
etaj jñānam iti proktam ajñānaṁ yad ato'nyathā

12. Fixity in self knowledge and seeing God as the object of true knowledge; this is declared to be knowledge and what is other than this, is ignorance.

ज्ञेयं यत्तत्प्रवक्ष्यामि, यज्ज्ञात्वाऽमृतमश्नुते ।
अनादिमत्परंब्रह्म, न सत्तन्नासदुच्यते ॥१३॥

jñeyaṁ yat tat pravakṣyāmi / yaj jñātvā 'mṛtam aśnute
anādimat paraṁ brahma / na sat tan nāsad ucyate

13. I shall speak to you at length about that which ought to be known, knowing which one attains to immortal bliss. The Supreme Brahman, the beginningless, is neither being nor non-being.

सर्वतःपाणिपादं तत्सर्वतोऽक्षिशिरोमुखम् ।
सर्वतःश्रुतिमल्लोके सर्वमावृत्य तिष्ठति ॥१४॥

sarvataḥ pāṇi-pādaṁ tat sarvato'kṣi-śiro-mukham
sarvataḥ śrutimal loke sarvam āvṛtya tiṣṭhati

14. It has hands and feet on all sides, with eyes, heads, and mouths in all directions, with ears everywhere–That stands pervading all in the universe.

सर्वेन्द्रियगुणाभासं, सर्वेन्द्रियविवर्जितम् ।
असक्तं सर्वभृच्चैव, निर्गुणं गुणभोक्तृ च ॥१५॥

sarvendriya-guṇābhāsaṁ / sarvendriya-vivarjitam
asaktaṁ sarva-bhṛc caiva / nirguṇaṁ guṇa-bhoktṛ ca

15. Though perceiving all sense objects, it is without the senses; Though attributeless, yet sustaining all; devoid of gunas, yet their enjoyer.

बहिरन्तश्च भूतानामचरं चरमेव च ।
सूक्ष्मत्वात्तदविज्ञेयं दूरस्थं चान्तिके च तत् ॥१६॥

bahir antaś ca bhūtānām acaraṁ caram eva ca
sūkṣmatvāt tad avijñeyaṁ dūra-sthaṁ cāntike ca tat

16. It exists without and within all beings and constitutes the unmoving and also the moving. Because of Its subtlety, it is incomprehensible; It is close at hand and stands afar too.

अविभक्तं च भूतेषु, विभक्तमिव च स्थितम् ।
भूतभर्तृ च तज्ज्ञेयं, ग्रसिष्णु प्रभविष्णु च ॥१७॥

avibhaktañ ca bhūteṣu / vibhaktam iva ca sthitam
bhūta-bharttṛ ca taj jñeyaṁ / grasiṣṇu prabhaviṣṇu ca

17. Indivisible, yet It exists as if divided in beings: It is to be known as sustaining beings; and devouring, as well as creating them.

ज्योतिषामपि तज्ज्योतिस्तमसः परमुच्यते ।
ज्ञानं ज्ञेयं ज्ञानगम्यं हृदि सर्वस्य विष्ठितम् ॥१८॥

jyotiṣām api taj jyotis tamasaḥ param ucyate
jñānaṁ jñeyaṁ jñāna-gamyaṁ hṛdi sarvasya vishiṣṭhitam

18. The Light itself of all lights, It is entirely beyond the illusionary Maya. This godhead is Knowledge and the One Thing worth knowing. The Goal of all knowledge it is, dwelling in the hearts of all.

इति क्षेत्रं तथा ज्ञानं, ज्ञेयं चोक्तं समासतः ।
मद्भक्त एतद्विज्ञाय, मद्भावायोपपद्यते ॥१९॥

iti kṣetraṁ tathā jñānaṁ / jñeyañ coktaṁ samāsataḥ
mad-bhakta etad vijñāya / mad-bhāvāyopapadyate

19. Thus the truth of the kshetra and knowledge and that which is worth knowing, have been briefly stated. Knowing this, My devotee enters into My being.

प्रकृतिं पुरुषं चैव, विद्ध्यनादी उभावपि ।
विकारांश्च गुणांश्चैव, विद्धि प्रकृतिसंभवान् ॥२०॥

prakṛtiṁ puruṣañ caiva / viddhyanādī ubhāv api
vikārāṁś ca guṇāṁś caiva / viddhi prakṛti-sambhavān

20. Know that both Prakriti and Purusha are beginningless; and know also that all modifications and gunas are born of Prakriti.

कार्यकरणकर्तृत्वे, हेतुः प्रकृतिरुच्यते ।
पुरुषः सुखदुःखानां, भोक्तृत्वे हेतुरुच्यते ॥२१॥

kārya-kāraṇa-karttṛtve / hetuḥ prakṛtir ucyate
puruṣaḥ sukha-duḥkhānāṁ / bhoktṛtve hetur ucyate

21. Prakriti is said to be the cause in the bringing forth of the body and the senses, while the individual self is said to be the experiencer of pleasure and pain.

पुरुषः प्रकृतिस्थो हि, भुङ्क्ते प्रकृतिजान्गुणान् ।
कारणं गुणसङ्गोऽस्य, सदसद्योनिजन्मसु ॥२२॥

puruṣaḥ prakṛti-stho hi / bhuṅkte prakṛti-jān guṇān
kāraṇaṁ guṇa-saṅgo'sya / sad-asad-yoni-janmasu

22. Purusha seated in Prakriti, senses objects of the nature of the gunas born of Prakriti; the reason of his birth in good and evil wombs is his contact with the gunas.

उपद्रष्टानुमन्ता च, भर्ता भोक्ता महेश्वरः ।
परमात्मेति चाप्युक्तो, देहेऽस्मिन्पुरुषः परः ॥२३॥

upadraṣṭānumantā ca / bharttā bhoktā maheśvaraḥ
paramātmeti cāpy ukto / dehe'smin puruṣaḥ paraḥ

23. And the Supreme Purusha in this body as the spirit is also called the Witness, the Guide, the Sustainer, the Experiencer, the Over Lord and the Absolute.

य एवं वेत्ति पुरुषं, प्रकृतिं च गुणैः सह ।
सर्वथा वर्तमानोऽपि, न स भूयोऽभिजायते ॥२४॥

ya evaṁ vetti puruṣaṁ / prakṛtiñ ca guṇaiḥ saha
sarvathā varttamāno'pi / na sa bhūyo'bhijāyate

24. He who thus knows the Purusha and Prakriti together with the gunas, though performing his duties in life, is not born again.

ध्यानेनात्मनि पश्यन्ति, केचिदात्मानमात्मना ।
अन्ये सांख्येन योगेन, कर्मयोगेन चापरे ॥२५॥

dhyānenātmani paśyanti / kecid ātmānam
ātmanā
anye sāṅkhyena yogena / karma-yogena cāpare

25. Some by meditation behold the Supreme spirit in the heart by their sharp intellect, others by the path of knowledge, others again by discipline of Action.

अन्ये त्वेवमजानन्तः, श्रुत्वान्येभ्य उपासते ।
तेऽपि चातितरन्त्येव, मृत्युं श्रुतिपरायणाः ॥२६॥

anye tv evam ajānantaḥ / śrutvānyebhya upāsate
te'pi cātitaranty eva / mṛtyuṁ śruti-parāyaṇāḥ

26. Others, not knowing thus, worship as they have heard from others. Even these go beyond death, devoted to what they have heard as the Supreme Refuge.

यावत्संजायते किंचित्सत्त्वं स्थावरजङ्गमम् ।
क्षेत्रक्षेत्रज्ञसंयोगात्तद्विद्धि भरतर्षभ ॥२७॥

yāvat saṁjāyate kiñcit / sattvaṁ sthāvara-jaṅgamam
kṣetra-kṣetrajña-saṁyogāt / tad viddhi bharatarṣabha

27. Arjuna, whatever being is born, animate or inanimate, know it to be from the union of kshetra and kshetrajna.

समं सर्वेषु भूतेषु, तिष्ठन्तं परमेश्वरम् ।
विनश्यत्स्वविनश्यन्तं, यः पश्यति स पश्यति ॥२८॥

samaṁ sarveṣu bhūteṣu / tiṣṭhantaṁ parameśvaram
vinaśyatsv avinaśyantaṁ / yaḥ paśyati sa paśyati

28. He alone truly sees, who sees the Supreme Lord, existing equally in all beings; sentient and insentient.

समं पश्यन्हि सर्वत्र, समवस्थितमीश्वरम् ।
न हिनस्त्यात्मनात्मानं, ततो याति परां गतिम् ॥२९॥

samaṁ paśyan hi sarvatra / samavasthitam īśvaram
na hinasty ātmanātmānaṁ / tato yāti parāṁ gatim

29. Seeing the Lord equally present everywhere, he injures not self by self, and so attains to the Supreme state.

प्रकृत्यैव च कर्माणि क्रियमाणानि सर्वशः ।
यः पश्यति तथात्मानमकर्तारं स पश्यति ॥३०॥

prakṛtyaiva ca karmāṇi kriyamāṇāni sarvaśaḥ
yaḥ paśyati tathātmānam akarttāraṁ sa paśyati

30. He alone sees, who sees that all actions are done by Prakriti alone and that the Self is the non-doer.

यदा भूतपृथग्भावमेकस्थमनुपश्यति ।
तत एव च विस्तारं ब्रह्म संपद्यते तदा ॥३१॥

yadā bhūta-pṛthag-bhāvam eka-stham anupaśyati
tata eva ca vistāraṁ brahma saṁpadyate tadā

31. When he perceives the separate existence of all beings rooted in the One and their spreading forth from That (One) alone, he then becomes Brahman.

अनादित्वान्निर्गुणत्वात्परमात्मायमव्ययः ।
शरीरस्थोऽपि कौन्तेय न करोति न लिप्यते ॥३२॥

anāditvān nirguṇatvāt paramātmāyam avyayaḥ
śarīra-stho'pi kaunteya na karoti na lipyate

32. Arjuna, being without beginning and devoid of gunas, this Supreme Self, immutable, though existing in the body neither acts nor is affected.

यथा सर्वगतं सौक्ष्म्यादाकाशं नोपलिप्यते ।
सर्वत्रावस्थितो देहे तथात्मा नोपलिप्यते ॥३३॥

yathā sarva-gataṁ saukṣmyād / ākāśaṁ nopalipyate
sarvatrāvasthito dehe / tathātmā nopalipyate

33. As the all-pervading Akasha (space), because of its subtlety, is not tainted, so the Self, existent everywhere, though dwelling in the body, is not tainted.

यथा प्रकाशयत्येकः, कृत्स्नं लोकमिमं रविः ।
क्षेत्रं क्षेत्री तथा कृत्स्नं, प्रकाशयति भारत ॥३४॥

yathā prakāśayaty ekaḥ / kṛtsnaṁ lokam imaṁ raviḥ
kṣetraṁ kṣetrī tathā kṛtsnaṁ / prakāśayati bhārata

34. As the one sun illumines all this world, so does He who abides in the kshetra, O Arjuna, illumines the whole kshetra.

क्षेत्रक्षेत्रज्ञयोरेवमन्तरं ज्ञानचक्षुषा ।
भूतप्रकृतिमोक्षं च ये विदुर्यान्ति ते परम् ॥३५॥

kṣetra-kṣetrajñayor evam antaraṁ jñāna-cakṣuṣā
bhūta-prakṛti-mokṣañ ca ye vidur yānti te param

35. They who thus, with the eye of knowledge, perceive the distinction between the kshetra and the kshetrajna and also the phenomenon of liberation of beings from the evolutes of Prakriti, they go to the Supreme.

ॐ तत् सत् । इति श्रीमद्भगवद्गीतासु उपनिषत्सु
ब्रह्मविद्यायां योगशास्त्रे श्रीकृष्णार्जुन संवादे
क्षेत्रक्षेत्रज्ञविभागयोगो नाम त्रयोदशोऽध्यायः ॥

Om Tat Sat. Iti Śrimad Bhagavat Gitasu Upanishatsu Brahmavidyayām yogaśastre Sri Krishnarjuna samvade Kṣetra Kṣetrañja Vibhāga yogonama thrayodashodhyayaḥ

Thus ends the thirteenth chapter named "Ksetra-Ksetrajna-Vibhaga-Yoga" (Creation and the Creator) of the Upanishad of the Bhagavad Gita, the scripture of yoga, dealing with the science of the Absolute in the form of the dialogue between Sri Krishna and Arjuna.

अथ चतुर्दशोऽध्यायः - गुणत्रयविभागयोगः

Chapter Fourteen: Guṇa-Traya-Vibhāga-Yoga

श्रीभगवानुवाच ।
परं भूयः प्रवक्ष्यामि, ज्ञानानां ज्ञानमुत्तमम् ।
यज्ज्ञात्वा मुनयः सर्वे, परां सिद्धिमितो गताः ॥१॥

śrī bhagavān uvāca
paraṁ bhūyaḥ pravakṣyāmi / jñānānāṁ jñānam uttamam
yaj jñātvā munayaḥ sarve / parāṁ siddhim ito gatāḥ

1. The Blessed Lord said: I shall discuss once more, the supreme wisdom which is above all knowledge and having acquired which all the sages have attained highest perfection after this life.

इदं ज्ञानमुपाश्रित्य, मम साधर्म्यमागताः ।
सर्गेऽपि नोपजायन्ते, प्रलये न व्यथन्ति च ॥२॥

idaṁ jñānam upāśritya / mama sādharmyam āgatāḥ
sarge'pi nopajāyante / pralaye na vyathanti ca

2. They who, having practised this wisdom, have entered into My being, are neither born again at the time of creation, nor are they disturbed at the time of dissolution.

मम योनिर्महद्ब्रह्म, तस्मिन्गर्भं दधाम्यहम् ।
संभवः सर्वभूतानां, ततो भवति भारत ॥३॥

mama yonir mahad brahma / tasmin garbhaṁ dadhāmy aham
sambhavaḥ sarva-bhūtānāṁ / tato bhavati bhārata

3. My womb is the Primordial Nature. In that I place the seed of all life; from thence, is the birth of all beings, O Arjuna.

सर्वयोनिषु कौन्तेय मूर्तयः संभवन्ति याः ।
तासां ब्रह्म महद्योनिरहं बीजप्रदः पिता ॥४॥

sarva-yoniṣu kaunteya mūrtayaḥ sambhavanti yāḥ
tāsāṁ brahma mahad yonir ahaṁ bīja-pradaḥ pitā

4. Whatever forms are created, O Arjuna, in all the wombs, the great Prakriti (Nature) is their womb and I the seed-giving Father.

सत्त्वं रजस्तम इति, गुणाः प्रकृतिसंभवाः ।
निबध्नन्ति महाबाहो, देहे देहिनमव्ययम् ॥५॥

sattvaṁ rajas tama iti / guṇāḥ prakṛti-sambhavāḥ
nibadhnanti mahā-bāho / dehe dehinam avyayam

5. Sattwa, rajas, and tamas – these gunas, O Arjuna, born of Prakriti, tie down the imperishable soul to the body.

तत्र सत्त्वं निर्मलत्वात्प्रकाशकमनामयम् ।
सुखसङ्गेन बध्नाति ज्ञानसङ्गेन चानघ ॥६॥

tatra sattvaṁ nirmalatvāt prakāśakam anāmayam
sukha-saṅgena badhnāti jñāna-saṅgena cānagha

6. Of these sattwa, being immaculate, luminous and free from flaws, binds, O Arjuna, by attachment to joy and wisdom.

रजो रागात्मकं विद्धि, तृष्णासङ्गसमुद्भवम् ।
तन्निबध्नाति कौन्तेय, कर्मसङ्गेन देहिनम् ॥७॥

rajo rāgātmakaṁ viddhi / tṛṣṇā-saṅga-samudbhavam
tan nibadhnāti kaunteya / karma-saṅgena dehinam

7. O son of Kunti, know rajas to be of the quality of passion, giving rise to cupidity and attachment; it binds the embodied soul, by attachment to action and its fruit.

तमस्त्वज्ञानजं विद्धि मोहनं सर्वदेहिनाम् ।
प्रमादालस्यनिद्राभिस्तन्निबध्नाति भारत ॥८॥

tamas tv ajñāna-jaṁ viddhi / mohanaṁ sarva-dehinām
pramādālasya-nidrābhis / tan nibadhnāti bhārata

8. And know tamas to be born of ignorance, stupefying all embodied beings; it binds fast, O Arjuna, through error, sloth and sleep.

सत्त्वं सुखे सञ्जयति, रजः कर्मणि भारत ।
ज्ञानमावृत्य तु तमः, प्रमादे सञ्जयत्युत ॥९॥

sattvaṁ sukhe sañjayati / rajaḥ karmaṇi bhārata
jñānam āvṛtya tu tamaḥ / pramāde sañjayaty uta

9. Sattwa propels one to happiness and rajas to action, O Arjuna; while tamas, verily, shrouding discrimination, incites one to error, sloth and sleep.

रजस्तमश्चाभिभूय, सत्त्वं भवति भारत ।
रजः सत्त्वं तमश्चैव, तमः सत्त्वं रजस्तथा ॥१०॥

rajas tamaś cābhibhūya / sattvaṁ bhavati bhārata
rajaḥ sattvaṁ tamaś caiva / tamaḥ sattvaṁ rajas tathā

10. Sattwa arises, O Arjuna, overpowering rajas and tamas; likewise rajas over sattwa and tamas; and tamas over sattwa and rajas.

सर्वद्वारेषु देहेऽस्मिन्प्रकाश उपजायते ।
ज्ञानं यदा तदा विद्याद्विवृद्धं सत्त्वमित्युत ॥११॥

sarva-dvāreṣu dehe'smin / prakāśa upajāyate
jñānaṁ yadā tadā vidyād / vivṛddhaṁ sattvam ity uta

11. When the light of intelligence and discrimination dawns in the body, senses and mind, then it should be known that sattwa is predominant.

लोभः प्रवृत्तिरारम्भः, कर्मणामशमः स्पृहा ।
रजस्येतानि जायन्ते, विवृद्धे भरतर्षभ ॥१२॥

lobhaḥ pravṛttir ārambhaḥ / karmaṇām aśamaḥ spṛhā
rajasy etāni jāyante / vivṛddhe bharatarṣabha

12. Greed, activity, the undertaking of selfish actions, restlessness, thirst for enjoyment – these arise when rajas is predominant, O Arjuna.

अप्रकाशोऽप्रवृत्तिश्च, प्रमादो मोह एव च ।
तमस्येतानि जायन्ते, विवृद्धे कुरुनन्दन ॥१३॥

aprakāśo'pravṛttiś ca / pramādo moha eva ca
tamasy etāni jāyante / vivṛddhe kuru-nandana

13. Dullness of the mind and senses, disinclination to perform one's obligatory duties, frivolity and stupor - these arise when tamas is predominant, O descendant of Kuru.

यदा सत्त्वे प्रवृद्धे तु प्रलयं याति देहभृत् ।
तदोत्तमविदां लोकानमलान्प्रतिपद्यते ॥१४॥

yadā sattve pravṛddhe tu pralayaṁ yāti deha-bhṛt
tadottama-vidāṁ lokān amalān pratipadyate

14. If one dies when sattwa is predominant, he attains to the spotless ethereal regions attained by men of noble deeds.

रजसि प्रलयं गत्वा कर्मसङ्गिषु जायते ।
तथा प्रलीनस्तमसि मूढयोनिषु जायते ॥१५॥

rajasi pralayaṁ gatvā karma-saṅgiṣu jāyate
tathā pralīnas tamasi mūḍha-yoniṣu jāyate

15. Meeting death in rajas, he is born among those attached to action; so dying in tamas, he is born in the species of stupid creatures.

कर्मणः सुकृतस्याहुः सात्त्विकं निर्मलं फलम् ।
रजसस्तु फलं दुःखमज्ञानं तमसः फलम् ॥१६॥

karmaṇaḥ sukṛtasyāhuḥ sāttvikaṁ nirmalaṁ phalam
rajasas tu phalaṁ duḥkham ajñānaṁ tamasaḥ phalam

16. The fruit of righteous action, they say, is Sattvika and joy, wisdom and dispassion; verily, the fruit of rajas is sorrow and ignorance is the fruit of tamas.

सत्त्वात्सञ्जायते ज्ञानं, रजसो लोभ एव च ।
प्रमादमोहौ तमसो, भवतोऽज्ञानमेव च ॥१७॥

sattvāt sañjāyate jñānaṁ rajaso lobha eva ca
pramāda-mohau tamaso bhavato'jñānam eva ca

17. From sattwa flows wisdom, and from rajas greed; error, delusion and ignorance arise from tamas.

ऊर्ध्वं गच्छन्ति सत्त्वस्थाः, मध्ये तिष्ठन्ति राजसाः ।
जघन्यगुणवृत्तिस्थाः, अधो गच्छन्ति तामसाः ॥१८॥

ūrddhvaṁ gacchanti sattva-sthā / madhye tiṣṭhanti rājasāḥ
jaghanya-guṇa-vṛtti-sthā / adho gacchanti tāmasāḥ

18. Those who abide in the quality of sattwa, go upwards; the rajasic dwell in the middle; and the tamasic, abiding in the temperament of the lowest guna, go downwards.

नान्यं गुणेभ्यः कर्तारं, यदा द्रष्टानुपश्यति ।
गुणेभ्यश्च परं वेत्ति, मद्भावं सोऽधिगच्छति ॥१९॥

nānyaṁ guṇebhyaḥ karttāraṁ / yadā draṣṭānupaśyati
guṇebhyaś ca paraṁ vetti / mad-bhāvaṁ so'dhigacchati

19. When the seer perceives no agent other than the gunas and knows that supreme spirit beyond the gunas, he enters into My being.

गुणानेतानतीत्य त्रीन्देही देहसमुद्भवान् ।
जन्ममृत्युजरादुःखैर्विमुक्तोऽमृतमश्नुते ॥२०॥

guṇān etān atītya trīn dehī deha-samudbhavān
janma-mṛtyu-jarā-duḥkhair vimukto'mṛtam aśnute

20. Having transcended the three gunas, out of which the body is evolved, this soul is freed from birth, death, decay and sorrow and attains to immortality.

अर्जुन उवाच ।
कैर्लिङ्गैस्त्रीन्गुणानेतानतीतो भवति प्रभो ।
किमाचारः कथं चैतांस्त्रीन्गुणानतिवर्तते ॥२१॥

arjuna uvāca
kair liṅgais trīn guṇān etān atīto bhavati prabho
kim ācāraḥ kathaṁ caitāṁs trīn guṇān ativarttate

21. Arjuna said: By what signs, O Lord, is he known who has gone beyond these three gunas? What is his conduct, and how does he go beyond the gunas?

श्रीभगवानुवाच ।
प्रकाशं च प्रवृत्तिं च, मोहमेव च पाण्डव ।
न द्वेष्टि संप्रवृत्तानि, न निवृत्तानि काङ्क्षति ॥२२॥

śrī bhagavān uvāca
prakāśañ ca pravṛttiñ ca / moham eva ca pāṇḍava
na dveṣṭi sampravṛttāni / na nivṛttāni kāṅkṣati

22. The Blessed Lord said: He who hates not the light (the effect of sattwa), activity (the effect of rajas), and delusion (the effect of tamas), when prevalent, O Pandava, nor longs for them when they have ceased.

उदासीनवदासीनो, गुणैर्यो न विचाल्यते ।
गुणा वर्तन्त इत्येव, योऽवतिष्ठति नेङ्गते ॥२३॥

udāsīna-vad āsīno / guṇair yo na vicālyate
guṇā vartanta ity evaṁ / yo'vatiṣṭhati neṅgate

23. He who, sitting like a witness, is moved not by the gunas, who knowing that the gunas operate among themselves, is Self-centered and swerves not.

समदुःखसुखः स्वस्थः समलोष्टाश्मकाञ्चनः ।
तुल्यप्रियाप्रियो धीरस्तुल्यनिन्दात्मसंस्तुतिः ॥२४॥

sama-duḥkha-sukhaḥ sva-sthaḥ sama-loṣṭāśma-kāñcanaḥ
tulya-priyāpriyo dhīras tulya-nindātma-saṁstutiḥ

24. Alike in pleasure and pain, Self-abiding, regarding a clod of earth, a stone and gold alike; the same to pleasant and unpleasant, firm, the same in censure and praise.

मानापमानयोस्तुल्यस्तुल्यो मित्रारिपक्षयोः ।
सर्वारम्भपरित्यागी गुणातीतः स उच्यते ॥२५॥

mānāpamānayos tulyas tulyo mitrāri-pakṣayoḥ
sarvārambha-parityāgī guṇātītaḥ sa ucyate

25. The same in honor and ignominy, the same to friend and foe, relinquishing the sense of doership in all undertakings – he is said to have gone beyond the gunas.

मां च योऽव्यभिचारेण भक्तियोगेन सेवते ।
स गुणान्समतीत्यैतान्ब्रह्मभूयाय कल्पते ॥२६॥

māñ ca yo'vyabhicāreṇa bhakti-yogena sevate
sa guṇān samatītyaitān brahma-bhūyāya kalpate

26. And he who worships Me with unswerving devotion, he, going beyond the gunas, is eligible for attaining Brahman.

ब्रह्मणो हि प्रतिष्ठाहममृतस्याव्ययस्य च ।
शाश्वतस्य च धर्मस्य सुखस्यैकान्तिकस्य च ॥२७॥

brahmaṇo hi pratiṣṭhāham amṛtasyāvyayasya ca
śāśvatasya ca dharmasya sukhasyaikāntikasya ca

27. For I am the ground of imperishable Brahman, the Immortal and Immutable, of everlasting dharma and of Absolute Bliss.

ॐ तत् सत् । इति श्रीमद्भगवद्गीतासु उपनिषत्सु ब्रह्मविद्यायां योगशास्त्रे श्रीकृष्णार्जुन संवादे गुणत्रयविभागयोगो नाम चतुर्दशोऽध्यायः ॥

Om Tat Sat. Iti Śrimad Bhagavat Gitasu Upanishatsu Brahmavidyayām yogaśastre Sri Krishnarjuna samvade Guṇa-Traya-Vibhāga-Yogonama chaturdashodhyayaḥ

Thus ends the fourteenth chapter named "Guna-Traya-Vibhaga-Yoga" (Three Qualities of Nature) of the Upanishad of the Bhagavad Gita, the scripture of yoga, dealing with the science of the Absolute in the form of the dialogue between Sri Krishna and Arjuna.

अथ पञ्चदशोऽध्यायः - पुरुषोत्तमयोगः

Chapter Fifteen: Puruṣottama-Yoga

श्रीभगवानुवाच ।
ऊर्ध्वमूलमधःशाखमश्वत्थं प्राहुरव्ययम् ।
छन्दांसि यस्य पर्णानि यस्तं वेद स वेदवित् ॥१॥

śrī bhagavān uvāca
ūrddhva-mūlam adhaḥ-śākham aśvatthaṁ prāhur avyayam
chandāṁsi yasya parṇāni yas taṁ veda sa veda-vit

1. The Blessed Lord said: They speak of an eternal Ashvattha (Pipal tree) rooted above and branching below whose leaves are the Vedas; he who knows it, is a knower of Veda.

अधश्चोर्ध्वं प्रसृतास्तस्य शाखाः गुणप्रवृद्धा विषयप्रवालाः।
अधश्च मूलान्यनुसंततानि कर्मानुबन्धीनि मनुष्यलोके ॥२॥

adhaś corddhvaṁ prasṛtās tasya śākhā guṇa-pravṛddhā viṣaya-pravālāḥ
adhaś ca mūlāny anusantatāni karmānubandhīni manuṣya-loke

2. Nourished by the gunas, below and above spread its branches; sense objects are its buds; and below in the world of man stretch forth the roots, propelling action.

न रूपमस्येह तथोपलभ्यते नान्तो न चादिर्न च संप्रतिष्ठा ।
अश्वत्थमेनं सुविरूढमूलमसङ्गशस्त्रेण दृढेन छित्त्वा ॥३॥
ततः पदं तत् परिमार्गितव्यं यस्मिन् गता न निवर्तन्ति भूयः ।
तमेव चाद्यं पुरुषं प्रपद्ये यतः प्रवृत्तिः प्रसृता पुराणी ॥४॥

na rūpam asyeha tathopalabhyate nānto na
cādir na ca saṁpratiṣṭhā
aśvattham enaṁ su-virūḍha-mūlam asaṅga-
śastreṇa dṛḍhena chittvā
tataḥ padaṁ tat parimārgitavyaṁ yasmin gatā
na nivarttanti bhūyaḥ
tam eva cādyaṁ puruṣaṁ prapadye yataḥ
pravṛttiḥ prasṛtā purāṇī

3 & 4. The form, origin, end and existence of this Tree is not perceived here. Having cut asunder this firm-rooted Ashvattha with the strong axe of non-attachment – then that Goal is to be sought for, going where the wise do not return again. And once there, seek refuge in that Primordial Being from whom streamed forth the eternal dynamism.

निर्मानमोहा जितसङ्गदोषाः अध्यात्मनित्या विनिवृत्तकामाः ।
द्वन्द्वैर्विमुक्ताः सुखदुःखसंज्ञैर्गच्छन्त्यमूढाः पदमव्ययं तत्
॥५॥

nirmāna-mohā jita-saṅga-doṣā
adhyātma-nityā vinivṛtta-kāmāḥ

dvandvair vimuktāḥ sukha-duḥkha-saṁjñair
gacchanty amūḍhāḥ padam avyayaṁ tat

5. Those wise men who are free from pride and delusion, having overcome the evil of attachment, ever dwelling in the self, with total desirelessness and liberated from the pairs of opposites like pleasure and pain, reach that highest Immortal state.

न तद्भासयते सूर्यो, न शशाङ्को न पावकः ।
यद्गत्वा न निवर्तन्ते, तद्धाम परमं मम ॥६॥

na tad bhāsayate sūryo / na śaśāṅko na pāvakaḥ
yad gatvā na nivarttante / tad dhāma paramaṁ mama

6. Neither the sun nor the moon, nor even fire can illumine that Supreme state, My abode, going where they never return.

ममैवांशो जीवलोके, जीवभूतः सनातनः ।
मनःषष्ठानीन्द्रियाणि, प्रकृतिस्थानि कर्षति ॥७॥

mamaivāṁśo jīva-loke / jīva-bhūtaḥ sanātanaḥ
manaḥ ṣaṣṭhānīndriyāṇi / prakṛti-sthāni karṣati

7. A portion of Myself, the external Jivatma, having become a living soul in the world, draws (to itself) the (five) senses and mind which rest in Prakriti.

शरीरं यदवाप्नोति यच्चाप्युत्क्रामतीश्वरः ।
गृहीत्वैतानि संयाति वायुर्गन्धानिवाशयात् ॥८॥

śarīraṁ yad avāpnoti yac cāpy utkrāmatīśvaraḥ
gṛhītvaitāni saṁyāti vāyur gandhān ivāśayāt

8. Just as the wind carries the scent of flowers, so the embodied self carries the six senses and their desires from whichever body it abandons to whichever body it migrates.

श्रोत्रं चक्षुः स्पर्शनं च, रसनं घ्राणमेव च ।
अधिष्ठाय मनश्चायं, विषयानुपसेवते ॥९॥

śrotrañ caksuḥ sparśanañ ca / rasanaṁ ghrāṇam eva ca
adhiṣṭhāya manaś cāyaṁ / viṣayān upasevate

9. While dwelling in the sense organs - the ear, the eye, the touch, the taste and the smell, as also the mind - the embodied Self experiences the sense objects.

उत्क्रामन्तं स्थितं वापि, भुञ्जानं वा गुणान्वितम् ।
विमूढा नानुपश्यन्ति, पश्यन्ति ज्ञानचक्षुषः ॥१०॥

utkrāmantaṁ sthitaṁ vāpi / bhuñjānaṁ vā guṇānvitam
vimūḍhā nānupaśyanti / paśyanti jñāna-cakṣuṣaḥ

10. The ignorant do not know the Self while transmigrating (from one body to another) or residing (in the same) or experiencing objects of the senses or when united with the gunas. But those who have the eye of wisdom realize It.

यतन्तो योगिनश्चैनं, पश्यन्त्यात्मन्यवस्थितम् ।
यतन्तोऽप्यकृतात्मानो, नैनं पश्यन्त्यचेतसः ॥११॥

yatanto yoginaś cainaṁ / paśyanty ātmany avasthitam
yatanto'py akṛtātmāno / nainaṁ paśyanty acetasaḥ

11. The Yogis striving (for perfection) behold Him dwelling in their heart ; but the impure and unwise, even though striving, see Him not.

यदादित्यगतं तेजो, जगद्भासयतेऽखिलम् ।
यच्चन्द्रमसि यच्चाग्नौ, तत्तेजो विद्धि मामकम् ॥१२॥

yad āditya-gataṁ tejo / jagad bhāsayate'khilam
yac candramasi yac cāgnau / tat tejo viddhi māmakam

12. The light in the sun which illumines the whole world, which shines in the moon and the fire – know that light to be Mine.

गामाविश्य च भूतानि, धारयाम्यहमोजसा ।
पुष्णामि चौषधीः सर्वाः, सोमो भूत्वा रसात्मकः ॥१३॥

gām āviśya ca bhūtāni / dhārayāmy aham ojasā
puṣṇāmi cauṣadhīḥ sarvāḥ / somo bhūtvā rasātmakaḥ

13. Permeating the earth with My energy, I support all beings, and I nourish all the herbs by becoming the nectarian moon.

अहं वैश्वानरो भूत्वा, प्राणिनां देहमाश्रितः ।
प्राणापानसमायुक्तः, पचाम्यन्नं चतुर्विधम् ॥१४॥

ahaṁ vaiśvānaro bhūtvā / prāṇināṁ deham āśritaḥ
prāṇāpāna-samāyuktaḥ / pacāmy annaṁ catur-vidham

14. Abiding in the body of all creatures as (the fire) Vaishvanara, I, united with prana and apana, digest the four kinds of food.

सर्वस्य चाहं हृदि संनिविष्टो मत्तः स्मृतिर्ज्ञानमपोहनं च ।
वेदैश्च सर्वैरहमेव वेद्यो वेदान्तकृद्वेदविदेव चाहम् ॥१५॥

sarvasya cāhaṁ hṛdi sanniviṣṭo mattaḥ smṛtir jñānam apohanañ ca
vedaiś ca sarvair aham eva vedyo vedānta-kṛd veda-vid eva cāham

15. I am seated in the hearts of all; memory and perception as well as their loss come from Me. I am verily that which is worth knowing by all the Vedas, I indeed am the source of the Vedanta and the Knower of the Veda am I.

द्वाविमौ पुरुषौ लोके, क्षरश्चाक्षर एव च ।
क्षरः सर्वाणि भूतानि, कूटस्थोऽक्षर उच्यते ॥१६॥

dvāv imau puruṣau loke / kṣaraś cākṣara eva ca
kṣaraḥ sarvāṇi bhūtāni / kūṭa-stho'kṣara ucyate

16. There are the Perishable and the Imperishable Purushas in the world. All beings are the Perishable and the embodied Self is called Imperishable.

उत्तमः पुरुषस्त्वन्यः, परमात्मेत्युदाहृतः ।
यो लोकत्रयमाविश्य, बिभर्त्यव्यय ईश्वरः ॥१७॥

uttamaḥ puruṣas tv anyaḥ / paramātmety udāhṛtaḥ
yo loka-trayam āviśya / bibharty avyaya īśvaraḥ

17. But there is yet another, the Supreme Person, called the Supreme Spirit, the immutable Lord, who pervading the three worlds, sustains them.

यस्मात्क्षरमतीतोऽहमक्षरादपि चोत्तमः ।
अतोऽस्मि लोके वेदे च प्रथितः पुरुषोत्तमः ॥१८॥

yasmāt kṣaram atīto'ham akṣarād api cottamaḥ
ato'smi loke vede ca prathitaḥ puruṣottamaḥ

18. I transcend the Perishable and even the Imperishable. Therefore am I celebrated as Purushottama, (the Highest Purusha)in the world and in the Veda.

यो मामेवमसंमूढो, जानाति पुरुषोत्तमम् ।
स सर्वविद्भजति मां, सर्वभावेन भारत ॥१६॥

yo mām evam asammūḍho / jānāti puruṣottamam
sa sarva-vid bhajati māṁ / sarva-bhāvena bhārata

19. Arjuna, he who, thus realizes Me, the Highest Spirit, he, knowing all, worships Me with all his being.

इति गुह्यतमं शास्त्रमिदमुक्तं मयानघ ।
एतद्बुद्ध्वाबुद्धिमान्स्यात्कृतकृत्यश्च भारत ॥२०॥

iti guhyatamaṁ śāstram idam uktaṁ mayānagha
etad buddhvā buddhimān syāt kṛta-kṛtyaś ca bhārata

20. Thus, has this most profound teaching been imparted by Me. Knowing this, one becomes wise and will have accomplished his life's mission, O descendant of Bharata.

ॐ तत् सत् । इति श्रीमद्भगवद्गीतासु उपनिषत्सु
ब्रह्मविद्यायां योगशास्त्रे श्रीकृष्णार्जुन संवादे
पुरुषोत्तमयोगो नाम पञ्चदशोऽध्यायः ॥

Om Tat Sat. Iti Śrimad Bhagavat Gitasu Upanishatsu Brahmavidyayām yogaśastre Sri Krishnarjuna samvade Puruṣottama-Yogonama panchadashodhyayaḥ

Thus ends the fifteenth chapter named "Purusottama-Yoga" (The Supreme Person) of the Upanishad of the Bhagavad Gita, the scripture of yoga, dealing with the science of the Absolute in the form of the dialogue between Sri Krishna and Arjuna.

अथ षोडशोऽध्यायः - दैवासुरसंपद्विभागयोगः

Chapter Sixteen: Daivāsura-Sampada-Vibhāga-Yoga

श्रीभगवानुवाच ।
अभयं सत्त्वसंशुद्धिर्ज्ञानयोगव्यवस्थितिः ।
दानं दमश्च यज्ञश्च स्वाध्यायस्तप आर्जवम् ॥१॥

śrī bhagavān uvāca
abhayaṁ sattva-saṁśuddhir jñāna-yoga-vyavasthitiḥ
dānaṁ damaś ca yajñaś ca svādhyāyas tapa ārjavam

1. The Blessed Lord said: Fearlessness, purity of mind, steadfastness in knowledge and yoga of meditation; charity, control of the senses, sacrifices, reading of the shastras, austerity, uprightness.

अहिंसा सत्यमक्रोधस्त्यागः शान्तिरपैशुनम् ।
दया भूतेष्वलोलुप्त्वं मार्दवं ह्रीरचापलम् ॥२॥

ahiṁsā satyam akrodhas tyāgaḥ śāntir apaiśunam
dayā bhūteṣv aloluptvaṁ mārdavaṁ hrīr acāpalam

2. Non-violence, truth, absence of anger, renunciation, tranquility, absence of calumny, compassion, uncovetousness, gentleness, modesty, absence of fickleness.

तेजः क्षमा धृतिः शौचमद्रोहो नातिमानिता ।
भवन्ति संपदं दैवीमभिजातस्य भारत ॥३॥

tejaḥ kṣamā dhṛtiḥ śaucam adroho nāti-mānitā
bhavanti sampadaṁ daivīm abhijātasya bhārata

3. Sublimity, forgiveness, fortitude, purity, absence of hatred, absence of pride; these belong to one born of a divine state, O descendant of Bharata.

दम्भो दर्पोऽभिमानश्च, क्रोधः पारुष्यमेव च ।
अज्ञानं चाभिजातस्य, पार्थ संपदमासुरीम् ॥४॥

dambho darpo'bhimānaś ca / krodhaḥ pāruṣyam eva ca
ajñānaṁ cābhijātasya / pārtha sampadam āsurīm

4. Ostentation, arrogance, self-conceit, anger as also harshness and ignorance, belong to one who is born, O Partha, of demonic qualities.

दैवी संपद्विमोक्षाय निबन्धायासुरी मता ।
मा शुचः संपदं दैवीमभिजातोऽसि पाण्डव ॥५॥

daivī sampad vimokṣāya nibandhāyāsurī matā
mā śucaḥ sampadaṁ daivīm abhijāto'si pāṇḍava

5. The divine qualities are conducive for liberation, the demonic for bondage; grieve not, O Pandava, you are born of divine qualities.

द्वौ भूतसर्गौ लोकेऽस्मिन् दैव आसुर एव च ।
दैवो विस्तरशः प्रोक्तः आसुरं पार्थ मे शृणु ॥६॥

dvau bhūta-sargau loke'smin daiva āsura eva ca
daivo vistaraśaḥ prokta āsuraṁ pārtha me śṛṇu

6. In this world, there are two types of beings, the divine and the demonic. The divine have been described at length; hear from Me, O Partha, of the demonic.

प्रवृत्तिं च निवृत्तिं च, जना न विदुरासुराः ।
न शौचं नापि चाचारो, न सत्यं तेषु विद्यते ॥७॥

pravṛttiñ ca nivṛttiñ ca / janā na vidur āsurāḥ
na śaucaṁ nāpi cācāro / na satyaṁ teṣu vidyate

7. The persons of demonic nature know not what to do and what to refrain from. They possess neither purity nor good conduct, nor truth.

असत्यमप्रतिष्ठं ते, जगदाहुरनीश्वरम् ।
अपरस्परसंभूतं, किमन्यत्कामहैतुकम् ॥८॥

asatyam apratiṣṭhaṁ te / jagad āhur anīśvaram
aparaspara-sambhūtaṁ / kim anyat kāma-haitukam

8. They say, "There is no Truth in this world, nor has it any moral foundation, nor a God. It has been brought about by mutual union, with lust for its cause; nothing else."

एतां दृष्टिमवष्टभ्य, नष्टात्मानोऽल्पबुद्धयः ।
प्रभवन्त्युग्रकर्माणः, क्षयाय जगतोऽहिताः ॥६॥

etāṁ dṛṣṭim avaṣṭabhya / naṣṭātmāno'lpa-buddhayaḥ
prabhavanty ugra-karmāṇaḥ / kṣayāya jagato'hitāḥ

9. Clinging to this false notion, these people of small intellect and fierce deeds, rise as the enemies of mankind for its destruction.

काममाश्रित्य दुष्पूरं दम्भमानमदान्विताः ।
मोहाद्गृहीत्वाऽसद्ग्राहान्प्रवर्तन्तेऽशुचिव्रताः ॥१०॥

kāmam āśritya duṣpūraṁ dambha-māna-madānvitāḥ
mohād gṛhītvā 'sad-grāhān pravarttante 'śuci-vratāḥ

10. Cherishing insatiable desires and holding evil ideas through delusion, they work with impure resolve, full of hypocrisy, pride, and arrogance.

चिन्तामपरिमेयां च, प्रलयान्तामुपाश्रिताः ।
कामोपभोगपरमाः, एतावदिति निश्चिताः ॥११॥

cintām aparimeyāñ ca / pralayāntām upāśritāḥ
kāmopabhoga-paramā / etāvad iti niścitāḥ

11. Beset with innumerable cares ending only with death, they remain wedded to gratification of sensuous pleasures as the highest joy.

आशापाशशतैर्बद्धाः कामक्रोधपरायणाः ।
ईहन्ते कामभोगार्थमन्यायेनार्थसञ्चयान् ॥१२॥

āśā-pāśa-śatair baddhāḥ kāma-krodha-parāyaṇāḥ
īhante kāma-bhogārtham anyāyenārtha-sañcayān

12. Held hostage to hundred ties of expectations, given over to lust and wrath, they strive to amass wealth by unjust means for sensuous pleasures.

इदमद्य मया लब्धमिमं प्राप्स्ये मनोरथम् ।
इदमस्तीदमपि मे भविष्यति पुनर्धनम् ॥१३॥

idam adya mayā labdham idaṁ prāpsye manoratham
idam astīdam api me bhaviṣyati punar dhanam

13. They say to themselves: "This much has been secured by me today; this desire I shall obtain; this is already mine and this wealth also shall be mine."

असौ मया हतः शत्रुर्हनिष्ये चापरानपि ।
ईश्वरोऽहमहं भोगी सिद्धोऽहं बलवान्सुखी ॥१४॥

asau mayā hataḥ śatrur haniṣye cāparān api
īśvaro'ham ahaṁ bhogī siddho'haṁ balavān sukhī

14. "That enemy has been killed by me and I shall slay others also. I am the Lord of all, I enjoy, I am successful, powerful, and happy.

आढ्योऽभिजनवानस्मि, कोऽन्योऽस्ति सदृशो मया ।
यक्ष्ये दास्यामि मोदिष्ये, इत्यज्ञानविमोहिताः ॥१५॥

āḍhyo'bhijanavān asmi / ko'nyo'sti sadṛśo mayā
yakṣye dāsyāmi modiṣya / ity ajñāna-vimohitāḥ

15. "I am wealthy and I have a large family. Who else is equal to me? I will sacrifice to gods, I will give in charity, I will enjoy." Thus are they deluded by ignorance.

अनेकचित्तविभ्रान्ताः, मोहजालसमावृताः ।
प्रसक्ताः कामभोगेषु, पतन्ति नरकेऽशुचौ ॥१६॥

aneka-citta-vibhrāntā / moha-jāla-samāvṛtāḥ
prasaktāḥ kāma-bhogeṣu / patanti narake'śucau

16. Bewildered as they are by many a fancy ideas, deluded and addicted to sense enjoyments, they fall down into the foulest hell.

आत्मसंभाविताः स्तब्धाः, धनमानमदान्विताः ।
यजन्ते नामयज्ञैस्ते, दम्भेनाविधिपूर्वकम् ॥१७॥

ātma-sambhāvitāḥ stabdhā / dhana-māna-madānvitāḥ
yajante nāma-yajñais te / dambhenāvidhi-pūrvakam

17. Intoxicated by wealth and fame, self-conceited, haughty, full of pride, they perform sacrifices just for putting up a show, disregarding injunctions.

अहंकारं बलं दर्पं, कामं क्रोधं च संश्रिताः ।
मामात्मपरदेहेषु, प्रद्विषन्तोऽभ्यसूयकाः ॥१८॥

ahaṅkāraṁ balaṁ darpaṁ / kāmaṁ krodhañ ca saṁśritāḥ
māṁ ātma-para-deheṣu / pradviṣanto'bhyasūyakāḥ

18. Given over to egoism, power, insolence, lust and arrogance, these evil people hate Me, (the self within), in their own bodies and those of others.

तानहं द्विषतः क्रूरान्संसारेषु नराधमान् ।
क्षिपाम्यजस्रमशुभानासुरीष्वेव योनिषु ॥१६॥

tān ahaṁ dviṣataḥ krūrān saṁsāreṣu narādhamān
kṣipāmy ajasram aśubhān āsurīśv eva yoniṣu

19. These malicious and sinful evil-doers, most degraded of men, I cast again and again into demonical wombs in this world.

आसुरीं योनिमापन्नाः, मूढा जन्मनिजन्मनि ।
मामप्राप्यैव कौन्तेय, ततो यान्त्यधमां गतिम् ॥२०॥

āsurīṁ yonim āpannā / mūḍhā janmani janmani
mām aprāpyaiva kaunteya / tato yānty adhamāṁ gatim

20. Failing to reach me Arjuna, these deluded souls are born again and again in demonic worlds, thus falling, into a still lower condition.

त्रिविधं नरकस्येदं, द्वारं नाशनमात्मनः ।
कामः क्रोधस्तथा लोभस्तस्मादेतत्त्रयं त्यजेत् ॥२१॥

tri-vidhaṁ narakasyedaṁ / dvāraṁ nāśanam ātmanaḥ
kāmaḥ krodhas tathā lobhas / tasmād etat trayaṁ tyajet

21. Lust, anger and greed are the triple gates of hell, ruining the self. Therefore one should avoid all these three.

एतैर्विमुक्तः कौन्तेय, तमोद्वारैस्त्रिभिर्नरः ।
आचरत्यात्मनः श्रेयस्ततो याति परां गतिम् ॥२२॥

etair vimuktaḥ kaunteya / tamo-dvārais tribhir naraḥ
ācaraty ātmanaḥ śreyas / tato yāti parāṁ gatim

22. The man who goes beyond these three gates of darkness, O son of Kunti, practices what is good for himself and thus attains to the Supreme Goal.

यः शास्त्रविधिमुत्सृज्य, वर्तते कामकारतः ।
न स सिद्धिमवाप्नोति, न सुखं न परां गतिम् ॥२३॥

yaḥ śāstra-vidhim utsṛjya / varttate kāma-kārataḥ
na sa siddhim avāpnoti / na sukhaṁ na parāṁ gatim

23. Having disregarded the injunctions of the shastra, if one acts under the impulse of desire, he attains neither perfection, nor happiness, nor the Supreme Goal.

तस्माच्छास्त्रं प्रमाणं ते, कार्याकार्यव्यवस्थितौ ।
ज्ञात्वा शास्त्रविधानोक्तं, कर्म कर्तुमिहार्हसि ॥२४॥

tasmāc chāstraṁ pramāṇaṁ te / kāryākārya-vyavasthitau
jñātvā śāstra-vidhānoktaṁ / karma karttum ihārhasi

24. Therefore, let the shastra alone be your authority in ascertaining what should be done and what should not be done. Having known what is said in the shastra, perform action as ordained in the scriptures.

ॐ तत् सत् । इति श्रीमद्भगवद्गीतासु उपनिषत्सु ब्रह्मविद्यायां योगशास्त्रे श्रीकृष्णार्जुन संवादे दैवासुरसंपद्विभागयोगो नाम षोडशोऽध्यायः ॥

Om Tat Sat. Iti Śrimad Bhagavat Gitasu Upanishatsu Brahmavidyayām yogaśastre Sri Krishnarjuna samvade Daivāsura Sampad-Vibhāga-Yogonama śodaśodhyayaḥ

Thus ends the sixteenth chapter named "Daivasura-Sampada-Vibhaga-Yoga" (Divine and Demonic Qualities) of the Upanishad of the Bhagavad Gita, the scripture of yoga, dealing with the science of the Absolute in the form of the dialogue between Sri Krishna and Arjuna.

अथ सप्तदशोऽध्यायः - श्रद्धात्रयविभागयोगः

Chapter Seventeen: Śraddhā-Traya-Vibhāga-Yoga

अर्जुन उवाच ।
ये शास्त्रविधिमुत्सृज्य, यजन्ते श्रद्धयान्विताः ।
तेषां निष्ठा तु का कृष्ण, सत्त्वमाहो रजस्तमः ॥१॥

arjuna uvāca
ye śāstra-vidhim utsṛjya / yajante śraddhayānvitāḥ
teṣāṁ niṣṭhā tu kā kṛṣṇa / sattvam āho rajas tamaḥ

1. Arjuna said: Those who are endowed with faith and those who, casting aside the injunctions of the shastra, perform sacrifice, what is their condition, O Krishna? (Is it) sattwa, rajas, or tamas?

श्रीभगवानुवाच ।
त्रिविधा भवति श्रद्धा, देहिनां सा स्वभावजा ।
सात्त्विकी राजसी चैव, तामसी चेति तां शृणु ॥२॥

śrī bhagavān uvāca
tri-vidhā bhavati śraddhā / dehināṁ sā svabhāva-jā
sāttvikī rājasī caiva / tāmasī ceti tāṁ śṛṇu

2. The Blessed Lord said: Threefold is the faith of the embodied, which is inherent in their nature – the satwic, rajasic, and the tamasic. Do you hear of it.

सत्त्वानुरूपा सर्वस्य, श्रद्धा भवति भारत ।
श्रद्धामयोऽयं पुरुषो, यो यच्छ्रद्धः स एव सः ॥३॥

sattvānurūpā sarvasya / śraddhā bhavati bhārata
śraddhā-mayo'yaṁ puruṣo / yo yac-chraddhaḥ sa eva saḥ

3. The faith of a man is according to his natural mental disposition, O descendant of Bharata. He verily is what his faith is.

यजन्ते सात्त्विका देवान्यक्षरक्षांसि राजसाः ।
प्रेतान् भूतगणांश्चान्ये यजन्ते तामसा जनाः ॥४॥

yajante sāttvikā devān yakṣa-rakṣāṁsi rājasāḥ
pretān bhūta-gaṇāṁś cānye yajante tāmasā janāḥ

4. Sattwic men worship the gods; rajasika, the demi gods and demons; and the tamasic men, the ghosts and the spirits.

अशास्त्रविहितं घोरं, तप्यन्ते ये तपो जनाः ।
दम्भाहंकारसंयुक्ताः, कामरागबलान्विताः ॥५॥

कर्षयन्तः शरीरस्थं, भूतग्राममचेतसः ।
मां चैवान्तःशरीरस्थं, तान्विद्ध्यासुरनिश्चयान् ॥६॥

aśāstra-vihitaṁ ghoraṁ / tapyante ye tapo janāḥ
dambhāhaṅkāra-saṁyuktāḥ / kāma-rāga-balānvitāḥ

karśayantaḥ śarīra-sthaṁ / bhūta-grāmam acetasaḥ
māñ caivāntaḥ śarīra-sthaṁ / tān viddhy āsura-niścayān

5 & 6. Those who practice severe penances not enjoined by the shastras, who are full of hypocrisy and egoism, endowed with pride of power and obsessed with desire and attachment, torture, senseless as they are, the body, and Me dwelling in the body within; know them to be of demonic disposition.

आहारस्त्वपि सर्वस्य, त्रिविधो भवति प्रियः ।
यज्ञस्तपस्तथा दानं, तेषां भेदमिमं शृणु ॥७॥

āhāras tv api sarvasya / tri-vidho bhavati priyaḥ
yajñas tapas tathā dānaṁ / teṣāṁ bhedam imaṁ śṛṇu

7. The food also which is agreeable to each of them is threefold, as also sacrifice, penance and charity. Hear their distinction as follows:

आयुःसत्त्वबलारोग्य सुखप्रीतिविवर्धनाः ।
रस्याः स्निग्धाः स्थिरा हृद्याः आहाराः सात्त्विकाप्रियाः ॥८॥

āyuḥ-sattva-balārogya sukha-prīti-vivarddhanāḥ
rasyāḥ snigdhāḥ sthirā-hṛdyā āhārāḥ sāttvika-priyāḥ

8. The Foods which promote vigour, longevity, intelligence, health, happiness and cheerfulness, which are sweet, bland, substantial and agreeable, are liked by the sattwic.

कट्वम्ललवणात्युष्ण तीक्ष्णरूक्षविदाहिनः ।
आहारा राजसस्येष्टाः, दुःखशोकामयप्रदाः ॥९॥

kaṭv-amla-lavaṇāty-uṣṇa- / tīkṣṇa-rukṣa-vidāhinaḥ
āhārā rājasasyeṣṭā / duḥkha-śokāmaya-pradāḥ

9. Foods that are bitter, acidic, salty, excessively hot, pungent, dry, and burning and are productive of suffering, grief and disease are liked by the rajasic.

यातयामं गतरसं, पूति पर्युषितं च यत्
उच्छिष्टमपि चामेध्यं, भोजनं तामसप्रियम् ॥१०॥

yātayāmaṁ gata-rasaṁ / pūti paryuṣitañ ca yat
ucchiṣṭam api cāmedhyaṁ / bhojanaṁ tāmasa-priyam

10. That which is stale, insipid, putrid, cooked overnight, refuse, and impure, is the food liked by the tamasic people.

अफलाकाङ्क्षिभिर्यज्ञो, विधिदृष्टो य इज्यते ।
यष्टव्यमेवेति मनः, समाधाय स सात्त्विकः ॥११॥

aphalākāṅkṣibhir yajño / vidhi-diṣṭo ya ijyate
yaṣṭavyam eveti manaḥ / samādhāya sa sāttvikaḥ

11. That sacrifice is sattwic which is offered by men desiring no fruit, as enjoined by scriptures, with their mind fixed on the sacrifice only, for its own sake.

अभिसन्धाय तु फलं, दम्भार्थमपि चैव यत् ।
इज्यते भरतश्रेष्ठ, तं यज्ञं विद्धि राजसम् ॥१२॥

abhisandhāya tu phalaṁ / dambhārtham api caiva yat
ijyate bharata-śreṣṭha / taṁ yajñaṁ viddhi rājasam

12. Arjuna, that which is performed, seeking for fruit and merely as a show, know it to be a rajasic sacrifice.

विधिहीनमसृष्टान्नं, मन्त्रहीनमदक्षिणम् ।
श्रद्धाविरहितं यज्ञं, तामसं परिचक्षते ॥१३॥

vidhi-hīnam asṛṣṭānnaṁ / mantra-hīnam adakṣiṇam
śraddhā-virahitaṁ yajñaṁ / tāmasaṁ paricakṣate

13. The sacrifice done with no respect to injunctions in which no food is offered, which is devoid of mantras, gifts and faith, is said to be tamasic.

देवद्विजगुरुप्राज्ञपूजनं शौचमार्जवम् ।
ब्रह्मचर्यमहिंसा च शारीरं तप उच्यते ॥१४॥

deva-dvija-guru-prājña-pūjanaṁ śaucam ārjavam
brahmacaryam ahiṁsā ca śārīraṁ tapa ucyate

14. Worship of the gods, the Brahmans, elders, gurus and wise men; purity, straightforwardness, continence and non-violence - this is called bodily penance.

अनुद्वेगकरं वाक्यं, सत्यं प्रियहितं च यत् ।
स्वाध्यायाभ्यसनं चैव, वाङ्मयं तप उच्यते ॥१५॥

anudvega-karaṁ vākyaṁ / satyaṁ priya-hitañ ca yat
svādhyāyābhyasanaṁ caiva / vāṅ-mayaṁ tapa ucyate

15. Speech which causes no annoyance to others and is truthful, as also agreeable and wholesome and the regular study of Vedas – these are said to form the austerity of speech.

मनःप्रसादः सौम्यत्वं मौनमात्मविनिग्रहः ।
भावसंशुद्धिरित्येतत्तपो मानसमुच्यते ॥१६॥

manaḥ-prasādaḥ saumyatvaṁ maunam ātma-vinigrahaḥ
bhāva-saṁśuddhir ity etat tapo mānasam ucyate

16. Cheerfulness of mind, kindliness, contemplation, self-control, honesty of motive – this is called the mental austerity.

श्रद्धया परया तप्तं, तपस्तत्त्रिविधं नरैः ।
अफलाकाङ्क्षिभिर्युक्तैः, सात्त्विकं परिचक्षते ॥१७॥

śraddhayā parayā taptaṁ / tapas tat tri-vidhaṁ naraiḥ
aphalākāṅkṣibhir yuktaiḥ / sāttvikaṁ paricakṣate

17. This threefold penance performed by steadfast men, with utmost faith, desiring no fruit, is said to be sattwic.

सत्कारमानपूजार्थं, तपो दम्भेन चैव यत् ।
क्रियते तदिह प्रोक्तं, राजसं चलमध्रुवम् ॥१८॥

satkāra-māna-pūjārthaṁ / tapo dambhena caiva yat
kriyate tad iha proktaṁ / rājasaṁ calam adhruvam

18. That penance which is performed with the object of gaining fame, honor, and worship, or by way of ostentaion, and yield only unstable and transitory fruits, are called rajasic.

मूढग्राहेणात्मनो यत्पीडया क्रियते तपः ।
परस्योत्सादनार्थं वा तत्तामसमुदाहृतम् ॥१६॥

mūḍha-grāheṇātmano yat pīḍayā kriyate tapaḥ
parasyotsādanārthaṁ vā tat tāmasam udāhṛtam

19. Austerity which is practised through perversity, with self-torture, or for the purpose of ruining others, is declared to be tamasic.

दातव्यमिति यद्दानं, दीयतेऽनुपकारिणे ।
देशे काले च पात्रे च, तद्दानं सात्त्विकं स्मृतम् ॥२०॥

dātavyam iti yad dānaṁ / dīyate'nupakāriṇe
deśe kāle ca pātre ca / tad dānaṁ sāttvikaṁ smṛtam

20. A gift given by a sense of duy to one who does no service in return, in a fit place and time and to a deserving person, that gift is said to be sattwic.

यत्तु प्रत्युपकारार्थं, फलमुद्दिश्य वा पुनः।
दीयते च परिक्लिष्टं, तद्दानं राजसं स्मृतम् ॥२१॥

yat tu pratyupakārārthaṁ / phalam uddiśya vā punaḥ
dīyate ca parikliṣṭaṁ / tad dānaṁ rājasaṁ smṛtam

21. And gift given reluctantly with an object of receiving in return, or looking for rewards, is held to be rajasic.

अदेशकाले यद्दानमपात्रेभ्यश्च दीयते ।
असत्कृतमवज्ञातं तत्तामसमुदाहृतम् ॥२२॥

adeśa-kāle yad dānam apātrebhyaś ca dīyate
asat-kṛtam avajñātaṁ tat tāmasam udāhṛtam

22. A gift given at the wrong place or time, to undeserving persons, without regard or with disdain, that is declared to be tamasic.

ॐ तत्सदिति निर्देशो, ब्रह्मणस्त्रिविधः स्मृतः ।
ब्राह्मणास्तेन वेदाश्च, यज्ञाश्च विहिताः पुरा ॥२३॥

oṁ tat sad iti nirdeśo / brahmaṇas tri-vidhaḥ smṛtaḥ
brāhmaṇās tena vedāś ca / yajñāś ca vihitāḥ purā

23. "Om, Tat, Sat": this has been declared as the three-fold designation of Brahman. By that were made the Brahmanas, the Vedas and the sacrifices at the cosmic dawn.

तस्माद् ओमित्युदाहृत्य, यज्ञदानतपःक्रियाः ।
प्रवर्तन्ते विधानोक्ताः, सततं ब्रह्मवादिनाम् ॥२४॥

tasmād oṁ ity udāhṛtya / yajña-dāna-tapaḥ-kriyāḥ
pravarttante vidhānoktāḥ / satataṁ brahma-vādinām

24. Therefore, the acts of sacrifice, gift and austerity, as enjoined in the scriptures, by the followers of the Vedas, always begin by uttering the divine name OM.

तदित्यनभिसंधाय, फलं यज्ञतपःक्रियाः ।
दानक्रियाश्च विविधाः, क्रियन्ते मोक्षकाङ्क्षिभिः ॥२५॥

tad ity anabhisandhāya / phalaṁ yajña-tapaḥ-kriyāḥ
dāna-kriyāś ca vividhāḥ / kriyante mokṣa-kāṅkṣibhiḥ

25. Uttering "Tat," without aiming for fruits, are the various acts of sacrifice, penance and charity performed by the seekers of liberation.

सद्भावे साधुभावे च, सदित्येतत्प्रयुज्यते ।
प्रशस्ते कर्मणि तथा, सच्छब्दः पार्थ युज्यते ॥२६॥

sad-bhāve sādhu-bhāve ca / sad ity etat prayujyate
praśaste karmaṇi tathā / sac-chabdaḥ pārtha yujyate

26. O Partha, the word "Sat" is used in the sense of truth and goodness; and so also, the word "Sat" is used in the sense of an auspicious act.

यज्ञे तपसि दाने च, स्थितिः सदिति चोच्यते ।
कर्म चैव तदर्थीयं, सदित्येवाभिधीयते ॥२७॥

yajñe tapasi dāne ca / sthitiḥ sad iti cocyate
karma caiva tad-arthīyaṁ / sad ity evābhidhīyate

27. Steadiness in sacrifice, penance and charity is also called "Sat": as also action for the sake of God, is called "Sat."

अश्रद्धया हुतं दत्तं, तपस्तप्तं कृतं च यत् ।
असदित्युच्यते पार्थ, न च तत्प्रेत्य नो इह ॥२८॥

aśraddhayā hutaṁ dattaṁ / tapas taptaṁ kṛtañ ca yat
asad ity ucyate pārtha / na ca tat pretya no iha

28. Whatever is offered in sacrifice and given in charity and whatever austerity is practiced without faith, it is called Asat, O Partha; it is naught and is of no avail here or hereafter.

ॐ तत् सत् । इति श्रीमद्भगवद्गीतासु उपनिषत्सु ब्रह्मविद्यायां योगशास्त्रे श्रीकृष्णार्जुन संवादे श्रद्धात्रयविभागयोगो नाम सप्तदशोऽध्यायः ॥

Om Tat Sat. Iti Śrimad Bhagavat Gitasu Upanishatsu Brahmavidyayām yogaśastre Sri Krishnarjuna samvade Śraddhā-Traya-Vibhāga-Yogonama sapthadaśodhyayaḥ

Thus ends the seventeenth chapter named "Sraddha-Traya-Vibhaga-Yoga" (Threefold Faith) of the Upanishad of the Bhagavad Gita, the scripture of yoga, dealing with the science of the Absolute in the form of the dialogue between Sri Krishna and Arjuna.

अथ अष्टादशोऽध्यायः - मोक्षसंन्यासयोगः

Chapter Eighteen: Mokṣa-Sannyāsa-Yoga

अर्जुन उवाच ।
संन्यासस्य महाबाहो, तत्त्वमिच्छामि वेदितुम् ।
त्यागस्य च हृषीकेश, पृथक्केशिनिषूदन ॥१॥

arjuna uvāca
sannyāsasya mahā-bāho / tattvam icchāmi veditum
tyāgasya ca hṛṣīkeśa / pṛthak keśi-niṣūdana

1. Arjuna said: I wish to know severally, O mighty-armed Sri Krishna, the truth of sannyasa, as also of tyaga.

श्रीभगवानुवाच ।
काम्यानां कर्मणां न्यासं, संन्यासं कवयो विदुः ।
सर्वकर्मफलत्यागं, प्राहुस्त्यागं विचक्षणाः ॥२॥

śrī bhagavān uvāca
kāmyānāṁ karmaṇāṁ nyāsaṁ / sannyāsaṁ kavayo viduḥ
sarva-karma-phala-tyāgaṁ / prāhus tyāgaṁ vicakṣaṇāḥ

2. The Blessed Lord said: The wise declare the renunciation of desire driven actions as sannyasa and the abandonment of the fruit of action as tyaga.

त्याज्यं दोषवदित्येके, कर्म प्राहुर्मनीषिणः ।
यज्ञदानतपःकर्म, न त्याज्यमिति चापरे ॥३॥

tyājyaṁ doṣa-vad ity eke / karma prāhur manīṣiṇaḥ
yajña-dāna-tapaḥ-karma / na tyājyam iti cāpare

3. Some wise men declare that all actions are touched by evil and should therefore be relinquished, whilst others (say) that the acts of sacrifice, charity and austerity should not be shunned.

निश्चयं शृणु मे तत्र, त्यागे भरतसत्तम ।
त्यागो हि पुरुषव्याघ्र, त्रिविधः संप्रकीर्तितः ॥४॥

niścayaṁ śṛṇu me tatra / tyāge bharata-sattama
tyāgo hi puruṣa-vyāghra / tri-vidhaḥ saṁprakīrttitaḥ

4. Arjuna, hear from Me the final truth about Tyaga. For Tyaga has been declared to be of three kinds.

यज्ञदानतपःकर्म, न त्याज्यं कार्यमेव तत् ।
यज्ञो दानं तपश्चैव, पावनानि मनीषिणाम् ॥५॥

yajña-dāna-tapaḥ-karma / na tyājyaṁ kāryam eva tat
yajño dānaṁ tapaś caiva / pāvanāni manīṣiṇām

5. The work of sacrifice, charity and austerity should not be given up, but it should indeed be performed; (for) they are purifying.

एतान्यपि तु कर्माणि, सङ्गं त्यक्त्वा फलानि च ।
कर्तव्यानीति मे पार्थ, निश्चितं मतमुत्तमम् ॥६॥

etāny api tu karmāṇi / saṅgaṁ tyaktvā phalāni ca
karttavyānīti me pārtha / niścitaṁ matam uttamam

6. O Partha, but even these acts, should be performed, without attachment to the fruits; this is My best and firm conviction.

नियतस्य तु संन्यासः कर्मणो नोपपद्यते ।
मोहात्तस्य परित्यागस्तामसः परिकीर्तितः ॥७॥

niyatasya tu sannyāsaḥ karmaṇo nopapadyate
mohāt tasya parityāgas tāmasaḥ parikīrttitaḥ

7. But the abandonment of obligatory action is not advised. Such renunciation due to delusion is declared to be tamasic.

दुःखमित्येव यत्कर्म, कायक्लेशभयात्त्यजेत् ।
स कृत्वा राजसं त्यागं, नैव त्यागफलं लभेत् ॥८॥

duḥkham ity eva yat karma / kāya-kleśa-bhayāt tyajet
sa kṛtvā rājasaṁ tyāgaṁ / naiva tyāga-phalaṁ labhet

8. For fear of bodily discomfort and pain, if one relinquishes action, thus doing a rajasic renunciation, he obtains not the fruit thereof.

कार्यमित्येव यत्कर्म, नियतं क्रियतेऽर्जुन ।
सङ्गं त्यक्त्वा फलं चैव, स त्यागः सात्त्विको मतः ॥९॥

kāryam ity eva yat karma / niyataṁ kriyate 'rjuna
saṅgaṁ tyaktvā phalañ caiva / sa tyāgaḥ sāttviko mataḥ

9. O Arjuna, when a prescribed duty is performed, only because it is ought to be done, without attachment to it and its fruit, such relinquishment is regarded as sattwic.

न द्वेष्ट्यकुशलं कर्म, कुशले नानुषज्जते ।
त्यागी सत्त्वसमाविष्टो, मेधावी छिन्नसंशयः ॥१०॥

na dveṣṭy akuśalaṁ karma / kuśale nānuṣajjate
tyāgī sattva-samāviṣṭo / medhāvī chinna-saṁśayaḥ

10. The relinquisher endowed with sattwa and a steadfast understanding and with his doubts dispelled, shirks not even a disagreeable work nor is he attached to an agreeable one.

न हि देहभृता शक्यं, त्यक्तुं कर्माण्यशेषतः ।
यस्तु कर्मफलत्यागी, स त्यागीत्यभिधीयते ॥११॥

na hi deha-bhṛtā śakyaṁ / tyaktuṁ karmāṇy aśeṣataḥ
yas tu karma-phala-tyāgī / sa tyāgīty abhidhīyate

11. Since actions cannot be entirely relinquished by an embodied being, he who relinquishes the fruits of actions is called a man of renunciation.

अनिष्टमिष्टं मिश्रं च, त्रिविधं कर्मणः फलम् ।
भवत्यत्यागिनां प्रेत्य, न तु संन्यासिनां क्वचित् ॥१२॥

aniṣṭam iṣṭaṁ miśrañ ca / tri-vidhaṁ karmaṇaḥ phalam
bhavaty atyāgināṁ pretya / na tu sannyāsināṁ kvacit

12. The threefold fruit of action – agreeable, disagreeable and mixed – accrues to non-relinquishers after death, but never to relinquishers.

पञ्चैतानि महाबाहो, कारणानि निबोध मे ।
सांख्ये कृतान्ते प्रोक्तानि, सिद्धये सर्वकर्मणाम् ॥१३॥

pañcaitāni mahā-bāho / kāraṇāni nibodha me
sāṅkhye kṛtānte proktāni / siddhaye sarva-karmaṇām

13. Learn from Me, O mighty-armed, these five causes for the accomplishment of all actions as declared by the wise which is the end and means of all actions.

अधिष्ठानं तथा कर्ता, करणं च पृथग्विधम् ।
विविधाश्च पृथक् चेष्टाः, दैवं चैवात्र पञ्चमम् ॥१४॥

adhiṣṭhānaṁ tathā karttā / karaṇañ ca pṛthag-vidham
vividhāś ca pṛthak ceṣṭā / daivañ caivātra pañcamam

14. The body, the agent, the various senses, the different functions of a manifold kind, and the presiding divinity - are the five factors for the success of an action.

शरीरवाङ्मनोभिर्यत्कर्म प्रारभते नरः ।
न्याय्यं वा विपरीतं वा पञ्चैते तस्य हेतवः ॥१५॥

śarīra-vāṅ-manobhir yat karma prārabhate naraḥ
nyāyyaṁ vā viparītaṁ vā pañcaite tasya hetavaḥ

15. These five are its causes - whatever action a man performs by his body, speech and mind and whether it is right or wrong.

तत्रैवं सति कर्तारमात्मानं केवलं तु यः ।
पश्यत्यकृतबुद्धित्वान्न स पश्यति दुर्मतिः ॥१६॥

tatraivaṁ sati karttāram ātmānaṁ kevalan tu yaḥ
paśyaty akṛta-buddhitvān na sa paśyati durmatiḥ

16. Notwithstanding this, he who through an impure mind, looks upon his self, the Absolute, as the agent – he is of perverse understanding and his mind does not see aright.

यस्य नाहंकृतो भावो बुद्धिर्यस्य न लिप्यते ।
हत्वापि स इमाँल्लोकान्न हन्ति न निबध्यते ॥१७॥

yasya nāhaṅkṛto bhāvo buddhir yasya na lipyate
hatvāpi sa imāl̐ lokān na hanti na nibadhyate

17. He who is free from the notion of doership, whose intelligence is not affected (by good or evil), though he kills these people, he kills not, nor is bound by sin.

ज्ञानं ज्ञेयं परिज्ञाता, त्रिविधा कर्मचोदना ।
करणं कर्म कर्तेति, त्रिविधः कर्मसंग्रहः ॥१८॥

jñānaṁ jñeyaṁ parijñātā / tri-vidhā karma-codanā
karaṇaṁ karma kartteti / tri-vidhaḥ karma-saṅgrahaḥ

18. Knowledge, the known and the knower - these three motivate action. Even so, doer, the organs and activity are the threefold basis of action.

ज्ञानं कर्म च कर्ता च, त्रिधैव गुणभेदतः ।
प्रोच्यते गुणसंख्याने, यथावच्छृणु तान्यपि ॥१९॥

jñānaṁ karma ca karttā ca / tridhaiva guṇa-bhedataḥ
procyate guṇa-saṅkhyāne / yathāvac chṛṇu tāny api

19. In the Sankhya philosophy, knowledge, action and agent are declared to be of three kinds only, according to the distinction of gunas: hear them also duly.

सर्वभूतेषु येनैकं, भावमव्ययमीक्षते ।
अविभक्तं विभक्तेषु, तज्ज्ञानं विद्धि सात्त्विकम् ॥२०॥

sarva-bhūteṣu yenaikaṁ / bhāvam avyayam īkṣate
avibhaktaṁ vibhakteṣu / taj jñānaṁ viddhi sāttvikam

20. That by which the one imperishable existence is perceived, undivided and equally present, in all beings, know that knowledge to be sattwic.

पृथक्त्वेन तु यज्ज्ञानं, नानाभावान्पृथग्विधान् ।
वेत्ति सर्वेषु भूतेषु, तज्ज्ञानं विद्धि राजसम् ॥२१॥

pṛthaktvena tu yaj jñānaṁ / nānā-bhāvān pṛthag-vidhān
vetti sarveṣu bhūteṣu / taj jñānaṁ viddhi rājasam

21. But that knowledge which sees in all beings various entities of distinct kinds as different from one another, know that knowledge as rajasic.

यत्तु कृत्स्नवदेकस्मिन्कार्ये सक्तमहैतुकम् ।
अतत्त्वार्थवदल्पं च तत्तामसमुदाहृतम् ॥२२॥

yat tu kṛtsna-vad ekasmin kārye saktam ahaitukam
atattvārtha-vad alpañca tat tāmasam udāhṛtam

22. Whilst that which is confined to one single body as if it were the whole, without reason, without foundation in truth, and trivial – that is declared to be tamasic.

नियतं सङ्गरहितमरागद्वेषतः कृतम् ।
अफलप्रेप्सुना कर्म यत्तत्सात्त्विकमुच्यते ॥२३॥

niyataṁ saṅga rahitam arāga-dveṣataḥ kṛtam
aphala-prepsunā karma yat tat sāttvikam ucyate

23. An ordained action done without love or hatred by one not desirous of the fruit and free from attachment, is declared to be sattwic.

यत्तु कामेप्सुना कर्म, साहंकारेण वा पुनः ।
क्रियते बहुलायासं, तद्राजसमुदाहृतम् ॥२४॥

yat tu kāmepsunā karma / sāhaṅkāreṇa vā punaḥ
kriyate bahulāyāsaṁ / tad rājasam udāhṛtam

24. But the action which is done desiring enjoyment, or with self-conceit and with much strain, is declared to be rajasic.

अनुबन्धं क्षयं हिंसामनवेक्ष्य च पौरुषम् ।
मोहादारभ्यते कर्म यत्तत्तामसमुच्यते ॥२५॥

anubandhaṁ kṣayaṁ hiṁsām anapekṣya ca pauruṣam
mohād ārabhyate karma yat tat tāmasam ucyate

25. That action is declared to be tamasic which is undertaken through sheer arrogance, without considering the consequence, loss of power and wealth and injury to others and oneself.

मुक्तसङ्गोऽनहंवादी, धृत्युत्साहसमन्वितः ।
सिद्ध्यसिद्ध्योर्निर्विकारः, कर्ता सात्त्विक उच्यते ॥२६॥

mukta-saṅgo 'nahaṁ-vādī / dhṛty-utsāha-samanvitaḥ
siddhy-asiddhyor nirvikāraḥ / karttā sāttvika ucyate

26. One who is free from attachment, non-egotic, endowed with firmness and vigour and unaffected by success or failure, is called sattwic.

रागी कर्मफलप्रेप्सुर्लुब्धो हिंसात्मकोऽशुचिः ।
हर्षशोकान्वितः कर्ता राजसः परिकीर्तितः ॥२७॥

rāgī karma-phala-prepsur lubdho hiṁsātmako 'śuciḥ
harṣa-śokānvitaḥ karttā rājasaḥ parikīrttitaḥ

27. He who is full of passion, attached to the fruits of action, oppressive, malignant, impure, easily elated or dejected, is called rajasic.

अयुक्तः प्राकृतः स्तब्धः, शठोऽनैष्कृतिकोऽलसः ।
विषादी दीर्घसूत्री च, कर्ता तामस उच्यते ॥२८॥

ayuktaḥ prākṛtaḥ stabdhaḥ / śaṭho naiṣkṛtiko 'lasaḥ
viṣādī dīrgha-sūtrī ca / karttā tāmasa ucyate

28. Uncultured, vulgar, arrogant, deceitful, malicious, indolent, slothful, and procrastinating, such an agent is called tamasic.

बुद्धेर्भेदं धृतेश्चैव, गुणतस्त्रिविधं शृणु ।
प्रोच्यमानमशेषेण, पृथक्त्वेन धनंजय ॥२९॥

buddher bhedaṁ dhṛteś caiva / guṇatas tri-vidhaṁ śṛṇu
procyamānam aśeṣeṇa / pṛthaktvena dhanañjaya

29. Hear now Arjuna, the three fold distinction of intellect and fortitude, based on the gunas (qualities) as I declare them exhaustively and severally.

प्रवृत्तिं च निवृत्तिं च, कार्याकार्ये भयाभये ।
बन्धंमोक्षं च या वेत्ति, बुद्धिः सा पार्थ सात्त्विकी ॥३०॥

pravṛttiñ ca nivṛttiñ ca / kāryākārye bhayābhaye
bandhaṁ mokṣañ ca yā vetti / buddhiḥ sā pārtha sāttvikī

30. The intellect which correctly determines the paths of work and renunciation, right and wrong action, fear and fearlessness, bondage and liberation, that intellect, O Partha, is sattwic.

यया धर्ममधर्मं च, कार्यं चाकार्यमेव च ।
अयथावत्प्रजानाति, बुद्धिः सा पार्थ राजसी ॥३१॥

yayā dharmam adharmañ ca / kāryañ cākāryam eva ca
ayathāvat prajānāti / buddhiḥ sā pārtha rājasī

31. That intellect which has a distorted apprehension of Dharma and Adharma and also of right and wrong action, that intellect, O Partha, is rajasic.

अधर्मं धर्ममिति या, मन्यते तमसावृता ।
सर्वार्थान्विपरीतांश्च, बुद्धिः सा पार्थ तामसी ॥३२॥

adharmaṁ dharmam iti yā / manyate tamasāvṛtā
sarvārthān viparītāṁś ca / buddhiḥ sā pārtha tāmasī

32. O Arjuna, that intellect which, wrapped in ignorance, regards Adharma as Dharma and views all things in a perverted light, is tamasic.

धृत्या यया धारयते, मनःप्राणेन्द्रियक्रियाः ।
योगेनाव्यभिचारिण्या, धृतिः सा पार्थ सात्त्विकी ॥३३॥

dhṛtyā yayā dhārayate / manaḥ-prāṇendriya-kriyāḥ
yogenāvyabhicāriṇyā / dhṛtiḥ sā pārtha sāttvikī

33. Sattwic, Arjuna is the fortitude by which the functions of the mind, the prana and the senses are controlled, unswervingly through yoga.

यया तु धर्मकामार्थान्धृत्या धारयतेऽर्जुन ।
प्रसङ्गेन फलाकाङ्क्षी धृतिः सा पार्थ राजसी ॥३४॥

yayā tu dharma-kāmārthān dhṛtyā dhārayate 'rjuna
prasaṅgena phalākāṅkṣī dhṛtiḥ sā pārtha rājasī

34. Rajasic, Arjuna, is the fortitude by which one regulates (one's mind) to dharma, desire and wealth, seeking the fruit of each from attachment.

यया स्वप्नं भयं शोकं, विषादं मदमेव च ।
न विमुञ्चति दुर्मेधा, धृतिः सा पार्थ तामसी ॥३५॥

yayā svapnaṁ bhayaṁ śokaṁ / viṣādaṁ madam eva ca
na vimuñcati durmedhā / dhṛtiḥ sā tāmasī matā

35. Tamasic, Arjuna, is that fortitude by which a stupid man clings to sleep, fear, grief, despondency and also vanity.

सुखं त्विदानीं त्रिविधं, शृणु मे भरतर्षभ ।
अभ्यासाद्रमते यत्र, दुःखान्तं च निगच्छति ॥३६॥

sukhaṁ tv idānīṁ tri-vidhaṁ / śṛṇu me bharatarṣabha
abhyāsād ramate yatra / duḥkhāntañ ca nigacchati

36. And now hear from Me, O bull of the Bharatas, of the threefold happiness that one learns to practice by habit and by which one comes to the end of suffering.

यत्तदग्रे विषमिव परिणामेऽमृतोपमम् ।
तत्सुखं सात्त्विकं प्रोक्तमात्मबुद्धिप्रसादजम् ॥३७॥

yat tad agre viṣam iva pariṇāme 'mṛtopamam
tat sukhaṁ sāttvikaṁ proktam ātma-buddhi-prasāda-jam

37. That which is like poison at first, but is like nectar at the end; that happiness is declared to be sattwic, born of the subtlety of intellect due to meditation on God.

विषयेन्द्रियसंयोगाद्यत्तदग्रेऽमृतोपमम् ।
परिणामे विषमिव तत्सुखं राजसं स्मृतम् ॥३८॥

viṣayendriya-saṁyogād yat tad agre 'mṛtopamam
pariṇāme viṣam iva tat sukhaṁ rājasaṁ smṛtam

38. That joy that arises from the contact of object with sense, at first like nectar, but at the end like poison, that happiness is spoken of as rajasic.

यदग्रे चानुबन्धे च, सुखं मोहनमात्मनः ।
निद्रालस्यप्रमादोत्थं, तत्तामसमुदाहृतम् ॥३९॥

yad agre cānubandhe ca / sukhaṁ mohanam ātmanaḥ
nidrālasya-pramādotthaṁ / tat tāmasam udāhṛtam

39. That happiness which begins with and results in self-delusion derived from sleep, indolence, and miscomprehension, that is declared to be tamasic.

न तदस्ति पृथिव्यां वा, दिवि देवेषु वा पुनः ।
सत्त्वं प्रकृतिजैर्मुक्तं, यदेभिः स्यात्त्रिभिर्गुणैः ॥४०॥

na tad asti pṛthivyāṁ vā / divi deveṣu vā punaḥ
sattvaṁ prakṛti-jair muktaṁ / yad ebhiḥ syāt tribhir guṇaiḥ

40. There is no being on earth, or in heaven among the devas, who is free from these three gunas, born of Prakriti.

ब्राह्मणक्षत्रियविशां, शूद्राणां च परंतप ।
कर्माणि प्रविभक्तानि, स्वभावप्रभवैर्गुणैः ॥४१॥

brāhmaṇa-kṣatriya-viśāṁ / śūdrāṇāñ ca parantapa
karmāṇi pravibhaktāni / svabhāva-prabhavair guṇaiḥ

41. The duties of brahmanas, kshatriyas, vaishyas and shudras, O Arjuna, are divided according to their inborn qualities (Gunas).

शमो दमस्तपः शौचं, क्षान्तिरार्जवमेव च ।
ज्ञानं विज्ञानमास्तिक्यं, ब्रह्मकर्म स्वभावजम् ॥४२॥

śamo damas tapaḥ śaucaṁ / kṣāntir ārjavam eva ca
jñānaṁ vijñānam āstikyaṁ / brahma-karma svabhāva-jam

42. Subduing of the mind and the senses, austerity, purity, forbearance, and also uprightness, study of scriptures, realization of truth, faith in a hereafter life –these are the natural duties of the brahmanas.

शौर्यं तेजो धृतिर्दाक्ष्यं, युद्धे चाप्यपलायनम् ।
दानमीश्वरभावश्च, क्षात्रं कर्म स्वभावजम् ॥४३॥

śauryaṁ tejo dhṛtir dākṣyaṁ / yuddhe cāpy apalāyanam
dānam īśvara-bhāvaś ca / kṣatraṁ karma-svabhāva-jam

43. Prowess, valour, fortitude, dexterity, and also not running away from battle, generosity and sovereignty are the natural duties of the kshatriyas.

कृषिगौरक्ष्यवाणिज्यं, वैश्यकर्म स्वभावजम् ।
परिचर्यात्मकं कर्म, शूद्रस्यापि स्वभावजम् ॥४४॥

kṛṣi-go-rakṣya-vāṇijyaṁ / vaiśya-karma svabhāva-jam
paricaryātmakaṁ karma / śūdrasyāpi svabhāva-jam

44. Agriculture, cattle-rearing, and trade are the duties of the Vaishyas, born of (their own) nature; and action consisting of service is the duty of the shudras, born of (their own) nature.

स्वे स्वे कर्मण्यभिरतः, संसिद्धिं लभते नरः ।

स्वकर्मनिरतः सिद्धिं, यथा विन्दति तच्छृणु ॥४५॥

sve sve karmaṇy abhirataḥ / saṁsiddhiṁ labhate naraḥ
sva-karma nirataḥ siddhiṁ / yathā vindati tac chṛṇu

45. Keenly devoted to their own natural duty, man attains the highest perfection in the shape of God realisation. Now hear how a person, engaged in his own prescribed duty, can attain perfection.

यतः प्रवृत्तिर्भूतानां, येन सर्वमिदं ततम् ।
स्वकर्मणा तमभ्यर्च्य, सिद्धिं विन्दति मानवः ॥४६॥

yataḥ pravṛttir bhūtānāṁ / yena sarvam idaṁ tatam
sva-karmaṇā tam abhyarcya / siddhiṁ vindati mānavaḥ

46. Worshipping Him, from whom evolve all beings and by whom all this is pervaded, with his own duty, a man attains perfection.

श्रेयान्स्वधर्मो विगुणः, परधर्मात्स्वनुष्ठितात् ।
स्वभावनियतं कर्म, कुर्वन्नाप्नोति किल्बिषम् ॥४७॥

śreyān sva-dharmo viguṇaḥ / para-dharmāt sv-anuṣṭhitāt
svabhāva-niyataṁ karma / kurvan nāpnoti kilbiṣam

47. Better is one's own duty, (though) devoid of merit than the dharma of another well-performed. He who does the duty ordained by his own nature incurs no sin.

सहजं कर्म कौन्तेय, सदोषमपि न त्यजेत् ।
सर्वारम्भा हि दोषेण, धूमेनाग्निरिवावृताः ॥४८॥

saha-jaṁ karma kaunteya / sa-doṣam api na tyajet
sarvārambhā hi doṣeṇa / dhūmenāgnir ivāvṛtāḥ

48. One should not relinquish, O Arjuna, the duty to which one is born, though it may be tainted with blemish; for, all undertakings are clouded by demerit, as fire by smoke.

असक्तबुद्धिः सर्वत्र, जितात्मा विगतस्पृहः ।
नैष्कर्म्यसिद्धिं परमां, संन्यासेनाधिगच्छति ॥४९॥

asakta-buddhiḥ sarvatra / jitātmā vigata-spṛhaḥ
naiṣkarmya-siddhiṁ paramāṁ / sannyāsenādhigacchati

49. He whose intellect is unattached everywhere, who has subdued his mind for enjoyment altogether of desires, he attains by renunciation to the supreme perfection, consisting of freedom from action.

सिद्धिं प्राप्तो यथा ब्रह्म, तथाप्नोति निबोध मे ।
समासेनैव कौन्तेय, निष्ठा ज्ञानस्य या परा ॥५०॥

siddhiṁ prāpto yathā brahma / tathāpnoti nibodha me
samāsenaiva kaunteya / niṣṭhā jñānasya yā parā

50. O son of Kunti, know from Me in brief, how such a man of perfection, attains to Brahman, that supreme consummation of knowledge and actionlessness.

बुद्ध्या विशुद्धया युक्तो, धृत्यात्मानं नियम्य च ।
शब्दादीन्विषयांस्त्यक्त्वा, रागद्वेषौ व्युदस्य च ॥५१॥

buddhyā viśuddhayā yukto / dhṛtyātmānaṁ niyamya ca
śabdādīn viṣayāṁs tyaktvā / rāga-dveṣau vyudasya ca

51. Endowed with a pure intellect; subduing the body and the senses with fortitude; discarding sound and such other sense-objects; abandoning attraction and hatred;

विविक्तसेवी लघ्वाशी, यतवाक्कायमानसः ।
ध्यानयोगपरो नित्यं, वैराग्यं समुपाश्रितः ॥५२॥

vivikta-sevī laghv-āśī / yata-vāk-kāya-mānasaḥ
dhyāna-yoga-paro nityaṁ / vairāgyaṁ samupāśritaḥ

52. Retiring to a lonely spot; eating but little; body, speech, and mind controlled; ever engaged in meditation and concentration; possessed of dispassion.

अहंकारं बलं दर्पं, कामं क्रोधं परिग्रहम् ।
विमुच्य निर्ममः शान्तो, ब्रह्मभूयाय कल्पते ॥५३॥

ahaṅkāraṁ balaṁ darpaṁ / kāmaṁ krodhaṁ parigraham
vimucya nirmamaḥ śānto / brahma-bhūyāya kalpate

53. Forsaking egoism, power, pride, lust, anger and luxuries; freed from the notion of "mine" and tranquil–he is fit for oneness with Brahman.

ब्रह्मभूतः प्रसन्नात्मा, न शोचति न काङ्क्षति ।
समः सर्वेषु भूतेषु, मद्भक्तिं लभते पराम् ॥५४॥

brahma-bhūtaḥ prasannātmā / na śocati na kāṅkṣati
samaḥ sarveṣu bhūteṣu / mad-bhaktiṁ labhate parām

54. Established in identity with Brahman - tranquil-minded, he neither grieves nor desires; the same to all beings, he attains to supreme devotion unto Me.

भक्त्या मामभिजानाति, यावान्यश्चास्मि तत्त्वतः।
ततो माम् तत्त्वतो ज्ञात्वा, विशते तदनन्तरम् ॥५५॥

bhaktyā mām abhijānāti / yāvān yaś cāsmi tattvataḥ
tato māṁ tattvato jñātvā / viśate tad-anantaram

55. By that supreme devotion he knows me in reality, what and who I am; then having known Me, he forthwith enters into My Being.

सर्वकर्माण्यपि सदा, कुर्वाणो मद्व्यपाश्रयः ।
मत्प्रसादादवाप्नोति, शाश्वतं पदमव्ययम् ॥५६॥

sarva-karmāṇy api sadā / kurvāṇo mad-vyapāśrayaḥ
mat-prasādād avāpnoti / śāśvataṁ padam avyayam

56. Even though performing all actions, the Karma Yogi taking refuge in Me, by My grace, he attains to the eternal, Imperishable State.

चेतसा सर्वकर्माणि, मयि संन्यस्य मत्परः ।
बुद्धियोगमुपाश्रित्य, मच्चित्तः सततं भव ॥५७॥

cetasā sarva-karmāṇi / mayi sannyasya mat-paraḥ
buddhi-yogam upāśritya / mac-cittaḥ satataṁ bhava

57. Mentally resigning all actions to Me, having Me as the highest goal, resorting to buddhi-yoga, do you always fix your mind on Me.

मच्चित्तः सर्वदुर्गाणि, मत्प्रसादात्तरिष्यसि ।
अथ चेत्त्वमहंकारान्न श्रोष्यसि विनङ्क्ष्यसि ॥५८॥

mac-cittaḥ sarva-durgāṇi / mat-prasādāt tariṣyasi
atha cet tvam ahaṅkārān / na śroṣyasi vinaṅkṣyasi

58. With your mind thus given to Me, you shall, by My grace, overcome all obstacles; but if from egotism you will not listen, you shall perish.

यदहंकारमाश्रित्य, न योत्स्य इति मन्यसे ।
मिथ्यैष व्यवसायस्ते, प्रकृतिस्त्वां नियोक्ष्यति ॥५९॥

yad ahaṅkāram āśritya / na yotsya iti manyase
mithyaiva vyavasāyas te / prakṛtis tvāṁ niyokṣyati

59. If, filled with egotism, you think, "I will not fight," vain is this your resolve; your prakriti will prompt you to act.

स्वभावजेन कौन्तेय, निबद्धः स्वेन कर्मणा ।
कर्तुं नेच्छसि यन्मोहात्करिष्यस्यवशोऽपि तत् ॥६०॥

svabhāva-jena kaunteya / nibaddhaḥ svena karmaṇā
karttuṁ necchasi yan mohāt / kariṣyasy avaśo 'pi tat

60. O son of Kunti, by your own karma, born of your own nature, what you, out of ignorance, desire not to do, you will helplessly perform.

ईश्वरः सर्वभूतानां, हृद्देशेऽर्जुन तिष्ठति ।
भ्रामयन्सर्वभूतानि, यन्त्रारूढानि मायया ॥६१॥

īśvaraḥ sarva-bhūtānāṁ / hṛd-deśe 'rjuna tiṣṭhati
bhrāmayan sarva-bhūtāni / yantrārūḍhāni māyayā

61. The Lord, O Arjuna, dwells in the hearts of all beings, causing them, by His Maya, to revolve, (as if) mounted on a machine.

तमेव शरणं गच्छ, सर्वभावेन भारत ।
तत्प्रसादात्परां शान्तिं, स्थानं प्राप्स्यसि शाश्वतम् ॥६२॥

tam eva śaraṇaṁ gaccha / sarva-bhāvena bhārata
tat prasādāt parāṁ śāntiṁ / sthānaṁ prāpsyasi śāśvatam

62. Take refuge in Him alone with all your being, O Bharata; by His grace you shall attain supreme peace (and) the eternal abode.

इति ते ज्ञानमाख्यातं, गुह्याद्गुह्यतरं मया ।
विमृश्यैतदशेषेण, यथेच्छसि तथा कुरु ॥६३॥

iti te jñānam ākhyātaṁ / guhyād guhyataraṁ mayā
vimṛśyaitad aśeṣeṇa / yathecchasi tathā kuru

63. Thus has this wisdom, more profound than all profoundities, been imparted to you by Me; pondering over it fully, act as you like.

सर्वगुह्यतमं भूयः, शृणु मे परमं वचः ।
इष्टोऽसि मे दृढमिति, ततो वक्ष्यामि ते हितम् ॥६४॥

sarva-guhyatamaṁ bhūyaḥ / śṛṇu me paramaṁ vacaḥ
iṣṭo 'si me dṛḍham iti / tato vakṣyāmi te hitam

64. Hear again My supreme word, most esoteric of all; because you are extremely dear to Me, therefore, will I speak what is good for you.

मन्मना भव मद्भक्तो, मद्याजी मां नमस्कुरु ।
मामेवैष्यसि सत्यं ते, प्रतिजाने प्रियोऽसि मे ॥६५॥

man-manā bhava mad-bhakto / mad-yājī māṁ namaskuru
mām evaiṣyasi satyaṁ te / pratijāne priyo 'si me

65. Give your mind to Me, be devoted to Me, worship Me, bow down to Me. Thus, you shall reach Me; truly do I promise to you, for you are very dear to Me.

सर्वधर्मान्परित्यज्य, मामेकं शरणं व्रज ।

अहं त्वा सर्वपापेभ्यो, मोक्षयिष्यामि मा शुचः ॥६६॥

sarva-dharmān parityajya / mām ekaṁ śaraṇaṁ vraja
ahaṁ tvāṁ sarva-pāpebhyo / mokṣayiṣyāmi mā śucaḥ

66. Relinquishing all your dharmas take refuge in Me alone; I will absolve you of all sins; worry not.

इदं ते नातपस्काय, नाभक्ताय कदाचन ।
न चाशुश्रूषवे वाच्यं, न च मां योऽभ्यसूयति ॥६७॥

idan te nātapaskāya / nābhaktāya kadācana
na cāśuśrūṣave vācyaṁ / na ca māṁ yo 'bhyasūyati

67. This gospel should never be spoken by you to one who is devoid of austerities or devotion, nor to one who does not render service, not in any case to one who finds faults with Me.

य इदं परमं गुह्यं, मद्भक्तेष्वभिधास्यति ।
भक्तिं मयि परां कृत्वा, मामेवैष्यत्यसंशयः ॥६८॥

ya idaṁ paramaṁ guhyaṁ / mad-bhakteṣv abhidhāsyati
bhaktiṁ mayi parāṁ kṛtvā / mām evaiṣyaty asaṁśayaḥ

68. He who with supreme love to Me will teach this deeply profound gospel to My devotees, shall doubtless come to Me alone.

न च तस्मान्मनुष्येषु कश्चिन्मे प्रियकृत्तमः ।
भविता न च मे तस्मादन्यः प्रियतरो भुवि ॥६६॥

na ca tasmān manuṣyeṣu kaścin me priya-kṛttamaḥ
bhavitā na ca me tasmād anyaḥ priyataro bhuvi

69. Among men, there is none who does dearer service to Me, nor shall there be another man on earth dearer to Me, than he.

अध्येष्यते च य इमं धर्म्यं संवादमावयोः ।
ज्ञानयज्ञेन तेनाहमिष्टः स्यामिति मे मतिः ॥७०॥

adhyeṣyate ca ya imaṁ dharmyaṁ saṁvādam āvayoḥ
jñāna-yajñena tenāham iṣṭaḥ syām iti me matiḥ

70. And he who will study this sacred dialogue of ours, by him shall I be worshipped through the wisdom sacrifice; such is My conviction.

श्रद्धावाननसूयश्च शृणुयादपि यो नरः ।
सोऽपि मुक्तः शुभाँल्लोकान्प्राप्नुयात्पुण्यकर्मणां ॥७१॥

śraddhāvān anasūyaś ca śṛṇuyād api yo naraḥ
so 'pi muktaḥ śubhāl̐ lokān prāpnuyāt puṇya-karmaṇām

71. And even the one who hears this, full of faith and free from malice, he too, liberated from sin shall reach the happy worlds of the righteous.

कच्चिदेतच्छ्रुतं पार्थ, त्वयैकाग्रेण चेतसा ।
कच्चिदज्ञानसंमोहः, प्रनष्टस्ते धनंजय ॥७२॥

kaccid etac chrutaṁ pārtha / tvayaikāgreṇa cetasā
kaccid ajñāna-sammohaḥ / pranaṣṭas te dhanañjaya

72. Have you listened to me, O Partha, with an attentive mind? Has the delusion of your ignorance been destroyed, O Dhananjaya?

अर्जुन उवाच
नष्टो मोहः स्मृतिर्लब्धा, त्वत्प्रसादान्मयाऽच्युत ।
स्थितोऽस्मि गतसंदेहः, करिष्ये वचनं तव ॥७३॥

arjuna uvāca
naṣṭo mohaḥ smṛtir labdhā / tvat prasādān mayācyuta
sthito 'smi gata-sandehaḥ / kariṣye vacanaṁ tava

73. Arjuna said: O Krishna, by your grace my delusion has fled and I have gained wisdom. I am firm; all my doubts are gone. I will do Your bidding.

संजय उवाच ।
इत्यहं वासुदेवस्य पार्थस्य च महात्मनः ।
संवादमिममश्रौषमद्भुतं रोमहर्षणम् ॥७४॥

sañjaya uvāca
ity ahaṁ vāsudevasya pārthasya ca mahātmanaḥ
saṁvādam imam aśrauṣam adbhutaṁ roma-harṣaṇam

74. Sanjaya said: Thus have I heard this mysterious dialogue between Vasudeva and the high-souled Partha, causing my hair to stand on end.

व्यासप्रसादाच्छ्रुतवानेतद् गुह्यमहं परम् ।
योगं योगेश्वरात्कृष्णात्साक्षात्कथयतः स्वयम् ॥७५॥

vyāsa-prasādāc chrutavān imaṁ guhyam ahaṁ param
yogaṁ yogeśvarāt kṛṣṇāt sākṣāt kathayataḥ svayam

75. By the grace of sage Vyasa have I heard this supremely esoteric gospel, the most profound Yoga, direct from Krishna, the Lord of Yoga, Himself declaring it.

राजन्संस्मृत्य संस्मृत्य, संवादमिममद्भुतम् ।
केशवार्जुनयोः पुण्यं, हृष्यामि च मुहुर्मुहुः ॥७६॥

rājan saṁsmṛtya saṁsmṛtya / saṁvādam imam adbhutam
keśavārjunayoḥ puṇyaṁ / hṛṣyāmi ca muhur muhuḥ

76. O King, remembering over and over again this mystic dialogue between Keshava and Arjuna, I rejoice.

तच्च संस्मृत्य संस्मृत्य रूपमत्यद्भुतं हरेः ।
विस्मयो मे महान्राजन्हृष्यामि च पुनः पुनः ॥७७॥

tac ca saṁsmṛtya saṁsmṛtya rūpam atyadbhutaṁ hareḥ
vismayo me mahān rājan hṛṣyāmi ca punaḥ punaḥ

77. And as I recall and remember that most wonderful form of Sri Krishna, great is my wonder, O King; and I rejoice again and again.

यत्र योगेश्वरः कृष्णो यत्र पार्थो धनुर्धरः ।
तत्र श्रीर्विजयो भूतिर्ध्रुवा नीतिर्मतिर्मम ॥७८॥

yatra yogeśvaraḥ kṛṣṇo yatra pārtho dhanurdharaḥ
tatra śrīr vijayo bhūtir dhruvā nītir matir mama

78. Wherever there is Sri Krishna, the Lord of Yoga and wherever is Partha, the wielder of the bow, there are goodness, victory, glory and unfailing righteousness: such is my conviction.

ॐ तत् सत् । इति श्रीमद्भगवद्गीतासु उपनिषत्सु ब्रह्मविद्यायां योगशास्त्रे श्रीकृष्णार्जुन संवादे मोक्षसंन्यासयोगो नाम अष्टादशोऽध्यायः ॥

Om Tat Sat. Iti Śrimad Bhagavat Gitasu Upanishatsu Brahmavidyayām yogaśastre Sri Krishnarjuna samvade Mokṣa-Sannyāsa-Yogonama ashtādaśodhyayaḥ

Thus ends the eighteenth chapter named "Moksa-Sannyasa-Yoga" (Liberation through Renunciation) of the Upanishad of the Bhagavad Gita, the scripture of yoga, dealing with the science of the Absolute in the form of the dialogue between Sri Krishna and Arjuna.

Amma's Websites

AMRITAPURI—Amma's Home Page
Teachings, Activities, Ashram Life, eServices, Yatra, Blogs and News
http://www.amritapuri.org

AMMA USA
About Amma, Meeting Amma, Global Charities, Groups and Activities and Teachings
http://www.amma.org

EMBRACING THE WORLD®
Basic Needs, Emergencies, Environment, Research and News
http://www.embracingtheworld.org

AMRITA UNIVERSITY
About, Admissions, Campuses, Academics, Research, Global and News
http://www.amrita.edu

THE AMMA SHOP—Embracing the World® Books & Gifts Shop
Blog, Books, Complete Body, Home & Gifts, Jewelry, Music and Worship
http://www.theammashop.org

IAM—Integrated Amrita Meditation Technique®
Meditation Taught Free of Charge to the Public, Students, Prisoners and Military
http://www.amma.org/groups/north-america/projects/iam-meditation-classes

AMRITA PUJA
Types and Benefits of Pujas, Brahmasthanam Temple, Astrology Readings, Ordering Pujas
http://www.amritapuja.org

GREENFRIENDS

Growing Plants, Building Sustainable Environments, Education and Community Building

http://www.amma.org/groups/north-america/projects/green-friends

FACEBOOK

This is the Official Facebook Page to Connect with Amma

https://www.facebook.com/MataAmritanandamayi

DONATION PAGE

Please Help Support Amma's Charities Here:

http://www.amma.org/donations

AMMA EUROPE

www.amma-europe.org

www.ingramcontent.com/pod-product-compliance
Lightning Source LLC
Chambersburg PA
CBHW071205090426
42736CB00014B/2720
9781680370201